FRESH HOPE FOR THE WORLD

FRESH HOPE
FOR THE WORLD

Moral Re-Armament in Action

EDITED AND INTRODUCED BY
GABRIEL MARCEL

TRANSLATED FROM THE FRENCH BY
HELEN HARDINGE

1724

LONGMANS

LONGMANS, GREEN AND CO LTD
6 & 7 CLIFFORD STREET, LONDON WI

THIBAULT HOUSE, THIBAULT SQUARE, CAPE TOWN
605–611 LONSDALE STREET, MELBOURNE CI
443 LOCKHART ROAD, HONG KONG
ACCRA, AUCKLAND, IBADAN
KINGSTON (JAMAICA), KUALA LUMPUR
LAHORE, NAIROBI, SALISBURY (RHODESIA)

LONGMANS, GREEN AND CO INC
119 WEST 40TH STREET, NEW YORK 18

LONGMANS, GREEN AND CO
20 CRANFIELD ROAD, TORONTO 16

ORIENT LONGMANS PRIVATE LTD
CALCUTTA, BOMBAY, MADRAS
DELHI, HYDERABAD, DACCA

Printed in Great Britain by
Northumberland Press Limited
Gateshead on Tyne

CONTENTS

v

CONTENTS

EDITOR'S NOTE

Quite apart from those whose evidence follows, many people engaged in Moral Re-Armament activities have helped to make the material of this book. One could not attempt to list them all here. They belong to widely different countries: France, Switzerland, India, Germany, England, Canada, the United States. But the book, no less than they, makes up a unity which testifies to the spiritual coherence of this team.

G. M.

TRANSLATOR'S NOTE

My thanks are due to the many friends and colleagues whose help in producing this translation has been invaluable: in particular to Jeanne Archard, Michael Hutchinson and Ian Cape for their work on the manuscript; also to Rozi Evans, Edric Cane, Basil Yates, Bill Stallybrass, Robin and Claire Evans, Mary Rutherford, Joyce Frecheville and Mary Rowlatt.

H. H.

Il ne se passe jamais rien de plus grand
en histoire qu'un changement d'espérance

HENRI GOUHIER

A Letter of Personal Reassurance to Three Anxious Friends

DEAR ROGER, PAUL AND TERRY,

EACH OF YOU has written independently to me to tell me how surprised and how sad you are to hear that I have thrown in my lot with Moral Re-Armament since visiting Caux last September. You have, of course, different points of view. You, Roger, are essentially a philosopher; you would by no means call yourself a believer, though you have always expressed a great respect for religion. You, Paul, are a Barthian Protestant. You, Terry, are just going to celebrate your first Mass in the country church where not so long ago you made your first communion. But though you have not openly said so for fear of hurting me, I realise very, very well that the three of you are shocked and even a little bewildered. 'He is getting old; a little *passé*.' That is the unexpressed thought which I have sensed behind all that you say. So I feel that I should reply to the three of you together.

Let me first set down the facts of my encounter with this movement. I think it was in 1933 that my wife and I first met what was then called the Oxford Group. It was in the home of my friend, André Davids, the painter. Robert and Diane de Watteville were there; also Pasteur Grosjean and Lucie Desoille, who later became my wife's best friend. They both died after the war and there was only a short interval between their deaths.

You can well imagine that what interested me was not the ideology proclaimed by the Group, that is to say its teaching about the four standards, taken in isolation—'Absolute honesty, absolute purity, absolute unselfishness and absolute love'—taken by itself, that was bound to seem to me rather naïve.

1

On the other hand, I could not help being struck by a rather remarkable coincidence. The year before I had written the essay entitled, 'Ontological Mystery; Its Nature and Concrete Approaches', which first appeared as an appendix to *The Broken World*.

Father de Lubac and Etienne Gilson rightly consider this to be one of my most significant writings, and had stressed the central value of recollection as an act of inner restoration. 'It is essentially,' I wrote, 'the process by which I realise myself as a single whole. The very word "recollection" suggests this; but this realisation, this recapturing of oneself, has more of the character of a "letting-go" or a surrender. It is a "surrender to . . ." or a "letting-go" without my being able to find any noun which can follow these propositions. The road ceases at the threshold. . . .

'In the heart of the stillness I face up to my life. In a sense, I stand back from it . . . and in this act of withdrawal, I take with me both what I am and possibly what my life is not. In this time of stillness the soul rests and waits. It does not look at or study any object. It is a time for inner refreshment and renewal. . . .'

We are here in the presence of that paradox which is a mystery, for through it the 'I into which I withdraw, ceases to belong to itself alone'.

Dear friends, I am sure that you will forgive these quotations. For they throw light on what was from the start the basic meeting point between the Group and myself. The fact was, that I was entirely ready to accept what for them remained the heart of the matter: that in a quiet time the voice to which we listen is no longer the voice of self.

But that was not all. There was also another point where I found myself seeing lived out in experience something which was in line with my own quest and my own conviction. I mean the encounter, or to put it more precisely, the act by which one person's consciousness (for want of a better word) can open up in the presence of another person's consciousness. The circumstances in which this happens are shown with great clarity in the following innumerable personal testimonies given by my friends.

You who know my writings well will recognise at once that this opening up in response to another person is exactly that *inter-subjectivity* which played such a central role in my later writings, though I do not think I had yet used this term at that period.

2

In view of all this you will hardly find it surprising that in the winter of 1933-34 my wife and I decided to hold small meetings of the Group in the flat into which we had recently moved in the Rue de Tournon. More and more people came to these meetings, which, I must admit, left me with mixed feelings. To start with, too many people just came to them out of curiosity, which inevitably spoilt the character of the meetings. Further, I blame myself for having often tried artificially to create opportunities for personal witness— even perhaps opportunities for reproaching myself. Altogether the personal element played too big a part in these meetings. And besides, at that time people considered (quite wrongly) that everything said ought to be what was called 'positive' which meant that critical reflection as such was considered to be negative, and therefore suspect.

During the following summer certain experiences, on which it now seems pointless to dwell, caused my wife and I to cease these activities with the Oxford Group of which I've been speaking, and we only occasionally kept in touch and learned of the evolution of the work and its transformation which led to the creation of Moral Re-Armament. In this way I was kept informed of the far-reaching and unforeseen developments which later profoundly altered the character of the movement.

In more recent years I was visited from time to time by people directly engaged in the work of Moral Re-Armament, who came to tell me what was going on in different countries.

I think I can say, however, that the turning point for me was my encounter last November in Tokyo with some American and Japanese who played a leading part in the events which are recorded in the third section of this book. The stories told me at Tokyo provided irrefutable proof of an extremely important fact, namely that the movement had now a direct impact on the political life of various countries in the Far East, and that statesmen—such as the President of the Philippines, the Prime Minister of Japan, and so on—were being directly influenced by it.

I had been invited to Caux more than once, but I had always declined the invitation. As a matter of fact, knowing my reactions, I was afraid of being set on edge, irritated or even exasperated by certain superficial features of the day-to-day life there, and in consequence finding myself less free to express my deep sympathy with the work which Moral Re-Armament was doing.

But I must admit that there was something dishonest and unjustifiable in this attitude. So you should not be surprised to learn that when I received in London last August a further invitation from my friend Lawson Wood, I decided that I must put an end to this kind of evasiveness and that my clear duty was to accept. Knowing how difficult travel is for me, they offered—with that generosity which is one of the magnificent characteristics of the people of Caux—to come and fetch me from Corrèze. I shall always recall with gratitude the marvellous trip which we made in one day through Auvergne and Velay, from the neighbourhood of Quercy to the borders of the Leman. But I am beginning to reminisce about things which have little to do with our purpose. . . .

I must now answer your questions, especially the chief objection, which, in somewhat different forms, appears in each of your three letters. What on earth could I be looking for in a movement like this? Or more specifically, how could a serious and exacting philosopher like myself so easily overlook the childishness which surely must be the hallmark of all this?

My immediate reply is that we must draw a very careful distinction (even though this distinction may be difficult to discern in practice) between childishness and simplicity. To my mind simplicity is a positive quality—the value of which goes almost entirely unrecognised in a world like ours that is on the verge of losing itself in its own complexity. One ought, really, to think out carefully which are the spheres where complexity is inevitable and the price of any real progress—and where it is literally disastrous and could even be said to checkmate itself. Wherever technique is supreme—and I am thinking especially of the technique needed to help forward man's operations on nature—it is hard to see how one can avoid complexity; indeed complexity seems to be the only way to achieve the ever greater precision that is necessary. This complexity applies both to the calculations and to the instruments that are made possible and efficient by these calculations. But the extraordinary thing, which very few people realise, is that the moment you enter the realm of the *human* everything becomes different. It is, of course, true that the word ' human ' is dangerously ambiguous. If I think of a man as a machine or as a system of mechanisms, I am certainly made to recognise the extreme complexity of his ' motor-processes '. Only, it must be carefully noted that the moment we do this we are ceasing to think of him as a *man*. I cannot think of him in this way without forgetting the essential point, that as a human being he is capable of conceiving—I do not say creating—values and ends, and of acting in conformity with or in opposition to them.

The moment you say this, however, you cease to think of a man as a machine. You will realise the importance of this if you recall that for my friends the fundamental experience is one of change, not just a subjective change, but a radical change of the personality. Here I could give you a hundred instances of what I mean, but you can readily refer to the personal testimonies which form Part One of this book. Take the story of R. D. Mathur. He is a young Indian who had given his whole self to the fight for independence. However, as you will see, once his country was liberated, it was not long before he had to recognise that his country's liberators were laying themselves open to the same charges as they had previously levelled against the British: they were not, in fact, maintaining either honesty or justice —the very things for which Mathur and his friends had fought. More important still, he realised that he himself had become just an ambitious man and that he was ending up by pursuing the high aims which he had set himself, no longer for their own sake or for the good of the people; but in reality *for his own benefit*. From that moment Mathur really started to become a new man.

I can imagine two objections being raised at this point: one by the philosopher and the other by the man of faith. I will come to them in a moment. But first I should like to draw your attention to the circumstances in which Mathur made his discovery. He did not make it alone, thinking things out quietly as we might have done in the silence of our studies. It came out of *contact with other men*; and everything points to the fact that it was because of this contact that his discovery was not a mere passing thought but left a lasting impression on his life, and that it became what I should like to call a water-shed or fresh well-spring in his life, something from which a whole series of actions sprang that would otherwise have been inconceivable.

So, Roger, if you say to me: ' There's nothing new in all this. The reflective life is full of examples of the same kind of thing,' I would ask you to pay special attention to what I have just said. Those of us who are of the reflective type have many ideas pass through our minds, and certainly it often happens that we see ourselves, or assess ourselves, in this or that situation but without this insight making any difference. Usually it changes absolutely nothing; but above all —and this is the vital point—if a man sees and assesses himself like this simply because he has acquired the habit of reflecting, he is still unable to enlighten others or be what I should like to call 'radio-active'. The point is, that these men and women whom I met at Caux have not been just changed; they have been endowed with a mysterious power, without their wills having any part in it. I am sorry to have to use the word 'power' as it almost always seems to invite misinterpretation. Perhaps a better phrase would be 'an active presence'—and you know what an important role this term 'presence' plays in my writings: a 'presence' which is a gift, a light, which acts almost without the person endowed with it being aware of it.

Then there is the other objection—yours, Paul. My phrase 'a new man' is almost certain to shock you. For, to a believer, a new man is a man who has been renewed inwardly by Grace, isn't he? Is not the most serious of your charges against Moral Re-Armament that it is a form of naturalism? You feel, do you not, that here we have created beings claiming to be invested with a power which belongs to God alone?

It seems to me that the right reply is this:

First of all, what we are dealing with here is not a theology, even of the most rudimentary kind, and still less a philosophy; it is an experience. And let me add at once, in every case, whether with Muslims or with Christians, a basic humility is maintained, which amounts to saying that this experience is always referred to God—and to God alone. You can be sure that, if one day R. D. Mathur finds that he has been a source of illumination, say, for a member of his family, he will at once go on his knees to thank God for having chosen to use such an unworthy instrument as himself. Further, I can assure you that if even a trace of self-satisfaction, vanity or presumption appears in someone's testimony, everyone at once detects and discounts it.

For instance, we heard one morning an African politician speak who had obviously missed the point, and was trying to use the movement to help him win his next election. Everyone immediately realised that he had still to grasp the ABC of the matter. I should like to add that the extraordinary joy which radiates especially from all the young people at Caux is in my opinion due to the fact that they have

—I shall not say *renounced* themselves, because the word renunciation has other overtones—but that they have once and for all given up the right to themselves. I know of no other place where you come into such clear touch with the only freedom which is worth while, the freedom of the children of God.

But no doubt, you, Terry, will take up the offensive at this point: 'God,' you will say. 'But what God? A rather flabby form of protestantism?' With complete certainty I reply, 'Absolutely not.' A young man from the Northern Cameroons, whose pure and fine face especially struck me, said this one day to us: 'I hesitated very much before coming here to Caux. I am a Muslim and my brothers said to me, "Be careful—they will try to convert you to Christianity." I came, all the same; and it has taken me only a few hours at Caux to realise that no one here goes in for proselytism of any kind, and I am completely reassured.'

The fact is that there is no attempt at conversion, for the very simple reason that there is no question of this being a religion or a sect. And yet no doubt you will object that there is all the same something here which transcends mere morality. For everyone claims to hear in their quiet time that which, if I dare not call it the Word of God itself, at least comes to them as Commands divine in essence.

At this point there are several observations which I think ought to be made. First, it is a fact that almost all those who, after meeting Buchman or one of his followers, have felt the need for a new level of thinking and living, even if they may have begun by interpreting this experience in terms of conscience only, have eventually come to recognise that they could not stop there; they have had to admit their dependence on a higher authority which they have called God. And those who have had a religious upbringing in their childhood have almost always gone back to their own Church, while the rest have chosen, I presume, the Church whose spirit most closely matched the new direction they had found for their lives. In any case they have considered their religious choice as following, or perhaps I should say crowning, their inner change. I feel it essential to emphasise this point, to put an end once and for all to the false idea which makes this out to be a new religion or a sect.

I fully realise the dilemma on whose horns Roger will try to impale me. 'Either,' he will say, 'we have here an affirmation which comes short of being strictly speaking religious—in which case we must not talk of guidance coming from God; or we insist on claiming that a changed man acts under a super-human impulsion, and then no matter what you say, we are in the realms of religion, and the question is, which religion?' It seems to me that this dilemma depends on an assumption which is not valid. To all appearances, the experience in question, of which you will find the most moving instances later on, could only be explained on the basis of a natural religion, which could serve as a 'common denominator' for Christians, Muslims and no doubt also Buddhists, etc.—not forgetting Japanese Shintoists—but which stops short not only of the revealed religions but even of all organised religion. However, if you insist on my giving my personal views on this very serious matter, I would say that in my opinion—and I speak for myself alone—it is not absolutely necessary to take literally the idea that it is God Himself who speaks to us during a quiet time. I would like to quote, in this connection, the words spoken by one of my favourite characters, Arnaud, in my play, Hungry Hearts.[1] He is speaking to Evelyne, his father's second wife, about a kind of pact he had made with a Being greater than himself in which he has promised not to try to probe the mystery which surrounds the death of his mother. 'Who did you make this pact with?' Evelyne asks. 'I feel no need,' he replies, ' to give a name to my partner. I only know that I am aware of His presence—not a human presence, not someone I can talk about, and yet someone apart from me, by whom I am known. He is there. He keeps watch.' I think personally, that that kind of reserve, that learned ignorance (docta ignorantia) is necessary here. When in a quiet time it is made clear to me, perhaps with the most gentle of promptings, that I ought to act in one way rather than in another, there is no doubt that someone greater than I has made this plain to me. But does the question, 'Who is it?' have any meaning here? As far as I am concerned, I would say that in this context the word 'God' has primarily a very special negative sense: it stands here for a refusal to put this question. Or rather, this refusal in itself is only as it were, 'the dark side of the moon', the aspect of unknowing, of a positive assertion which cannot be made explicit without its true nature being distorted. I do not think I need to cite Jaspers' idea of cyphers in order to made it clear that what we are treating here is something beyond the categories

[1] Cœurs Avides by Gabriel Marcel (Les Editions de la Table Ronde, 1952), p. 149.

of discourse, beyond this world of Who? and Which? The word 'transcendence' has been deplorably misused for years; but it would be in place here, because it exactly describes this 'going-beyondness' about which we have been speaking.

At the same time it is only honest to add that very probably neither Frank Buchman nor his followers would themselves accept the reservations which I have just expressed. I have voiced them only because I felt I should make clear my own position; but I do not think that we should attach too much importance to such a divergence of views. It can easily be explained by the fact that I am a philosopher; and a concern for strict intellectual accuracy which is proper for me is not necessarily incumbent, I feel, upon those people of whose unquestionably genuine stories I am continually speaking in these pages.

It should also be noted, on the other hand, that the absolute character of the four standards depends on this same going-beyondness or transcendence, which is essential here. And it is worth while noticing that here is, in another form, that same simplicity which I spoke about at the beginning. No doubt, this simplicity is only open to those who have rediscovered that child-like frame of mind, the essence of which has been so marvellously expressed in our day by a writer like Péguy.

You must surely have been struck by a remarkable feature of this point in history that we have reached: it is a moment when although in one sense the problems of the world are becoming infinitely complicated, in another and more profound sense they are becoming extremely simple. For we are being brought ever more clearly face to face with a basic choice: a choice, not for individuals only, but for the whole of humanity: the choice between life and death. For the first time in human history wholesale suicide has become a real possibility. And the only way to decide against suicide is to decide to abide by a basic pact whose terms are rooted in the ultimate nature of man —a nature which, be it noted, reveals itself only to moralists and not to any kind of scientist whatever. The progress of the de-humanising techniques which are at work in the world today only blinds us to that true nature of man. Dr. Frank Buchman's great merit, on the other hand, is that he has done everything to make that nature clear. You ask me what I think of him. I have met him only once or twice and I have never had consecutive conversation with him. But every-

B

thing that I have learned about him, and everything that I have noticed about the people—and they are innumerable—upon whom he has directly or indirectly left his mark, has inspired me with the deepest respect for him. This impact which he has had upon countless people's lives—an impact which has been at once discreet and yet permanent in its effect—is the hallmark of his vocation. Above all he has been, in the richest sense of the word, a man of goodwill, a pioneer and leader for all those who have understood and pondered his example.

I would also like you to think over this carefully. In Moral Re-Armament there reigns an atmosphere of simplicity regained. Thanks to it, a number of leaders from the young countries of Asia and Africa are evidently rediscovering unity between morals and politics—whereas in our aged and palsied world this unity usually seems a will-o'-the-wisp, except when it re-appears in a perverted form produced by the ideologies of Marxism and National Socialism with their teaching that the end both justifies and allegedly sublimates the means.

Of course it is always arguable that these statesmen from the young countries will soon become mere politicians. That is certainly possible and even likely. But I for my part maintain that all the same we ought to acclaim this magnificent and unique moment when simplicity has not yet been tarnished by ulterior motives, disillusion or resentment. This is one of the supreme cases where it is our duty not to try to anticipate events—a duty which I have often emphasised (much more in my plays than in my philosophical writings) perhaps because I have been so conscious in myself of a corroding propensity to foresee and to expect the worst. Moreover, the aim of a book like this should be to do all it can to arrest a decline which we have no right to judge inevitable.

If you read the third part of this book, you cannot fail to be struck by the number of heads of state, from Chancellor Adenauer onwards, who in these days have come to adopt the central teachings of Dr. Buchman and his followers.

But there still remain some questions which two of you have raised in your letters and to which I should like to reply. Both Paul and Terry attack what they call the 'palatial atmosphere'. I would ask them to realise that the huge hotel at Caux, built in one of the worst periods of architecture, bears no relation to the taste and spirit of the people we have been talking about. Advantage was taken of the chance to buy it at a low cost when it was on the point of being demolished, as it no longer paid its way. People thought, no doubt very rightly, that the most important considerations were its situation, which is certainly magnificent, and its accessibility from various large international centres. Other factors were its size and its large number of bedrooms. As far as I know, the much more simple building which has been created for Moral Re-Armament on Mackinac Island, Michigan, is much closer to the real spirit of the movement.

The worst mistake one could make—and I say this all the more strongly because I nearly fell into it myself—would be to imagine that the movement is financially dependent on a handful of millionaires living in the United States, Scandinavia or elsewhere. The facts seem to be that the money—and the sums needed are certainly large —comes almost entirely from people of modest means who, after meeting this movement, feel led to give not their surplus but often what they can ill afford. In other words we find here an organism which depends for its existence entirely on Faith (just as in Turin, where, as is well known, great charitable institutions are run on the same basis). My friends have told me sometimes they do not know where the next day's meals are going to come from, and they admit to the troubled feelings to which such uncertainty gives rise; but then suddenly the gift arrives, which frees them from anxiety.

Here, again, I can imagine your objections. You, Roger, will tell me that this kind of thing is irresponsible and that it goes against the elementary principles on which any sound undertaking is run. You will probably add that you think it very shocking that a group of people like this should have to depend from day to day for their very existence upon the chance generosity of others.

Let us pause for a moment, if we may. This question of dependence and non-dependence seems to me fundamental. I have always felt the need for security as strongly, possibly more strongly than anyone; so, I must admit, my immediate reaction is just like yours. I am naturally prone to think that as far as possible everyone ought to provide for himself and to earn his living by his own labour. But we do need to recognise, all the same, that this idea of self-sufficiency is bourgeois in the most narrow sense of the word. You will protest. You will remind me that even on communistic principles everyone is equitably rewarded for the services he renders to society. But my answer must be that in a capitalist society, just as in a communist one, we are dealing with a God-less world, where religion really seems to be just an addition or superstructure; and that is why it gives grounds for the suspicions and accusations levelled against it by the Marxists. For our friends, it is quite different. The basis of their action is the affirmation or fundamental insistence that *God comes first.* In that perspective the idea of the independence of the individual and even more of his self-sufficiency loses much of its meaning; it even becomes suspect. My friends are convinced that God has a plan for each one of us, and that our task is to discover that plan in quiet. From the moment we understand this, we only need to start out, absolutely confident that the means will be given us without stint. The opposite would be a contradiction in terms. Instead of the secular conception of independence, you have here the Gospel conception of the freedom of the children of God. One cannot but see that this resembles such experiences as those of the Little Brothers and Little Sisters of Father de Foucald. Here also, under the leading of Providence, each one is expected to discover his own road, that is to say, his vocation—a word which here recovers its full original meaning.

I am well aware that your reaction, Terry, is a very different one from Roger's. You will observe, rather tartly, that the moment people start talking about a community life based on Faith, similar to that, say, lived by the Mendicant Orders, all the ambiguities reappear. 'Which Faith?' you will ask. I think that the reply must be that the men and women of Moral Re-Armament, for in this context they are not thinking in terms of the differences between the confessional faiths to which they personally belong, will most probably not consider themselves bound to answer this question; they think of themselves as engaged in something quite new, in an adventure which does not need at all to be given a doctrinal form. I would add that, to my way of thinking, this should, rather, be considered in the perspective of a lived-out oecumenical experience and that this should be enough to cause us to welcome this idea gratefully. I am thinking again of our young Muslim from the Cameroons. His stay at Caux meant that for some days he *fraternised* with Christians. I am emphasising the word 'fraternise' because it is another of those many words which have been debased by usage and have lost their original meaning. Here it actually means sharing in the common experience of brotherhood being lived out. This is something far beyond what is ordinarily called tolerance. (I have lately had occasion to draw attention to the ambiguous and even questionable meanings which attach to that word.) It is love. My young Muslim friend did not only feel 'tolerated' but understood and the quality of his own faith acknowledged.

I should like to make one further comment—mankind is now undergoing the most terrible crisis that it has faced throughout the length of recorded history. The greatest experts have not merely proved incapable of solving the basic problem, that is, of establishing a peace worthy of the name; it even seems that they are incapable of realising how inconceivably serious the situation is. An English diplomat who came to Caux from Geneva told me how the conference on the peaceful uses of nuclear energy was bedevilled all the time by ulterior militaristic motives. Now, when orthodox medical methods fail one has a perfect right, one is even in duty bound, to call in healers. And I would say that we have here a kind of rescue squad whose effectiveness cannot be ignored and must on no account be underestimated. And, just as all the best healers say that the strange power with which they have been endowed is a gift from on high, so you will find among all our friends that humility the secret of which has been lost to a world which is becoming daily more and more the slave of techniques. That loss is far from accidental. The word humility has no meaning in a world that is entirely obsessed by techniques and 'know-how'. Granted, there certainly are surgeons, for instance, who pray before starting a particularly delicate and dangerous operation. But in so far as they do this, they cease to behave as pure technicians; in fact, they proclaim the inadequacy of technique alone.

'But,' you will reply, ' does not Moral Re-Armament also make use of techniques? What about these films and plays which they take from continent to continent—are these not techniques, and techniques of a kind that we French have little faith in? '

This is another point on which I should like to try to make myself clear. I saw four of these plays while I was at Caux. They seemed to me of rather uneven quality and none of them fully satisfied me. But the assessment which I or any other professional dramatic critic might make of these plays is really beside the point. They have to be evaluated from a quite different point of view. I think that Buchman and his associates have made a real discovery. They have realised that people nowadays are far more profoundly influenced by seeing something acted than you could ever expect them to be by hearing a sermon. And what has happened has conclusively proved how right they were. Think of that Japanese play, for instance, given in the Philippines. The thousands of people who saw it had the most terrible reasons for hating those powerful neighbours of theirs of whose cruelties their own children had been the victims during the war. I do not think anyone disputes the fact that the performance of this play has helped to melt the Filipino's very justifiable resentment and to open up the way to reconciliation. Many other instances could be quoted of the remarkable moral effectiveness of these plays and the film *Freedom*. So, if we French come along and say that all this seems very stupid to us and that we should never have been converted by such childish stuff, the question arises whether we are not condemning ourselves out of our own mouths. For in actual fact we are being swayed by a fear of the opinions of others which, as we know only too well, so often deadens the best impulses of our hearts. I would person-ally like to add this: I agree that most of the plays I saw appeal to people of a different mentality from ours. But that in no way rules out the possibility of other plays being written—by Frenchmen, Italians, or even Portuguese—plays which would perhaps strike us as being less naïve and less didactic, but would nevertheless awaken us Latins to a higher moral life and sensitivity. It cannot be said too often that this higher moral sensitivity in life is the thing which matters. Many stories were told me of persons whose lives had been transformed originally as a result of meeting this work, these might be made into plays of great dramatic quality in the hands of a gifted writer. But the tragedy is that the most gifted dramatists in our land—and I am thinking of Anouilh as well as of Sartre in his early plays (his best)—in one way or another have used their talents in the service of forces which tend to the disintegration of man. Montherlant is different: but it is so long since he lost the spirit of childhood that you could hardly imagine him now writing a work of faith. What we really need is a young dramatic writer who combines the pure vision of Péguy with the universality of Claudel. Alas, this is a highly unlikely combination.

In conclusion I shall repeat what I have already said publicly at Caux: What strikes me before all else is that you find there the global and the intimate linked together in a surprising way. Ordinarily speaking, an epithet implying 'world-wide' is always suspect, for instance when people talk of world opinion or world-wide success. When I hear that word it always sounds to me as if it was written in headlines in one of the popular newspapers. You get the feeling that people are using it to make their hearers gape in awe. But here it has quite a different sense. An event took place at Caux that I thought very extraordinary but which was apparently quite usual and which illustrated for me very strikingly what I had already come to consider during the previous days as the distinctive characteristic of Caux. There was a wedding in the main meeting hall. The Norwegian bridegroom and his American bride had got to know each other as they campaigned side by side during a long tour through Asia. The young bride, who had apparently a wonderful voice, had used it in the service, I would not say of the team or of the movement, but of the poverty-stricken peoples of India, Kashmir and Burma, in order to bring them light and hope. I will not attempt to describe in detail the marvel of this wedding and above all of the reception that followed it. It was given to us to see gathered from all parts of the earth, people of different races and colours, bringing in their songs and dances their grateful homage to this chosen couple. You might have thought that there was a risk of this becoming the kind of thing which could have made copy for *Match* or *Jours de France*, but truly it was just an intimate festival lit from within by the glowing devotion of that young couple, who, you felt, were quite overwhelmed by the strength of the affection which greeted them on every side. I can bear witness that we all sensed that we had attained a higher dimension, the dimension of the heart, or to be more exact, the dimension where heart and mind meet: we saw, before our eyes, *this world, this vast world, becoming a family.*

It is on this picture that I would like to bring my over-long letter to its close. I do not hope to have convinced you, but I do hope I have said enough to make you at least read carefully the personal testimonies which follow. It will be already something if the scarcely-disguised disdain which I sensed in your letters has been tempered by an element of doubt, and if you are ready to admit that there is something here new and strange, which at least deserves to be looked into more closely.

GABRIEL MARCEL
Member of the 'Institut Français'

15

PART ONE

Decisive Encounters

IT IS NOT INTENDED in this book to add anything to the rainbow of political ideas. It is neither an exposition of principles nor a pronouncement on doctrine. It is all actual experience.

It is concerned with facts. We could, from these facts, have tried to reach a philosophy, but this we leave to the reader. What interests us is not so much each individual case, as the extraordinary identity of result that they reveal.

A new world conscience is evolving. Without a shot being fired and without tumult, a revolution is taking place among the nations which is transforming the thinking of individuals and so sweeping away the wreckage of a world in ruins. A new hope is seen. A fresh renaissance starts to emerge.

This renaissance begins in human hearts. We will follow in detail the journey through life of these people from different sections of society, from all nations, from all races, from all religions and from different political points of view. The repetition of similar experiences, under different conditions, in the physical world, allows one to deduce a law. That is why, at the beginning of this work, we start with particular examples. All whose stories are told here suddenly found their lives set on a fresh course, because of an arresting encounter. However different their stories are, something happened, in each case, which drew them into strong fellowship with each other for the future.

We have asked many people to recount this for us. We will let them speak for themselves and tell us what happened in their own lives.

A SOCIALIST WELCOMES THE WORLD

This word Socialism meant a great hope for the world, the hope that equality and peace would one day rule everywhere on earth. Both as a young girl and as the mother of a family, it was to Socialism that I turned. I really believe I was born a Socialist. Instinctively I have always felt for and wished to share the sufferings of others. I have had a great desire to improve conditions for women and have wished to protect them and their children and make them less defenceless. When I was fourteen my pocket money and my leisure hours were devoted to work on behalf of young unmarried mothers who were left alone to bring up their children. I was outraged by the working conditions and low salaries of many of the women. I became convinced that Socialism would remove the scourge of alcoholism, prostitution and war against which I fought so hard. If Socialism was really lived out it would free people from all this and that was why I believed in it.

The working-class mothers of my generation were ready to suffer any privation, from unemployment to hard work, so that the children should not go hungry—anything so that Socialism should triumph. In 1936 the victory of the Popular Front meant a quite unprecedented hope in the hearts of many women. Many good results followed, including paid holidays and the limitation of working hours.

My husband and I lived with our five children in a little house in the depth of the country at the village of Camoins, in the South of France, near Marseilles. It was a very old house with four rooms and plenty of sunshine. There was no electricity and we had lamps. A big fig tree grew near the house and its roots made all the floor of the kitchen uneven. One day we had to send for a bricklayer to take away the roots and put cement down on the floor.

All round on the different farms there were thousands of cherry trees and in times of unemployment we would go picking cherries. For this we would receive enough money to give the children something to eat and also to make two hundred pounds of jam for the year. It would be the same for harvesting peas or haricot beans.

My husband worked in the merchant navy, but there was such a decline in the economic conditions at this time that he would often be out of work for months on end. At school he had been a pupil of Marcel Cachin, who taught Marxism to generation after generation. After this he was one of the founder members of the Union of Maritime Workers at a time when trade unionism offered more dangers than advantages.

I worked as a night nurse. The shift was twelve hours, there was a tram journey of an hour both coming and going, which made fourteen hours, and I earned twelve francs a night. On my return home I would look after the children and for a long time I never had more than four hours sleep out of the twenty-four. But this was life, this was the struggle, and it seemed natural. I would not, for anything in the world, have changed places with women who had everything they needed to make life easy. As neither I nor my husband can bear to see a child abandoned without a home we have, over the years, rescued and brought up nine other children as well as our own.

After the Socialist victories of 1936 and in spite of all our hopes, war broke out a second time and a war in which civilians were exposed to dangers as great as those of the armed forces. All the French know, as I do, what followed: we had the occupation, hunger, the Resistance and fight.

The South of France was very hard hit through lack of food. One day the Préfet stopped the issue of all bread rations throughout our district. The population had already been deprived of so much that it was absolutely essential to get these ration tickets re-issued. I called on the women. Four thousand of them took part in a demonstration and we marched to the Préfet's office. It had been agreed that there should be complete silence and that not a single word should be spoken. The whole procession was utterly silent. We arrived before the railings of the Préfet's house and I succeeded in my request to be taken in to see him. I asked for bread. 'Are you not afraid?' asked the Préfet. 'You know I have the power to arrest you?' I did not feel particularly reassured, but I replied, 'I should be afraid if I was in your place, Monsieur le Préfet. If you do not agree, I would not give much for your life.' He capitulated.

The day of the allied landings came and there were the last battles. We lived then in Aubagne and for four days the French troops passed along the main road while the Germans, entrenched on the heights, harassed them without respite. We had installed a first-aid post in a stables and day and night we looked after the wounded, both civil and military, French and German, by the light of acetylene lamps. We were using dressings drawn from the stores of the Maquis and everyone helped, even the children. I shall never forget a big German boy who was brought to us with a terrible stomach wound. He was a hopeless case. My daughter, aged fifteen, looked at him and then at me, and said, 'I am thinking of his mother.' And then he died.

Our liberation brought with it great suffering. We were free of the Germans but where was the freedom of Frenchmen? Victory was poisoned by hates, bitterness and the pursuit of private revenge and the peace we had desired so much was but a lie, for there was no peace of heart.

It was at this moment that the political parties were reforming. I belonged to the Socialist party and so I naturally remained with them. Lists were being compiled for the elections and women's names were put forward for the first time. They asked for my name as wife and mother and also on account of my part in the Resistance. I gave it in order to help towards a Socialist victory and my name came third on the list of the first constituency of the Bouches-du-Rhône.

On the evening of polling day, tired by the electoral campaign, we all went to bed early, but at six in the morning, the former Socialist Mayor of Aumagne, a great friend, woke us with a ring at the door bell. I opened the door. 'I am the first to congratulate you,' he said. I was so far from thinking there could be such a great number of votes in our favour that I did not at once understand what he was congratulating us for, and my husband had to intervene and say, 'You could at least ask the Mayor to come in.'

At the Assembly, we had hoped, the women had hoped especially, to make a common effort together. But already the parties were getting entrenched in their positions and disillusion was growing. Although I worked with all my strength for the Socialist cause, yet I had a profound realisation that in spite of our victories, war, drunkenness and prostitution were still rampant.

One day at the National Assembly, two gentlemen came to look for me in my office. I learned this afterwards from a colleague in Parliament who belonged to another party and who advised me to see them. They came although they were not at all sure how I would receive them. They immediately came to the point, which was Moral Re-Armament, and they invited me to come to Caux, one of the great

20

ideological world centres. I had heard of this from various rumours, some pleasant and some unpleasant, circulating in the French Midi (South) and I replied quite definitely that I already had quite other ideas in my head and enough of them to prevent my taking up theirs. As they insisted and appeared not to understand me, I got up and, opening the door, said, 'Gentlemen, I am sorry I have no time to waste with you. Will you please go?'

It was difficult for them to do otherwise. I was to learn that one of the characteristics of these people was perseverance. This came from a deep conviction that certain persons were perhaps those who really could do something for their country.

So, with much patience, they went on telephoning, asking for appointments, and coming to my office. Tired of this insistence, I asked my secretary to say I was away. We had christened them 'regular nuisances'. If they rang on the telephone, my secretary would give me a sign and I would be 'out'.

Another time it was a young girl who came to my office. We were getting ready to go away to the Black Forest to the Socialist holiday camps. It meant moving hundreds of children and great feats of organisation were needed, and then people would come and interrupt me with talk about Moral Re-Armament; I thought, 'These people live up in the clouds. They have no idea what it is like living in a country where we are only just emerging from the sufferings of war. We do, at least, have our feet on the ground.'

A little later I had a telephone call from an unknown lady who invited me to lunch with some members of the English Labour Party who were passing through Paris, and I was glad to accept this invitation: it was my first meeting since the war with English Socialists. I found a nephew of Chamberlain's and Members of Parliament amongst them. They were on their way to Caux and invited me to go too. I found fresh reasons for refusing: I had too much to do: I had to look after my children who were ill after their years of privation. 'Bring your children with you,' they replied, and after a long discussion I ended by accepting.

This was during the month of September 1947. My first impression of Caux was not favourable. First of all, the impressive setting made me think that this must be an undertaking on the part of the capitalists to keep the workers quiet. As a Socialist I could not under any circumstances become associated with something that might harm the workers. And there was another thing, the Germans were at Caux. Their presence was unendurable and if one of them got up to speak I would leave the hall. Finally, there was much talk of God, and in my opinion God was a matter for personal conviction and had nothing to do with world problems.

All sorts of questions occurred to me: Where did the money come from? Were the aims we heard about the real ones? Should I stay here at all? My doubts grew and I packed my bags.

It is often said that the night brings counsel. It was impossible for me to sleep that night. I decided I needed to stay until I could be quite certain I had discovered what lay behind all that I saw, so that I could fight effectively against these people wherever I found them in the future. This lasted three weeks and it would have been impossible to find anyone more suspicious than myself. I searched for the catch in it as though I were looking for a needle in a haystack, but nowhere could I find the capitalist power behind it; the money simply came from those who were convinced that the ideas put forward at Caux could bring something fresh to the world. I remember especially a young man who saved every penny for months until he had enough to buy a bicycle. He had at last been able to realise this dream of his. But he decided to re-sell the bicycle so as to give his money to Caux. Two young girls who had inherited from an uncle who had died following deportation, gave the whole of their inheritance so that the spirit of Caux might reach Germany. Another day enough chairs arrived from Finland to furnish the whole dining-room—and this meant a lot of chairs. Finland, although ruined by the war, wished to take a part.

I witnessed a thousand other similar events and after three weeks of research could find nothing that confirmed my fears. On the contrary, if we all had this quality of life and of sacrifice, humanity would see being realised the great hopes that the beginnings of Socialism had given to the world.

As a Socialist I had always thought of changing the structure of society. For the first time I saw that this change in people would inevitably bring a change in the structure through the suppression of selfishness and pride. One of my first meetings at Caux was with a representative of management from the north of France. At the end of a meal we had gone out on to the terrace to talk. He told me all he thought about the Socialists and for my part I gave him our opinion of his colleagues. Not a very subtle opinion, but one that could be summarised as follows: the employers in the textile industry in the north of France are all sharks! In no other setting in the world could we have said the things we did to each other without the argument becoming angry and embittered. There, on the contrary, we had in common our care for the welfare of France. We also had a way opened before us by this formula, one of the best I have ever heard in my life: do not look to see who is right but what is right. We both decided to set to work to see that this spirit becomes a reality in our country. And we have kept our word.

It was during my stay at Caux that I met Frank Buchman for the first time, the man who started Moral Re-Armament. What first strikes you about him is the tranquil look in his eyes. He is never hurried. One feels that his life corresponds exactly with his belief. He transmits the feeling of certainty to you, that if you will accept change you can have a part to play in the transformation of the world. We talked of European unity. He asked me a simple question, 'What kind of unity do you want for Europe?'

I had so great a hate of Germany that I had worked for her complete destruction. During the war I rejoiced when I heard the noise of the bombers on their way out towards the German towns. I could never forget the day on which I had seen one of the burying pits opened up and I had looked on those bodies of my old friends, from the Resistance, atrociously mutilated by the tortures they had undergone. After all the horrors I had seen I no longer knew how to cry.

'What kind of unity do you want for Europe?' For the first time I considered how hate can destroy but not construct and that my own hatred was a negative force.

At this point in the narrative of Iréne Laure it is worth while to let Peter Petersen, a young German who was at Caux with her, take up the story.

At the age of seven he had become one of Hitler's youth and been given training for four years in a special School for National Socialism. He was wounded while he was with the crack division of the German Army and he was imprisoned after the war by the British authorities because he still held to his convictions. 'In 1947 many were dying of hunger in the German towns which had been destroyed and millions of Germans were trying to prove (by any means in their power) that they had never heard of National Socialism.

'The whole world considered that Germany should give some proofs of a new outlook before she could once more be admitted in the company of civilised nations. But it was just at this time Frank Buchman got from the allied powers the special permit needed to invite 150 Germans to Caux. I was among them.

'I had always worn a uniform and I arrived at Caux in an outfit of my grandfather's that was both too short and too big. We were met by a French chorus with a German song, a song which foretold the true destiny of Germany. We were already past masters at defending ourselves when we were accused. But here the doors were wide open for us and we were completely disarmed. Three days after my arrival at Caux I learned of the presence there of Madame Iréne Laure, the Secretary of the Socialist Women of France. I also learned that she had wanted to leave the moment she had seen the Germans because the S.S. had tortured her own son in an effort to force him to give away the names and addresses of members of the Resistance. A violent argument broke out amongst us Germans: we could no longer escape the question which divided us at home: who was guilty? We all recognised that this Frenchwoman had a right to hate us, but we were determined, if she expressed this hatred, to reply with stories of the French occupation in the Black Forest.

'A week later Madame Laure asked to speak at one of the main meetings. We were sitting as far back as possible in the hall, very ill at ease and wondering whether we should not do better to leave. Madame Laure spoke three phrases which were to mark a turning point in our lives, both as individuals and as Germans. "I have so hated Germany that I wanted to see her erased from the map of Europe. But I have seen here that my hatred was wrong and I wish to ask the forgiveness of all the Germans present." She sat down again. I was dumbfounded. For several nights it was impossible for me to sleep. All my past rose up in revolt against the courage of this woman. But we knew, my friends and I, that she showed us the only way open to Germany if that country wanted to join in the reconstruction of Europe. The foundations of this Europe should be—Madame Laure had shown us this—forgiveness. One day we went to her and expressed our deep sorrow and our shame at what she herself and her people had suffered through our fault. We promised her that we would consecrate our lives and work so that these conditions could never again be reproduced in any part of the world.'

Returning to Madame Laure's narrative:

It was the first time that we were able to build on a forgiveness that was not just sentimental but that had the rock-like foundations of an ideology we held in common. If all the treaties had become scraps of paper it was because men had stayed what they were. This time there was a chance to build soundly. A year later I and my husband and my son left for Germany. We travelled for two months all through the Western Zone. We met representatives of different political parties in and out of the twelve provincial governments. At this time there was no Federal Government. In addition we had private and official interviews, gave Press conferences and spoke on the radio; altogether there were two hundred meetings in eleven weeks.

One day we were motoring through a town when I noticed a sign-post by the side of the road on which was written 'Ravensbrück Camp'. An arrow sign pointed the way. I suffered a shock: Ravensbrück—the camp for women where so many friends from the Resistance had died and from which some had returned unrecognisable. I had a feeling of anguish and the question in my mind was, 'Are you betraying your friends of the Resistance?' We had now passed through the town and the car was travelling fast. A great sense of inner peace possessed me. They seemed to speak to me saying, 'No, we did not die that hate should live on, our bodies do not cry out for revenge. We died martyrs that the world might find unity.' I arrived at my destination in peace because I knew that, no matter what might be said, the world must find this unity.

This conviction was strengthened by a sight that is indelibly engraved in my mind. It was in Berlin one evening when the women were finishing their day's work. Since dawn with only their bare hands they had been clearing away the ruins of the city. Their feet and hands were covered in blood and there was no longer any expression on their faces. They had simply become beasts of burden. I knew on that day the degree of degradation into which hate causes humanity to fall.

During my stay at Caux I came to understand that the key to what

25   C

I saw and also to the task before me lay in the time of silence that was practised by each person : in this silence a searching of conscience takes place and you see yourself as you are and what your motives are, also you see what you could become if you accepted change. One thinks one is somebody and discovers that one is not. One measures oneself against absolute standards, black on white. It is this that gives strength to the Quiet Time. Otherwise one comes out of a time of meditation with a vague feeling of personal uplift, but without having faced the reality of life. It is through these times of silence and in obeying what was deepest in myself that I have been able to accomplish things that were humanly speaking, for me, impossibilities.

I had this experience when I returned home after my first visit to Caux. I was full of hope and enthusiasm for these ideas and I naturally started talking about them. To my great astonishment nobody listened. Victor, my husband, left the room and the children disappeared, looking sceptical. It was impossible to say anything and I was left talking to the walls !

But I understood during one of these times of quiet in the morning that what mattered was not what others were going to decide for their lives, but whether I stayed faithful to these principles or not. In the end it was this faithfulness which interested them.

Sometimes this has to be shown in the simplest of ways. My eldest daughter did her hair in the fashion of the day with a bunch of curls over her forehead. This was not to my taste and every morning I would make a critical comment on the subject; every morning this brought an uncomfortable moment to the family circle. But in my quiet time one day came the thought, ' Leave her alone about her hair ! She can quite well do it her own way.' One or two days passed and I said nothing. On the third day my daughter came out of her room with her hair done in the way I liked and she said, ' You know, Mamma, I was not so keen about those curls really, but I wanted to aggravate you a bit.'

Often we, the parents, wish to impose on our children our tastes, our habits of speech, our way of life, and the studies which we choose for them, and when the children react against this, they often end by doing the opposite of what they really want to do.

If only we got off our pedestal, apologised when we were wrong, and told our children what we had been like when we were sixteen or eighteen, what family scenes would be avoided ! I know, because of having lived through it all. And if I know many children who make their parents weep, I know as many parents who make their children suffer and take the heart out of their children.

At the office also, it was necessary to start with the simplest things. To give an example: how often we teach secretaries to lie when speaking on the telephone and to write in letters things that are not exact. To keep their jobs they are obliged to obey us. I had to apologise for having asked them to do this. It was thus that those around me, sceptical to begin with and later interested, became curious to know more. My husband came to Caux with me first, and then to a meeting at Le Touquet where the employers' representative I had met in Switzerland had also come, accompanied by hundreds of workers, foremen and employers from the north of France. The meetings took place in a hall where the Casino had parties; this had been damaged by the war, so that we had to put up a tarpaulin to replace a wall that was missing. That autumn, late in the season, the wind blew with great fury through the town.

'We were walking along the front by the sea,' continues Victor Laure. 'Everything was in ruins—houses fallen in, hotels destroyed. I was struck by seeing these results of the madness of men tearing each other to pieces. To maintain their prestige, their hold over other men, they refuse to give an inch; then war breaks out and they have to accept all the consequences. Each follows his desires and projects, clinging to the framework of his preconceived ideas and refusing to listen to others. Men no longer see each other as men, their image of each other is deformed by the prejudices created by their professed beliefs. Yes, these ruins were the result of fights and also of lack of understanding between man and his fellow. I also realised that for anything new to rise from the debris, the intervention of a higher power was needed.

'I decided to have a good look at the four absolutes that had been presented to me: absolute honesty, absolute purity, absolute unselfishness and absolute love. In a world that I saw being reborn, thanks to Moral Re-Armament, I wanted to live according to these standards. But I did not feel I had the strength to do this. I had no faith and therefore no support. Then, as though in spite of myself, I knelt down and asked God to help me take up this quality of living, and also that I might persevere. I was very astonished to have made this prayer to

Heaven, but I felt stronger afterwards and more able to face the four standards which for me were quite new. To change the world, the best way is to change yourself. I went to the fight with no plan and no idea what to expect, but ready to do what this new faith told me to do, and that is why I went forward.

'It was the first step that was to take me, after forty-five years of Marxism, back to the faith of my fathers, the Roman Catholic religion. In doing this, I saw the necessity to conform to the natural law of the Church. Devotees of Marxist doctrines, my wife and I had only had a civil marriage. In the thirtieth year of our married life, I had a longing to have our marriage blessed by the Church. A priest from the outskirts of Paris who had been Chaplain in the Foreign Legion gave us this blessing. "It is not every day," said our son, "that a man of twenty-five is present at the wedding of his parents!"

'I am on the Good Road and that is why I stay on it.'

Our son Louis, continues Iréne Laure, decided to come with us to Germany. After all he had suffered during the war, he had made up his mind to enjoy himself to the full and have everything he wished for. Nobody could control him. He had started, in Paris, an export-import business that did very well, and he made as much money as he wanted. Success, pleasure, a motor-car, he had everything.

When we were in the Ruhr, there was a meeting at Moers, and I found myself on the platform with a group of Germans. Near me were two French people, one of whom had lost twenty-two members of his family, and the other fifteen, in the gas chambers. Louis heard me ask forgiveness for my past hatreds and commit myself to fight for a different future. I saw his look. I shall never forget it. He looked at the same time astonished, terribly upset and, I think, horrified. He left the hall and that evening went back to France.

He came back later and went with us as far as Berlin, travelling by the airlift. He had seen that there was a power at work that was able to change the course of history; that amusements and pleasures would never have the strength to create anything new, and that if all the youth of France lived as he did, without faith, and recognised no authority, the country would be lost.

After several sleepless nights he came to wake us up, knocking at the door at five in the morning. He had decided to make a trial of this new way, a trial which was finally to convince him completely that it really was worth while to change.

To begin with he asked my forgiveness for all the stupid things he had done, and the anxieties he had given me. It is true that often on the nights when I could not sleep I would wonder anxiously how all these troubles would end. But to forgive him was easy, for the hearts of mothers are made so that it is often the bad boys they prefer! Later he told me of his decision to pay up all his arrears of taxation because he had defrauded the Revenue. It was quite a large sum and there was also the risk of incurring penalties, and I knew all that facing up to this meant for him. Finally he resolved to put all his private life in order.

He carried all these decisions through and became a different man. Neither his relations nor anyone else could recognise him.

One day Frank Buchman sent for him, and three other young people, one French, one Swiss and one American. He gave into their hands the job of taking this new spirit to the whole of Brazil, almost a continent in itself! And so our 'three musketeers', not one of whom spoke a word of Portuguese, left for South America. After two and a half months, they returned in a special aeroplane which brought to the MRA Assembly the first delegation from Brazil. There were forty-five people representing all walks of national life, the armed forces, trade unionists, industrialists and politicians. From one man to another, from one industry to another, from the Port of Santos to that of Rio, the contagious spirit spread as you can read in the story of Damasio Cardosa.

It is thus that I found myself enlisted in a world force and engaged in a far greater revolution than I had previously thought possible, and one that took me into thirty different countries. Everywhere I met the heads of the Trade Union and Socialist Movements; in Calcutta, in homes where no Europeans had ever set foot, in America, in Finland, where the temperature was 30 or 40 degrees below zero.

I remain convinced of the value of the Socialist ideal but I know also that the future depends on the spirit with which it is applied, and on the quality of life that the Socialists of France and of the world have the wisdom to accept so that the world may find the unity it expects from them. Frankly speaking, in Asia and in the Middle East, I have seen the workers' leaders tackling appalling conditions of misery and poverty which seem insoluble, and I have wondered whether there exists in Europe or America the Socialist who has realistically envisaged the application of Socialism on a world scale. One who would never be satisfied to act within the limits of his own district only or the frontiers of his own country.

I asked myself this question: who will give the remedy to the scourges from which all humanity suffers? To what should we hold? To what else, except that which goes to the root of the matter and that we all know about but have not yet tried?

Ten years ago I thought it would be so slow that we should always arrive too late. But from year to year I have seen a real avalanche gathering speed in every country.

I know that the power that was able to change my husband and my son, and that was also able to change a politically minded woman like me, will attack evil, where its roots go deep, in human nature. This power can cure the world.

IRÉNE LAURE
Former Deputy for the Bouches-du-Rhône

REVOLUTION IN THE PORT OF RIO

That morning, I felt determined to go the whole way, and nothing could stop me. It was high time that the port management, in its test of strength against the trade unions, realised the sort of man it had to deal with. Would this necessitate using the same methods as a year before? At that time the port had been held up by a strike for fifty-four days. I must admit it was a stupid dispute, for everything could have been settled so easily. But at the beginning of the strike I had been suspended for thirty days. My comrades in the union of which I was Vice-President had decided that they would start work again only if I were reinstated; the management had had to give way to satisfy them. Encouraged by this victory they were skilfully manœuvred into taking a further step: the port manager had out-raged us by my unjustified suspension; the men would return to work only if he were dismissed and replaced by someone else!

The deadlock had been complete. The authority of the government, which is responsible for the port, was at stake; so was the dignity of thousands of dockers. That is why the port had been paralysed for more than fifty days. The ships were forming longer and longer queues in the huge Bay of Guanabara, which is said to be big enough to hold the largest merchant fleets in the world. In the end it really looked as if it were harbouring them all! But meanwhile the fruit and vegetables intended for the provisioning of the capital were rotting in the ships and on the wharves and had to be thrown into the sea. After a struggle of seven weeks, the government had finally given in and the port manager had to leave.

That gives you some idea of the atmosphere!

Everyone in the port calls me Damasio. I was born in Amazonas, that fabulous region in the north of Brazil. There is Indian blood in my veins. For over twenty years I have worked in the docks of Rio de Janeiro. Though I have never been either a Communist or a Fascist or anything like that, I have always rebelled against injustice. That is why I have never hesitated to fight for my comrades, especially when their rights or their dignity as men were threatened by anyone at all, whoever he was, whether a minister, the port manager or the President of the Republic himself!

So that morning I was feeling particularly bellicose. Once more we had sent out strike orders. My anger was directed not only at the port manager, but at the head of the baggage depot, Nelson Marcellino de Carvalho. The brief that I had compiled against him was shattering: to begin with, he was a 'boss', and that was enough to make him my enemy. But besides, he was one of the chief officials of the Port-workers' Union of Brazil. This union, which claimed to represent all the port workers, had in fact lost its influence. Nobody had any confidence in its committee. We considered the representatives were drawn merely from the bureaucrats and high officials. The majority of the workers considered it a bosses' institution. Furthermore, my comrades and I, despite the law, it is true, had founded a new union which had succeeded in asserting its authority from end to end of the docks. But instead of dying a natural death the Portworkers' Union of Brazil was resisting, and Nelson had just announced that, in defiance of the strike instructions, he intended to open his baggage depot, so that all the men needed to run it could go in. Two ships were arriving from abroad that day with foreign diplomats on board, and it was apparently essential to the good reputation of Brazil that they should be able to disembark with all their luggage. I did not worry about such considerations. 'If the diplomats want to leave the ship,' I had said, 'let them do so with whatever aid they can find. My men will do nothing to help them.'

I had had Nelson warned that if he tried to work he would be risking his life. The private settling of accounts was an everyday affair in the port. I had prepared myself for the fray; adding a second revolver to the one which I always carried, as well as a knife, I had gone to the depot at the head of a group of well-armed comrades. When we arrived I went straight up to Nelson; at the slightest movement on his part I would shoot.

I expected violent reactions: to my great surprise, he spoke quietly. He told me how sorry he was that we were enemies, when in point of fact we were both fighting for our workmates. But we were setting about it in the wrong way. He talked to me of a new job that awaited all the port workers and required their unity; to my amazement, he even went so far as to admit that he himself had made mistakes and that the Portworkers' Union was not without blame. He had realised that, to bring something new into the situation one must not always wait for the other person to change; you had to start with yourself, and he was in the process of reviewing his whole life from this fresh perspective.

At that moment something happened to me. I am sure it was a miracle in my life. That I was stopped in my attack and able to hear out what Nelson had to say to me was proof of it. I could not believe my ears, while all the time I wondered what might be behind it: was it cowardice? Or a trick? In my eyes, Nelson had been, up till then, merely an ambitious man, and his supposed union activity at the heart of the Portworkers' Union seemed to me to be aimed only at the defence of his own personal interests and those of officials like him. Yet he had spoken a completely new language. If he was sincere, it was worth making a closer study of his suggestions, which might perhaps avoid bloodshed. So I promised to come back and see him next day. On looking back now, I have no doubt whatsoever that, without the new factor introduced by Nelson, the wife of one of us would today be a widow and the other wife would be filled with bitterness because her husband would be in prison.

The next day he told me the reasons for his surprising attitude. A week before, he had been at a meeting at which industrialists and workers had told how they succeeded in settling the conflicts between them when they renounced self-interest and their personal ambitions. On the morning of our encounter, Nelson had arrived at the port ready to defend his life dearly. But when he saw me, he had remembered what he had heard at that meeting. 'I felt a great calm and even peace in my heart,' he told me. 'There was no fear, no hatred, no arrogance, no antipathy in me; I had only one desire; to win your friendship and confidence so that together we might unite the port workers.' He suggested to me that a few of the most active members from the two unions which we represented should meet and get to know each other. The workers of a textile factory in São Paulo were just organising a big demonstration to present the results of applying these new ideas among themselves; it was a good opportunity.

The following Saturday, forty of us set out for São Paulo. It was already a triumph that we had even agreed to travel together; some wouldn't hear of getting into the same coach as their worst enemies. During the 270-mile journey, we looked at each other out of the corners of our eyes. Some had brought their wives with them, others their revolvers.

We were welcomed by men of different classes, races and countries, in the home of an industrialist whose example was to play a decisive part in my change. In obedience to his undertaking to live above the level of his personal interests, he had stopped giving bribes to certain officials on whom his contracts depended. I did not think it was possible for an industrialist to do anything whatever in the interests of the workers. But this man proved to me that this was not so. This meeting was attended both by leading workers from the great port of Santos, of whose heroic struggles we all knew, and by a young Frenchman, full of fire and wit, whose mother, Iréne Laure, had been the secretary of the Socialist Women of France and whose father had been a pioneer of the trade union movement. He never spared himself, and for some months he had been living with the dockers in Santos, working out the ideas of which we had been told that day. Twenty-nine of the thirty-seven Union Presidents of Santos had just signed a manifesto addressed to the Governor of their State assuring him of their full support in creating an atmosphere which would put an end to the divisions between classes and nations without resorting to violence.

All these men brought to our notice a worthwhile purpose for which to unite. After two days spent in this atmosphere of brotherhood, the barriers between our two groups began to fall. On our return we were friends with a common aim.

This was the first step. A few months later, Nelson and I set out for a world assembly of Moral Re-Armament at Caux, with forty other Brazilians. We were going to see this ideology at work in other continents.

In the port the new ideas were tenaciously discussed. 'As I am, so is my nation.' This truth suggested many necessary changes. It was sure to clash not only with deep-rooted habits, but with all that years of bitterness, hatred, dishonesty, dissolute living, and despair, too, had left in thousands of consciences. Would it not be easy for people of evil intentions to mobilise all these forces so as to block the way against ideas that were so uncomfortable? I was one of the first to realise this, to my own cost. Everyone in the port knew that I had gone to Caux with Nelson; the Press had published the speeches which we had made there in the presence of many of the personalities of Europe and of the whole world; we had committed ourselves to fight side by side to make these ideas strong in the port and in the country. Frank Buchman had said to us: 'Brazil's destiny is to export not only good coffee, but good ideas.'

On my return from Caux, I found an explosive situation in the port of Rio. The unofficial union, of which I was still Vice-President, was stirring up a strike. It was an action with political objectives which had nothing to do with the interest of the working class and which created division in the port.

Convinced that this agitation was unjustified, I decided to tour the port with a dock railway motor tractor on which we had placed a Brazilian flag and a banner bearing the aggressive slogan: 'Boycott the strike.' From wharf to wharf we explained to our comrades the facts of the situation. On our arrival at Shed 7, the tractor was surrounded by a group of excited dockers who were expecting me there and a scuffle started. They seized hold of me and held me fast while one of them knocked me out with a bottle. I woke up in hospital with eleven stitches in my scalp. I was considered lucky to have escaped with my life. On seeing me fall, one of my friends had rushed forward and, drawing his revolver, had yelled: 'The first man who touches Damasio again, I'll shoot!'

Unfortunately, someone had run to my flat and told Nair, my wife, that I had been assassinated. Nair, who was pregnant, had collapsed,

34

and under the shock of violent emotion, had given birth to our sixth child two months too soon; as a result of this premature birth, the child had deformed legs. The following days were among the hardest of my life. The thought of my child made me mad with rage. It seemed to me that there was only one thing to do, to give free rein to the wave of bitterness and hatred that was welling up in me, to forget all about Moral Re-Armament and satisfy my thirst for revenge. But God, who had not wanted me to die, did not want me to kill either. He had a plan for me. One day when quietly and in silence I was looking for the answer to my despair, a thought came to me very clearly: 'During their life, men have to choose between two roads— the one of rebellion and the other of obedience to God. By their obedience they can remake the world. By their rebellion they will certainly destroy it. You must choose now; tomorrow it will be too late.' It was then I decided that instead of trying to take vengeance on my aggressor, I would try to make a friend of him. By the time I had recovered, the whole port knew I was looking for my man. But each time he saw me, he slipped away, as he had grave doubts about the sincerity of my intentions! In the end, I met him and we made it up.

After that I was expelled from the union of which I was the Vice-President and which I had served unstintingly. The decision was so arbitrary that it shook a large number of our militant members, although they were devoted to our President. He would not tolerate any deviation from the line which had been laid down; he was encouraged in this by those who were making use of the union to satisfy their political ambitions or to promote their long-term plans for the continent.

The situation was extremely serious. My former President practically controlled the port. Groups of armed men laid down the law in the docks, and certain shipping companies, to avoid trouble, paid them 'under the counter' whatever they demanded. Corruption and theft became so widespread that the insurance companies fixed higher and higher rates for goods destined for Rio and threatened to suspend the contracts. Many importers preferred to send their goods to Santos, 250 miles further south, and bring them back to Rio by lorry.

And yet, at the very moment when the forces of destruction seemed to be winning, a still greater force was about to show itself—the very one which had made a free man of me on my hospital bed.

People were talking about what had happened to me, and many were beginning to open their eyes. If it was dangerous to try to live in an honest way in the docks, was it not proof that certain people had an interest in maintaining the existing state of affairs? Nelson and I were fighting to recreate a unity in the port which would make it a strength to the country and not a perpetual source of trouble and difficulties. This was what the majority of the dockers also wanted.

My comrades and Nelson's were meeting more and more frequently so as to find out more about this ideology and to discover how to put it into practice.

There was a long way to go. We had picked up the habit, for example, of never going out unarmed; one had to be ready for anything. I remember that one day we had arranged a lunch party in the respectable Swiss Club in Rio de Janeiro to talk of our experiences to some new friends. The first man to arrive obviously thought that, since the subject was Moral Re-Armament, he would not need his revolver and left it in the cloakroom. A few minutes later some fifteen weapons had been left in a row there, and the porter rushed up to one of the organisers of the lunch and asked, 'What type of re-armament do you advocate, exactly?'

Gradually, as we discovered the possibility of changing our adversaries instead of liquidating them, the need to be armed became less and less. All the same, it needed some courage to give up carrying a weapon, as it meant all possibility of defending oneself in case of attack was out of the question. It took me some time to decide on this myself. I said to myself, 'Sell your two revolvers, a knife will be enough!' An incident which might have had a tragic ending drove me to give that up too. One day some comrades accosted me and made all sorts of offensive remarks about me. To start with, I was able to restrain myself; but all at once, one of them was so grossly insulting to me that I forgot all my good resolutions and, drawing my knife, I stabbed him in the shoulder. That day there was a Moral Re-Armament meeting, and I went there feeling utterly desperate. When I was asked what was going on, I replied that I had 'fallen a little short on unselfishness'! Actually, I was longing for the earth to swallow me up. Fortunately, after a few days in hospital, my victim recovered, but I had been so unhappy over this incident, that I thereupon decided never to carry any weapon.

We were all unanimous in condemning dishonest politicians who use their position to enrich themselves. But on looking at it more closely, we had to admit that we were not so different from them. It was a widespread habit in the port to 'take a commission' in certain quantities of goods, especially of foodstuffs. We made the needs of our families an excuse, but some went so far as to use lorries to take their 'commissions'. Obviously we could never demand honesty in the government if we did not show it in our own life. One of my close friends—a magnificent fighter who had distinguished himself in the War of Liberation in Italy where he fought with the Brazilian Expeditionary Corps—saw this clearly. His first thought was to 'cut down to normal' the quantities taken as commission so as to reduce them to a 'reasonable' level. Very soon he had to admit that a standard was valid only if it was absolute, and he completely stopped his doubtful practices. The effect was immediate; in his warehouse his workmates followed his example.

Some of us had given up drinking; that clarified our minds so that we could understand what was really going on in the port and in the country.

Nelson, too, was undergoing a radical change. His father, I knew, had been one of the pioneers of the trade union movement in Brazil. But Nelson's ambition up till then had been to live in a flat in Copacabana—the fashionable part of Rio—to own a car and to give his daughter a good education. Now, his main pre-occupation was to spread throughout the country the spirit which was beginning to take root in the port. In the old days, one of his great passions was horse-racing. An appreciable proportion of his income was spent on betting. On the day when he decided to cut it out, we knew for certain that Nelson was no longer the same man.

In his baggage warehouse there was no lack of temptation. One day a stranger approached him and offered him a million cruzeiros if he would agree to shut his eyes for a moment while a case was smuggled through. Nelson was just wondering how to find the necessary cash to pay back the loan which he had raised from a bank, and that million represented a real fortune to him. But he at once thought of all the men for whom he felt responsible: his comrades in the port, the Brazilian Members of Parliament, the statesmen of South America and of the whole world. What could he say to them if he gave in now? He told his tempter to go to hell!

37

Our families were backing us in this fight. For the first time our wives were not merely tolerated but welcome. Up till then, in all our activities there had been no room for them. We expected from them good meals ready on time, shirts well ironed, and all the attention to which we thought we had a right. Speaking frankly, I myself had been living for more than twenty years with my companion Nair, who had borne me seven children, but my sense of responsibilities towards her had never extended to making her my wife. Thought came to me one day during a time of quiet: 'Put your affairs in order in the eyes of God and of men.' For me it was a revolutionary decision. We live right next to the port in a group of workers' flats called 'Vila Portuaria'. It is lived in by hundreds of dockers' families and you always meet swarms of children there. I knew well that my decision would not pass unnoticed. My wife and I wanted to use this event to give a new conception of living to these families, many of whom live as we had done up till then.

The wedding took place one Saturday morning. For the civil wedding our witnesses were one of the big industrialists of Sao Paulo and his wife; I had travelled to Caux with them in 1953 and their new attitude had won us. All our children attended the religious ceremony, dressed in white like their mother. The priest was an old man of over eighty. He gave us to understand that he had never in his life blessed such a marriage!

Nair and I went to confession for the first time in years. In fact for my part it was the first time in my life, and I did not know how to set about it. The priest had allowed for only a limited time on the morning of the wedding. But how would I have time to tell him everything with a past like mine? Suddenly I had an idea: I would give him the main points and ask for absolution, promising to come back later to tell him the rest!

Some months before, at Buenos Aires, I had had the privilege of meeting a distinguished bishop, Monsignor de Andrea. I had told him of the decision I had made to get married. The real reason for it was that I could not take part in a struggle which has its basis in personal change if I did not change first myself. The bishop gave me his blessing in advance. His attitude moved me a lot, and it was this that helped me most to go ahead in obeying my convictions.

These events led me to find a faith, and so it was that my wife and I returned to the Church.

38

We had invited our witnesses and friends to lunch in our home; our flat has only three rooms and there are already nine of us living in it! But everything had been prepared for the occasion : there were new curtains at the windows, the walls had been recently repainted, and friends had lent us the crockery which we needed. An old friend of the family had even taken possession of the kitchen and prepared some delicious chickens 'a la Bahia', such as you can eat only in Brazil. The only difficulty was that there was not enough room for everyone at the table, so we had to eat in relays. But luckily we have a large balcony, and we live on the seventh floor, with an extensive and enchanting view over the Bay of Guanabara. So nobody complained.

In the evening there was a big celebration in the 'Vila Portuaria', attended by several hundreds of dockers and their families. I had the chance to say a few words about the meaning of this event. Then some of my new friends spoke: Nelson, my former mortal enemy; Carlos Pinto, the Secretary-General of the Portworkers' Union of Brazil, who told how in the old days, simply because he belonged to a rival union to mine, he hated me without knowing me; and a young industrialist whose revolutionary spirit is a constant challenge to me. The ladies had prepared a superb cake and fruit drinks. It was an unforgettable evening.

A few days after our wedding, the port welfare worker took me aside. She said to me, 'You are keeping me busy ! Now that you have got married, the others want to do likewise.'

Thus from man to man and from family to family a new spirit was spreading through the port. The effects in the union were not slow to make themselves felt.

One after another, my former President's chief henchmen left him and, like myself, rejoined the Portworkers' Union of Brazil, the legal union. They were convinced that the old methods had only served to divide and corrupt the port workers. They had found an objective which gave purpose to their struggle. The Portworkers' Union of Brazil for its part took a new lease of life from this influx of fresh blood and vitality. Its leaders themselves underwent a profound change with the help of Nelson and others, and the honesty of their policy gained the confidence of an increasing number of dockers. In 1953, the year that I went to Caux, the Portworkers' Union of Brazil was moribund. Four years later, the authority of this organisation was recognised throughout the port, and the rival union had disappeared. The unity of the workers had become a fact.

It was a victory, but it entailed a big responsibility. We had to reorganise the union so that it could adapt itself to the new circumstances. At the beginning of 1957, in accordance with its new statutes, the first really democratic elections were held in the port. Previously they had been a mere farce, because in my old union voting used to take place by show of hands, and all those who did not follow the leader's word of command were in for a bad time. As to the old Portworkers' Union of Brazil, its committee had been recruited from among fifty councillors who themselves did the electing, in such a way that the union members took no part in it at all.

This time the election of the new executive committee was to be completely democratic: the state electoral tribunal was asked to supervise it; the voting was to take place in the docks, so that all might take part, and of course by secret ballot. The election campaign was lively. The executive committee of the Portworkers' Union of Brazil offered themselves for re-election and asked the dockers to ratify their policy of 'honesty and work'. They announced in their programme their intention not to make promises which could not be fulfilled. 'The form of the elections is as important as the result itself,' said our President. 'We want to prove to the government that it is possible to be honest in politics.'

The election was a triumph. There was not the smallest incident. In the evening the votes were counted; the outgoing committee was re-elected. One of my friends, Henrique, found himself once more President of the Portworkers' Union of Brazil.

Joel, a Socialist, who had been to Caux in 1954, came second. When the results were announced, Henrique was cheered by all those present; he expressed his feelings simply, adding that he was determined to serve the whole port and all the workers. Joel rushed up to give him a hearty slap on the back and declared: 'Henrique's victory is a victory for me and my friends. The majority has decided. I am happy to give Henrique my votes. We are united by a common programme of absolute honesty, purity, unselfishness and love.' The whole hall applauded him. The next day, Rio newspapers announced the news, marvelling at the democratic spirit shown in these elections. The great daily *Correio da Manha* devoted three columns to the event and said, 'For the first time in Brazil a group of public servants has held an election within the framework of electoral justice.' In Parliament, a Member exclaimed, 'These dockers are giving us a lesson in democracy!'

A few days later, the next executive committee was officially installed. It was a great day, and I could not help thinking back over the way we had come during these few years. The day began with a Mass: at seven o'clock in the morning the church was full, and several of our comrades had to get up at three o'clock in order to arrive in time. The same evening, a big celebration took place, in which both winners and losers took part. There were flowers, speeches, refreshments . . . but no alcohol, in accordance with a decision by the executive committee. This gave our celebration a happy and natural atmosphere and at the same time a poise and dignity which delighted all present. A Government representative said to us at the end, 'In the course of my duties I have been present at countless union celebrations, but never yet have I seen so much dignity and harmony.'

Thus an idea has seized hold of a few men and influenced the life of a whole community. Through it we have found our unity again, and we know its price. Corruption has begun to decrease, and the executive committee of the Portworkers' Union of Brazil has decided that it will no longer automatically protect dockers accused of dishonesty.

Since 1954, there has not been a single strike in the port. It is true that work stopped for five minutes in 1955 on the occasion of what we called 'God's strike'. It was the eve of the international Eucharistic Congress which was held that year at Rio de Janeiro. The suffragan bishop had the thought to suggest a pause during work throughout the country, so that everyone might think of the significance of this Congress. When he asked for our co-operation, we agreed at once, and he appointed Nelson president of the executive commission responsible for organising the demonstration. On the day and at the time fixed the bishop was among us in the docks. It was the first time that had ever happened! While work stopped, he said a few words and read a moving prayer which he had written specially for this occasion. I was at his side, and I could not help smiling, when I noticed that the bishop, whose words were relayed over loudspeakers from one end of the port to the other, used the very same microphone that I had used a few years previously, to give strike instructions to my men.

In 1956, six of us, among them the President of the Portworkers' Union of Brazil, set out for the Argentine with the backing of the Minister of Transport and of the port management: the latter had undertaken to cover part of our travelling expenses. At the 'Casa Rosada' in Buenos Aires, General Aramburu, President of the provisional government of the Republic of Argentina, received us and was keenly interested in what we had to tell him. 'What we need here above all is a conviction,' he said, 'and conviction is possible only where there is faith. You are doing exactly what is needed.'

Quite recently, Nelson, Carlos Pinto and I set out for Washington, where we had interviews with leading Americans, including senators and high officials of the State Department. Never before had we imagined that one day simple dockers like ourselves could talk to men whose decisions affect so many countries.

That is our story. It all began the day I found myself confronting Nelson with hatred in my heart. That encounter, which might have been fatal in its effects, on the contrary brought about an understanding which now enables us to unite men. Today, Nelson and I are fighting side by side. We have a cure for hate, ambition and selfishness. We know that God can inspire and guide us. It is certainly not easy to live by these absolute moral standards. But I know that it is the only way to inspire others to do so, and that only thus will I see my country change and the world change. That is what fills me with enthusiasm for this revolution.

Damasio Cardoso

A FRENCH INDUSTRIALIST'S
BALANCE SHEET

If, on a fine day in the month of August 1952, I set out with my wife for Caux, it was only because I wished to get away from the demands of a friend who was constantly urging me to get to know Moral Re-Armament. In fact, I knew hardly anything about it, and had no wish to know more.

Who was I?

I was the chairman of an iron and steel company with a personnel of about 7,000. I was married and the head of a family of eight children.

What were my problems?

In my private life they came from the fact that I had, as a widower with three children, married a widow, herself the mother of five. We were accordingly faced with the difficulty of integrating the two families, with all the frictions this is bound to cause.

What were my main preoccupations on the professional side?

First, a problem many industrialists have in common—the deep misunderstanding between employer and employee. But there was also another matter, equally serious, that was beginning to perplex me: the prospect of the first Common Market coming to birth, the coal and steel pool, which raised, on a long or short-term basis, the problem of the future of the industry of the Loire area, where most of my business lay. It was a problem of life and death for us.

As I made my way up to Caux, I did not even consider whether there might be any connection between what I was going to find there, and the worries that preoccupied me. Yet it was there that I was to discover, if not the answer to all my questions, at least a key which would enable me to solve the majority of my human problems.

I had even less inkling as to who among the people I would be conversing with would enlighten me. For it was not my talks with industrialists who faced tasks and responsibilities similar to my own, nor the meetings at Caux (some of which, however, impressed me deeply), that gave me the real shock which has turned my life upside-down for the past six years. I felt this shock most deeply in the course of the simple, almost child-like conversations which I managed to carry on, despite the language difficulty, with two German workers, formerly militant Communists in the Ruhr, who had since given up everything to fight for Moral Re-Armament. Neither they nor I touched the great heights of philosophy or economics. Our tastes would have been unlikely to lead us to that point, nor would the presence of an interpreter, whom we needed despite my slight knowledge of German.

How can I express in words, to intellectuals as sceptical and as complicated as I could be myself, the conviction of these simple people who were radiant with an inner light, and according to whom it is possible to change human relationships by a return to moral prin-

43

ciples? How, above all, can I express my perplexity when, in reply to my self-professed deep experience of social relations and my conviction that it was Utopian to claim to modify human relations by the simple effect of a heart-to-heart contact, I heard as their sole retort: '*Haben Sie versucht?*' . . . 'Have you tried?'

No, I had not tried. I had often attempted to convince others of the superiority of my intellectual reasoning, but seldom to recognise where I had been wrong, or to look for what is right.

I thought this was what I should do. But I was quite annoyed and not a little embarrassed.

On the way back from Caux, my wife and I stopped beside a little stream and, sitting on the grass, we wondered where to begin . . . whether by admitting those points where I had been wrong, or by telling others that I thought it possible to find a common meeting ground beyond the bounds of official protocol and impersonal relationships, which would establish a fresh intercourse?

A few days later, I took the bull by the horns and called a special meeting of the works council of my firm's most important factory of about 5,000 workers. I shall never forget that occasion, when I explained what I had felt at Caux, my conviction that it was possible to create a new climate among men in seeking what is right, and where I apologised for any mistakes that I might have made. I shall never know what worried me most, as I confronted the stony faces of my listeners: my fear of ridicule, or the sense that the step I was taking would be ineffective.

For up till then my relations with these delegates had been somewhat strained; I had been divided from them by all the misunderstandings inherent in the separateness of the classes, whose differing points of view are as fixed as they are irreconcilable. . . . 'That is what I understood at Caux,' I said in conclusion. 'I am not asking you to believe me, or to share my conviction that it is possible for everyone to find a new solution based on personal change. I only ask you to agree to come with me to Caux and hear what they have to say.'

I only knew later, much later, what was going on at that moment in the hearts of some of my listeners. Those who were willing to tell me have declared that they were shattered. And yet they were tough fellows.

The meeting was adjourned. Uneasy over my boldness, I awaited the decision of the council members. After a quarter of an hour's deliberations, they informed me that they had unanimously agreed to go to Caux with me.

Of course, it was too good to be true. . . . On the very evening of that meeting, which was one of the most moving moments of my professional career, and indeed of my life, outside forces in the union had come into play and directives which went out from an anonymous source imposed their veto where earlier the heart had spoken. The most important union forbade its delegates to go with me. The others confirmed their acceptance.

It is difficult for me to say what has resulted over the past six years from those few moments of truth amongst men and from that journey together, because to try to delineate such things in black and white is a betrayal of the truth and depth of human feelings.

People have often asked me to draw up a balance-sheet of the positive results of identifying myself unreservedly with this work of Moral Re-Armament since August 1952. This I can say in all sincerity, that it is in my morning quiet time, when I try to discover the just way, regardless of any self-interest, that I have found the solution to serious industrial problems.

It is in the course of these meditations, imbued with the spirit of Caux, that the seeds of certain decisions have been sown and have borne fruit, and I would like to mention only the most striking of them.

Firstly, there was a free distribution of shares to the employees of my firm. Then there was the decision to amalgamate the four main iron and steel concerns of our region. This was in order to realise one of the biggest achievements in concentrating and rationalising industrial output, involving a total of 15,000 workers. The key to the problem was for me to give up the first place and take the second. Then there was an undertaking which no firm, to my knowledge, has ever made, not to resort to any dismissal of workers during a difficult period of industrial concentration which lasted for four years. Should I not also mention the settlement of a company agreement, in which there was the exceptional clause whereby employees agreed to forgo wage increases in order to re-establish the financial stability of the firm, and the undertaking given by the same employees, at another time, not to strike during a fixed period?

Each one of these facts is perhaps not extraordinary in itself,

45

though it is certainly unusual. It is above all the accumulation and regular succession of them since my return from Caux that makes me sure that their cause is a deep-rooted one.

Their origin lies in the challenge given me one day by two miners from the Ruhr and also in the extraordinary impression made on me by those few minutes of acute perception and intensity of life, when, in the course of a meeting of the works council, I felt as though the veil that hid us from each other was torn down.

I do not know whether all this is due to Moral Re-Armament. But I am sure that nothing would have happened without it. Nothing would have happened without that deep change in my heart and in my wife's during those August days of 1952. For, from that day, an average happy couple have been transformed into a strong team.

And this team has given birth to another one, a group of men and women which has met faithfully with us every month for the last five years, whenever we move from Paris to the town, in the centre of France, where the factories of our firm are situated. There we meet with workers, foremen and engineers from our factories, who, together with their wives, are united through Moral Re-Armament in the same fundamental belief. They have also grasped, in their family life and with their fellow-workers on the shop floor, how much this search of theirs for honesty and their care for others can transform their vision of the world and their relations with other men. Not only do they come with us to Caux every year, but they have also been several times together to other towns, so that their team, welded together by mutual trust in one another, can have an opportunity to tell others what they believe.

Director of an Iron and Steel Firm

NOTHING IS IMPOSSIBLE FOR HER

You find these busy, proud, dominating women in every country—even in Holland. And I was one of them. It was quite obvious to me that God had given me a gift for organising and directing; I organised and ruled dozens of committees and was president of a large number of organisations. I also made free use of my talents at home, and was astonished that my husband and children seemed to be lacking in enthusiasm. I was still more surprised that in spite of all my energy and hard work, nothing changed very much in the world.

One day I met some people who had obviously found something that I was seeking for myself: things around them changed, really became different. So I went up to one of the ladies and said, 'I realise you have something that I lack and for which I am searching. What must I do? How do I begin?' She said, 'It is very simple. We try to live four absolute moral standards in our lives—absolute honesty, absolute purity, absolute unselfishness, absolute love.' I said, 'Oh, that will be very easy. It is the way I have always lived.' 'There is something else too,' she said. 'We try to listen to God every morning and write down our thoughts.' I replied, 'Now that will be very difficult because, you see, I am so busy. Immediately after breakfast the telephone begins to ring, people come to see me: then I must go to my committee meetings. I am afraid that is out of the question.' She said, 'Yes, but it is before breakfast you must do it, not afterwards.' 'You don't know me. It is absolutely impossible. During the day I am full of energy, but I need a great deal of sleep. I am made like that and I fall ill if I have to get up early.'

'I thought you were looking for something . . .'

'Oh yes, I am . . .'

'Well, if you can't find the time, it would be better to think no more about it.'

She was quite right. I wanted what these people had, but I couldn't even sacrifice an hour's sleep for it. Suddenly, I made up my mind and went out and bought an alarm clock. The next morning it went off with a terrific noise, just an hour before our normal time of getting up. My husband jumped out of bed shouting, 'What on earth is the matter? What is happening?' I said, 'I'm going to be silent for an hour.' He simply roared with laughter and said, 'Oh, your latest craze.' And he wouldn't have anything to do with Moral Re-Armament. But I was so passionately interested in the discovery, because all kinds of new thoughts were coming into my mind which had never been there before, that I kept up the habit of waking an hour earlier for a whole month. At the end of a month, my husband said to me, 'Is this Moral Re-Armament of yours no longer having meetings?' I replied, 'Yes, of course.' 'Can you get me an invitation?' he asked. 'I thought you didn't want to hear it mentioned!' 'Yes, but something that can get you out of your bed an hour before you have to must be something very remarkable indeed and I would like to take a closer look at it.' And so he too adopted the idea.

One morning at the beginning of 1940 the thought came to me quite clearly to go to America to tell the women of America what was happening in Europe.

My country was mobilised. France was already at war. I had a feeling that in America they didn't realise what was happening and that we were really preparing for a world war. Soon afterwards I read an article about the plans being made for a big women's conference in Washington on the causes of war, and its cure. The most important women in America were coming to it, and also delegates from other countries.

The only possible boat was leaving from Genoa the following Friday. The conference was due to begin on the Tuesday after that. I went at once to see the American Consul-General about a visa. He said, 'I'm afraid it is absolutely impossible: apart from that, do you realise, Madam, that this journey is very dangerous? You would be sailing over mine-fields.' I said to him, 'I think that God wants me to go to America and I am determined to take part in this women's conference.' Finally he said, 'All right, I will give you a visa. I think you are a very courageous woman.'

With this visa I went to the French. The French diplomat said, 'Absolutely impossible. Absolutely impossible. It will take three weeks before I could get you a visa.' I said 'What is impossible for man is possible for God: so that if God wants me to go to America, and I am convinced that He does, I will get this visa. You will obtain it if you will only ask for it.' At last I persuaded him and he got it. I caught the boat that left Genoa the following Friday for America.

When I arrived in America, Frank Buchman, who knew about my plan, arranged for me to be presented to Mrs. Roosevelt, and when she had introduced me to the conference, I asked the chairman if I might be allowed to speak.

At first she said it was impossible as the whole programme had been completed long before, but in the end she let me speak for five minutes, and I went on for an hour, telling all these women about the conditions we were living in and the sort of realities people have to face in time of war. After I had spoken, many of the women came up and invited me to repeat what I had said in other cities in America.

When I arrived in San Francisco I met Frank Buchman again and it was there I heard that the Germans were marching into Denmark, and I knew that Holland would probably be the next country to be invaded. I went to Frank Buchman and told him how much I wanted to cut short my journey and return to be with my husband and children, although earlier I had felt clearly to go and speak to the women of Canada as well. He said, 'Let us be quiet and think about it.' Then he helped me to see that I should carry out my original conviction even at the risk of never going back to Holland again.

I met Frank again in New York. 'Well, Frank,' I said, 'I think now I should go home because on 17th May we shall be celebrating our fortieth wedding anniversary. I really think it is time to go back.' Frank said, 'Let us be quiet.' I suddenly thought of something and said, 'I should like to stop in Rome on the way, because I can obtain a private audience with the Pope, and I would like to ask him what to do about the women of Italy.' Frank said, 'Let us think about that in silence.' We were quiet a minute and Frank said, 'No, not this time. Go straight home.' I went home on an Italian boat, and we stopped in Naples, and I thought, 'Well, now I'm half a day's journey from Rome. Why don't I go there?' But I couldn't. I had to go on. I arrived home on 9th May at 6 o'clock. That evening, and during the night and in the early morning, the Germans crossed our frontiers. We were at war. If it had not been for the absolute clarity of Frank's direction, I would not have been home in time. And I could not have accomplished all those things I found waiting to be done.

Immediately after I got home, German officers arrived to go through the house and then moved into the rooms that suited them. The Nazis began to build a huge concentration camp right on our doorstep. Thousands of my countrymen, men, women and children, were imprisoned as political prisoners. Everyone who did something that the Germans did not like was put in this concentration camp and at the head of this camp was a very cruel man, who tortured his prisoners and just shot people if he was in a bad mood. Also his latest hobby was to starve his prisoners to death. Everyone knew about it and sometimes we saw the prisoners coming out to work on the roads; they were living skeletons and many people died every day of starvation. I couldn't sleep any more for thinking of them.

One morning I thought, 'Well, I can ask God what to do. I am sure God can tell me.' Then I prayed, and in the morning I had two thoughts. One was to have no fear whatever, and to walk straight into the camp and to ask to speak to the Commandant. The second was that nobody is entirely bad, that even this man had something good left in his heart which could still be touched; and that I could find out what it was. At first my husband was appalled and would not let me go. But I felt sure that God had inspired these thoughts and I went to the camp.

The Commandant was so astonished that a Dutch lady, of her own free will, dared to walk into his camp, that he asked me to come to his office and there I sat talking with him for two hours. At last I found out that his soft spot was his love for his only son, who was fighting at that moment in Russia. This was my clue, and I said to him, 'Well, your son can be killed, but he can also be put in a concentration camp, in Russia, and what would you think if someone came to help him?' He said, 'Naturally, I would be very glad.' I said, 'Well, I feel absolutely sure that if you give me permission to send in food to my countrymen, your son will be helped in Russia.' At first he said, 'Oh, that's quite unnecessary. They get the most wonderful food in the world here. This is more like a convalescent home than a concentration camp.' And I knew how many died every day. So I simply looked at him and said, 'Well, if you tell me so I have to believe you. But I think they could do with a little more.' Finally he said, 'All right, you may send in food.'

And so I came home very triumphant and I said to my husband, 'You see, nobody has hurt me, and here I have his promise that we may send food to these poor prisoners.' My husband said, 'That's wonderful, but how are you going to do it?' Because at that time we had very little to eat ourselves and were severely rationed. I had the thought that if God had asked me to go to the camp, He would also find the necessary food. We could begin by all eating a little less and saving every morsel of food. This we did, and the neighbours joined in and in ten days' time everybody in Holland had heard what I was doing because it was the only camp where this permission had been given. People came from all over the place with every bit of food they could spare out of their meagre rations. My whole house was transformed into a food market. The food was good. In a few weeks we were sending between one thousand and twelve hundred huge parcels of food every day from our home to the camp. Then I had a second thought—to make only sandwiches, so as to avoid our big pieces of cheese, bread, butter and meat being sent to Germany. As sandwiches get stale and rancid so quickly it would be necessary to distribute them to the prisoners.

This went all right for a few months and then, all at once, the Commandant did something that the Germans didn't like and he was dismissed. A second man came immediately and sent back my parcels. He wouldn't have anything to do with them. So I had to go to the camp a second time, and I ended by talking him over. Then a third one came who was absolutely determined not to see me in case I should get the better of him. This state of affairs lasted several days, the food was accumulating in the house, people were dying again, and I could do nothing because he simply refused to see me.

I decided to listen to God, and there came into my mind the story of the poor widow who puts her case before the judge and this judge refuses to listen. But she comes every day and the judge gets so exasperated by her perseverance that he gives in. I thought, 'This is what I must do.' So I bombarded the new commandant with letters and telephone calls and sent people to him to ask him why he would not see me, until at last he was so angry that he said, 'All right, I will see her, but in her own house,' thinking I would not do that. Many Dutch people would have been astonished that I should agree to receive a man like that in my own home.

At first I didn't know what to do, but I asked for guidance again and the thought came, 'Does the good opinion of people mean more to you than the lives of those prisoners?' I would have to admit it if I refused his request. So I said, 'All right, let him come.' My husband went out of the house protesting, 'I'm not going to receive that man.' On the appointed day I sat waiting for him. He came, bringing six of his officers with him to support him in the fray, and they all came in armed with sabres and looking very fierce, and at first my heart sank and I thought, 'They are going to take me.' But immediately it was as though a voice spoke to me saying, 'Have no fear, it is the Commandant that matters. The others don't count.' And so I asked them very kindly to sit down, and offered them tea or coffee. The Commandant refused. And he kept on saying, 'No, no, no, I don't want to hear anything about that.' And so we sat for three solid hours, and I couldn't get anything out of him other than, 'No, no, no.' And I was absolutely at a loss what to do. I prayed fervently and silently; I simply had to win over this man. I had a sudden thought, and straight out I said to him, 'Well, now we have been fighting for the whole afternoon, and you keep on saying, "No, no, no." But I know that you have a good heart and deep in your heart you want to give me the permission I seek.' And I saw the officers making faces in order not to burst out laughing at the idea of his having a good heart. He got very nervous, fidgeted in his chair, looked around him, and looked back at me and then burst out laughing himself, and said, 'All right, you have won.'

He kept his word, till the very end, when the Allied forces entered Holland and liberation was near. The prisoners were terrified. One day I got a little note scribbled in pencil by one of them saying, 'We are living in mortal fear because we have heard that 500 of us will be shot dead on the spot, and all the hostages, including the women and children, are to be taken to Germany. And you know what that means. You are the only one who can save us. We beg you to come and plead our case, but you must know that the approaches to the camp are all filled with soldiers with machine guns who have orders to shoot at sight everybody who has no official reason for coming.'

This was a difficult moment. I realised the danger, but my husband and I had guidance together and once again I was completely convinced that I had nothing to fear. It was my life or the prisoners'. God would look after me. At last my husband let me go. I went through the woods and immediately saw a group of soldiers pointing their machine guns at me and calling me to halt. I called back at them that I wanted to speak to them and continued calmly walking towards them. They were so astonished that they let me come near. I told them what I wanted to do. In this way I was able to walk up to group after group until I reached the last sentry, who agreed to telephone the Commandant, and I heard the Commandant yelling back through the telephone, 'Tell her I have no time. I can't speak to her. I have no time.' I took hold of the telephone myself and talked straight to him and told him that I had heard the rumour that he was going to shoot 500 of the prisoners, and that this was an inhuman act and that I was there to beg for their lives. He gave me his word that not one of them should be executed. I said, 'But what about the hostages? Those hostages have done nothing, they are not prisoners of war and not political prisoners, and it would be an absolutely inhuman act to take them to concentration camps in Germany.' He said, 'Well, what do you want me to do?' 'Let them go free. I will come and fetch them and see that they go home safely.' After some thought he said, 'All right, you may come tomorrow and take them away.'

The next day I gathered together all the friends I could who had some kind of vehicle and we went to the camp under the protection of a small Red Cross flag. The women and children were allowed to leave and we packed them off quickly in case he might change his mind; then we fed them and gave them new clothes, and sent them back home. Then it was the men's turn. So we got all the hostages out. All the other prisoners, who numbered about 5,000, were sent to concentration camps in Germany. Alas, very few came back.

Another extraordinary event took place after the war. I got a letter from this third commandant, saying that he himself was now in a French prison and that he wanted to know what had become of us; he knew that our home had been under fire, that a battle had been fought in the town and we had all been living in our cellars for thirty-five days and nights. Were we all alive? And he finished his letter saying, 'I would like to know, because I remember with great respect all that you did.' The final phrase of the letter was, 'Yours gratefully'. I asked myself why this man felt so grateful to us. But I understood that having been in a concentration camp himself now, he knew what suffering meant, and was grateful that he had allowed some good to be done. After some months I got a letter from a lawyer in France asking if I could say something in the man's favour, because he was going on trial as a war criminal. I immediately wrote back that in my opinion he deserved only slight punishment because he had not only given us permission to feed our fellow countrymen, but he had had the courage to take the decision on his own initiative, contrary to orders, to allow the hostages to go free.

A long time afterwards I saw in a magazine the photographs of three war criminals. He was one of the three. Two of them were condemned to death; he himself had been sentenced to some years in prison. So his life was saved as well.

This was how I learned that one must always follow the inspirations which flash into the mind during these times of quiet and listening, even when they seem to be in the realm of impossibility. If you obey Him, God comes to your aid.

LOTTIE VAN BEUNINGAN
The Netherlands

AN INDIAN FACES INDEPENDENCE

At the foot of the Himalayas lies one of the former princely states of India. To the north-east rise the snow-covered mountains over the Tibetan and Chinese borders. To the east, beyond the chain of the Himalayas, are Burma and Thailand with their ancient Buddhist culture; and further to the south-east is Indo-China. A short distance to the north is the U.S.S.R. and westwards begins the great Islamic girder which stretches from Pakistan down to Nigeria and Ghana.

My father was tutor to the Maharajah of this state and when I was born he suggested to my father that I should bear his name. We lived a simple life in a quiet city, where, because of our closeness to the royal family, everyone treated us with great respect.

I have four brothers and four sisters and we all lived in the same home. My father and mother are both orthodox Hindus. All their lives they kept the discipline of their faith, and they had spent an hour every morning in prayer, in the old Hindu fashion, before we children got out of our beds.

My mother spent most of her day looking after us nine children. But although we were a nice and respectable family all was not well within our four walls. I can still remember the raised voices of my father and mother arguing about the children and the rude tone with which we spoke to the servants who so faithfully and affectionately cared for us.

My father never beat me but I was always afraid of him. There was something in his way of speaking and looking that affected me more than a beating would have done. In fact, apart from the great care he took over my education and clothes, I never experienced any other tokens of affection from him. In contrast I was always very fond of my mother, who took upon herself the difficult task of presenting our requests to my father.

I grew up and became aware of all that was going on around me.

54

I can still see the streets of my city and the country round, where men and women slept on the pavements mixed up with the cows that roamed the streets and slept by them. I can still see people looking in the dustbins in the evening to find something to eat before lying down on the stones to sleep. This upset me and I remember rushing to my mother one day and asking her, 'Why do these people have to live like that, Mother, when we have these soft beds and all the other comforts?' Mother put me off, saying, 'You are too young to understand all this. Go and play outside.'

Even though I left the room, the question in my heart remained unanswered. It continued to haunt me until I entered the university. There we spent hours in the café during our free periods, discussing what were the causes of this poverty, injustice and inequality in the country. The one reply that seemed to come from every side was that it was the British who were responsible, that they had exploited us and taken away all our wealth to raise their own standard of living. 'You have never seen an Englishman lying on the streets in India or in his own country,' said one of the students to me. That remark unleashed strong feeling in me. That day I decided that if I really loved my people and my country I must do something against social injustice. Whatever it cost me, I would plunge into the struggle for the independence of my country along with other revolutionaries who were doing the same.

From that time on I had one aim to which I devoted all my time, and I used to leave the house at six in the morning and get back at eleven at night. We boys and girls from the university spent hours discussing and laying plans for the revolution. We sweated over writing pamphlets against the British, and then secretly handed them out on the streets while one of us kept watch in case a C.I.D. man or police officer was seen to be approaching. I remember one evening standing in a dark corner and putting leaflets in the pocket of every passer-by. Others of us would fill envelopes with a mixture of chemical products which were inflammable, then seal them up and put them in the letter boxes, particularly the ones near government offices. After a few hours the whole box would catch fire.

We thought of nothing but making our country free, which would mean the beginning of social justice and better living conditions for all our people. Our passion for this cause made us take great risks.

One day 7,000 students were moving in procession through the streets of New Delhi, shouting revolutionary slogans. Suddenly the leaders came face to face with a British officer on a motor-bike followed by four lorries loaded with police. The officer ordered us to stop the procession. I answered back, 'We are just expressing our desire for freedom.' His reply was: 'I'm not interested in all your nonsense; I will give you ten minutes in which to disperse. After that I will not answer for the consequences.' A few of us who had organised the procession consulted together. We decided to risk everything if that would help our country. We came back and told the officer that we had decided to go on with the demonstration and would accept any consequences.

The police opened fire. Men were killed and amongst them some of my closest friends. That day I learned to hate. I had thrown myself into the struggle through love for my country and my people, and now this was replaced by a savage hatred and desire for revenge.

Day by day, month by month, the struggle went on. My hate grew ever stronger till the day arrived when we were to get our independence. It was a tremendous fulfilment. Thousands of Indians were shouting for joy; for the first time we had the right to fly the national flag.

I sat in my room and with my father and mother listened on the radio to the ceremony during which the powers of government were transferred. At midnight it was over. The bells rang in all the Temples and I thanked God from the depth of my soul. I wept for joy and the thought came to me, 'Now we can build together an India where no one will be hungry and justice will reign. Those who have given their lives for this will see from their place in Eternity the achievement of their aims.' I thought of Mahatma Gandhi and how fortunate we were to have a leader like him.

Scarcely six months later he was taken from us. I began then to get disillusioned because the patriots rushed for the best jobs and felt they had a right to be in power. People forgot about the ordinary man.

I was not sparing in my criticism of our leaders. They, on their side, blamed the way we behaved and we fell into a vicious circle.

I felt completely at a dead end until the day when I said to myself that without political power it was impossible to serve one's country. That day I decided that I would do all I could to become a minister and enter the government. Having reached that position I would be able to do for the ordinary man what no one else was bothering to do.

I set out to achieve this aim regardless of anyone else, elbowing my way and plotting, and ending up by doing exactly the things for which I had blamed the others.

In 1950, with the help of some friends and certain national leaders, I founded the United Nations Student Organisation of India. I was conscious of the vacuum in the hearts of young men like myself who, having achieved independence, had nothing else to live for and suffered from a sense of frustration. An organisation of this kind could mobilise our energies for the unity and peace of the world. I also thought that political divisions made it necessary that both in the world and in my own country our activities should be non-political, but that cultural exchanges would help us to reach our aims.

At about this time, a campaign was started in India to win over the hearts and minds of the young to the ideology of communism. I was completely ignorant of the extent of these efforts.

We began to get in touch with the different Western Embassies in New Delhi in order to tell them about Indian culture, and they talked to us about theirs. It was useful work. We never went to the Russian or Chinese Embassies because I knew they had something else besides culture.

While we were struggling against the British for the freedom of our country, the communists had co-operated with us; they were already thinking what ideas would control India after she had achieved independence. For a long time, therefore, I had worked closely with the Indian communists with one aim in view—independence.

During the war an interesting thing happened. There was a period during which the Allies fought against Russia, who was then an ally of the Nazis. Then the change-over came and Britain and Russia united to fight Nazism. All the communists who had so far been under arrest were released by the British Government in India, and men like Gandhi and others who did not co-operate with the British were put in prison in their place. Then the communists encouraged us to co-operate with the British in the war effort—in fact to do the opposite of what they had advised up till that time.

I was, above all, a nationalist—I refused to follow them and we parted company. For me my country's independence was more important than the war. I became anti-communist, because I realised

57   E

that their first interest was not India's independence but the triumph of the ideas of Marx and Lenin in the world.

One day I received a letter signed by a lady who was cultural attaché at the Soviet Embassy. The letter said, 'We are aware of the part that the youth of India are playing in the United Nations and for the peace of the world. The youth of the Soviet Union has much to learn from the youth of India and we should be very pleased if you would come to our Embassy and tell us something about your great culture.'

This letter had a considerable effect on me. It was easy enough for the Western Embassies to convince us of their superiority; because it was true we didn't have television sets, washing-machines or jet planes, but that didn't bring us any closer to the West. This letter from the Russian cultural attaché for the first time gave me hope that even we Indians had something to offer to the world. Suddenly all my national pride came to the surface and I said to myself, 'Here, at last, is the chance to prove to the communists that our culture is superior to theirs.'

I collected twenty-five of the most brilliant students of the university who had no more intention than I had of becoming communists. We began to imbibe the philosophy of Marx and Lenin, so as to be masters of the situation, and able to discuss and hold our own in the intellectual fencing which would take place. We were on tip-toe when the great day arrived.

We were greeted in the Indian way, the palms of the hands together, and our hosts spoke fluent Hindi. We were shown into a magnificent room where six tables had been prepared for us with the greatest care. At each of these tables three of us sat down next to three girls from the Embassy staff. We were served vodka and black Russian cigarettes with gold tips. For many of us young students it was a heady experience to be received in this way and to drink vodka and get a taste of all these things for the first time in our lives.

We sat there for three-and-a-half hours and in that three-and-a-half hours the word 'communism' was never once mentioned. When I came away I said to myself that, after all, these men were very civilised human beings and maybe Russia and communism are not as frightful as the Western world made them out to be, and my hatred of communism died.

Next morning in the university restaurant, where we used to meet and discuss everything over a cup of tea or coffee in a cloud of cigarette smoke, everyone was talking about the 'wonderful evening reception'. I began to feel very self-important as the man who had organised an evening that had become the topic of discussion for the whole university.

Then I went a step further. I picked up the telephone to thank the lady at the Russian Embassy and we arranged to hold further monthly meetings with more of our students at the Russian Embassy for cultural exchanges, and I made the same arrangements with the Chinese Embassy.

Some of the men who were invited at this time to these two Embassies are today amongst the best-trained fighters for communism in India, and hold important positions in the Government, Press and trade unions of my country.

Some months later in Europe, I was to meet three of these young men at the University of Paris. I tackled them straight away on the subject of their political activity. 'What are you doing in this bourgeois city of Paris? Why don't you go to Moscow?' They replied: 'Men like you who are not yet convinced about communism ought to go to Moscow. We are here for a definite reason—to meet, convince and train the nationalist leaders of North Africa, so that they can go back to that continent committed to our way of thinking.'

This shook me. I suddenly woke up to the fact that even during the period when I was making anti-communist speeches, they had made use of my weak points, such as my taste for drink and expensive cigarettes and my vanity and ambition, in order to seek out and train communists who would know how to win not only my country but also another continent besides our own.

I was busy at the centre of my student organisation, with the legislative elections and a seat in Parliament in my mind which would be a stepping-stone to higher things. But the better known I became, and the nearer I got to my objective, the less interested I seemed to be in the ordinary man. Deep inside I was not satisfied: I was coming up against problems of jealousy, competition and place-seeking which were dividing us, and each was wasting his time and energies trying to get ahead of the other. I was making speeches about the United Nations Charter and the peace of the world, but the fourteen members of our Executive Council could find no concord amongst themselves, and every meeting left us more divided and confused.

At that time, in spite of our divisions, we convened the Conference of Asian Students to find solidarity and unity. I was on my way to the hall, where Mr. Nehru was to preside at the opening meeting, when a friend of mine stopped me to ask if it would be possible to get invitations for three friends from the West. I was able to arrange this, so that they were present at the conference.

At the end of the first session everybody hurried out to see the Prime Minister and other distinguished guests to their cars. Then I walked back to the hall to see if everything was all right. To my great surprise I found my friend and his three guests obviously still waiting for me, for they came quickly to meet me. They said, 'We just stayed behind to thank you and to say how deeply we appreciated being invited.'

I was astonished. Such a thing coming from the white races was unexpected. The kind of people from the West that I was accustomed to see on our streets had a pipe in their mouth, a whisky bottle in their hip pocket and a pretty girl at their side, and they put on an air of superiority, looking down on us as much as to say: 'You natives!' These people thought of our country solely in terms of getting as much out of it as possible.

This view of things obviously gave me little liking for Western democracy or for the Western way of life.

Then they took two invitation cards from their pockets and invited me to a play called *Jotham Valley* that was being shown in New Delhi. Saying how busy I was with the conference I told them I did not think it was possible for me to see the play. 'We quite understand,' they said. 'In that case give the cards to two of your friends. But we hope to welcome you, and thank you again for inviting us today.'

The next day one of my appointments in New Delhi was cancelled. When I looked in my diary to see what else I had to do, I found the *Jotham Valley* invitation and as I was free, and the theatre was close by, I walked in just in order to pass the time. I was interested at once. There was catchy music and in many places the dialogue was humorous. The story was about two brothers who began by hating each other and finally found a deep love for each other.

As I watched, I thought how much the relationship between myself and my father resembled that between the brothers. We lived under the same roof but I never felt comfortable in his presence, and we had grown further and further apart over the years.

Occupied solely in the struggle for my country's independence, and with other political activities, I had no longer had time to think about God or morals. Whenever that subject cropped up, I used to brush it aside, saying to myself that I would think about it when I was sixty and had nothing else to do. Morals and God were dull enough subjects, even rather embarrassing, and yet, all at once, as I sat watching this play, something began to spark inside me, which I cannot explain. I began to recognise something in the faces of these actors, something that reflected their joy in living and the adventure of life. They were not professionals. They were seeking a new way of life, more satisfying than ours. Their voices and faces showed that they had already found it.

That evening at home, for the first time, I asked myself where I was going, what were my aims and my motives. Sentences from the play kept coming into my mind: 'God has a plan. He loves you and He loves your nation. Life can never be dull with Him; but it can be full of worries and confusion and purposeless without Him.' All these thoughts kept turning over in my mind.

Next morning I woke up with a longing to take all my time to sort out these things in my own heart and mind. After the play one of the actors had suggested to me that I should sit quietly with a piece of paper and a pencil and examine my life in the light of the four moral standards of absolute honesty, purity, unselfishness and love, so that the channel between God and me should be cleared. Then little by little I would find His full and satisfying plan for my life and become part of His plan for my nation.

I wanted to try it. I had always thought of myself as a fairly decent fellow. Certainly, when the interests of my country demanded it, I had not hesitated to do the dishonest thing. Comparing myself with others I didn't think I was too bad, and I even knew others who had done much worse things than I had.

But that morning, as I looked back on my life, I realised that I had turned my back on God and was aimlessly running around. Then I took a look at my behaviour towards my father, and for the first time I was ashamed of the lies I had told. It was obvious that the present state of affairs would continue indefinitely unless I talked to my father. Without waiting, I opened the door to go into his room; he was there in front of me . . . and I pulled the door to behind me and went out again. I could not face it. I made another attempt the next day, but talked with him about everything except the things I wanted to tell him.

At that point an inner voice was saying, 'Don't be silly, this is just a phase and it will blow over.' Another voice said, 'Today you are face to face with a choice which will involve your whole life. You can find a new peace, a new purpose and a new passion, and help your country to find the answer to her troubles.' As hours went by, my struggle with myself became more violent. Exhausted from the conflict, I prayed and said to God, 'I do want to make a fresh start but I am afraid and I need Your strength.' As I stood up I knew that the fear of my father and all bitterness against him had gone, and that I loved him. I found I could sit down beside him and tell him things which I had carefully kept from him and which I had hoped to keep secret for the rest of my life. There was a silence. Neither of us knew what to say. Then I said, 'This is the kind of son I have really been, I have had three personalities: what I thought I was, what others told me I was, and what I really am.'

That day I discovered myself for the first time. I also said that I was determined to be different and to make a fresh start, and that I needed his help and the help of God.

Suddenly I felt close to my father as though a great wall and barrier broke between us. There was a power at work in my heart and in his. It could not be expressed in words but I was happy and full of life.

I had found an aim for my life and God used me, not only in my family, but in my country and in the rest of the world.

For the first time I had had a spiritual experience and felt deeply that it had also a universal application. I no longer thought that faith was all very well when you reached sixty years of age; for me it had become an immediate need, a basic necessity of life. And it was from the West, whose films have glorified violence and crime, divorce and drink, that had come this wonderful idea which my country could use to create national unity. We were even, strange as it may seem, challenged to live what Mahatma Gandhi taught us.

Every last shred of bitterness had gone. That does not mean that I was won to the West: democracy as practised in the Western countries did not interest me very much, but I was no longer an enemy of the West, seeking revenge for a painful past.

A little later I had an invitation to come to Europe. I was the first of our family to leave my country and my mother found it hard to let me go. As the time of separation got near I often found her in tears. When I left I asked her what gift I could bring her back from Europe. Her reply was that of a typical Indian mother when her children leave for the West: 'I do not want anything, but make me three promises, first of all that you will never eat beef—remember that your religion forbids it; that you will never accept alcoholic drinks or cigarettes, I know these are part of the Western way of life and that many young Indians find it normal to accept them and so break their mothers' hearts; and that you will never have a close relationship with any European girl.'

Thanks to the experience of the months that had gone before I was ready to promise these things. I have found strength through these decisions which I took for my mother's sake to resist some of the most dangerous temptations the Western world could offer. I understood many things, and I began to feel a real affection for the Western nations growing in me as I saw the problems they were up against. I had been like a frog in a pool, who thinks only of his pool and imagines it is the whole universe.

Of course I am still a nationalist. I love my country more than ever and long to see that every Indian finds justice and equality and the best possible way of life. But I know that can only happen if I see the needs of the world as a whole, and if I love other nations as much as my own.

In the course of our journeys we found ourselves staying at Addis Ababa in the same hotel as seventy-three Chinese artists from the Pekin Opera. In the evening we were invited to see this opera, and the next day to a reception given in honour of the Chinese delegation. The first person to whom we were introduced was the head of the delegation. We had a fascinating conversation. I said to him, 'I am myself a revolutionary and I have followed the social development of our Chinese neighbours ever since the revolution. Have you been able to eliminate selfishness in your social life?' He answered with a smile, 'Oh, we got rid of all the selfish people by making a present of them either to Formosa or America.' 'A good answer,' I went on, 'we did somewhat the same, we got rid of the British, but we have since realised two things: that the British took their selfishness with them to some other part of the world; and we find now they are gone and we begin to govern ourselves that we are by no means lacking in selfishness. We have only succeeded in transferring the disease from one part of the body to another: the poison is still there.'

The Chinese offered me a cigarette. 'We don't smoke,' I said, 'all our pocket money goes into the revolution which can bring a cure to selfishness.' This statement was hailed with a burst of laughter, as the leader of the Chinese delegation was a chain smoker. He was obviously longing to know to what revolution I was referring. We talked to him of the great revolution which dared to deal with human nature and change it and bring a cure to selfishness in Americans, English, Indians and Chinese. A light of hope came in his eyes when we brought up this major problem of the communist world: how can you create a society without class problems except by creating a new type of man, freed from selfish preoccupations and self-interest?

My heart is full of gratitude for one man from the West, Frank Buchman. Around him are gathered men and women of all races, nations and classes who are giving back hope, faith, unity and health to the world. The most precious possession I have is a faith that is strong enough to meet the crisis in the world today.

I believe we are faced with a choice which either way demands our whole being; communism and a world in which man rules all-powerful, or freedom and a world where man is guided by God. It is normal living for men and nations to be guided by God. So a new world can be created.

What a magnificent adventure to have a part in such a task!

R. D. MATHUR
India

TWO ESCAPES TO FREEDOM

I was born in a town on the Algerian Coast, Bougie, which was at one time the capital of all the Eastern Maghreb, that is to say of all Algeria, and a centre of cultural enlightenment for the whole of North Africa. The inhabitants have for a long time called the town Little Mecca, on account of the number of saints who lie buried there.

This splendid past, told in Arab poems, filled me with so much pride that as a child I would learn them by heart when I found them in the library of my home.

My father's family were magistrates and Imams. The memory of my great-grandfather is still venerated. My mother bears the name of Abdel-Mumin El-Muhades, the Emperor.

I owe my first knowledge of Arabic to my father. He entrusted me at the right moment to a Koranic school, where I learned the whole of the Koran at the age of eleven. Then I studied French in a state school whose director prepared me for the teachers' training college. However, as I desired to study both cultures I went to the Medersa where, after six years of work, I got a diploma which gave me a choice between the law or teaching. My father wanted me to be a magistrate, because he was one; but I chose to be a teacher, because I wanted to meet the great needs of the people for education.

When I got my appointment I organised, in addition to my official work, classes for children who had been abandoned. But I was prevented from continuing this voluntary work by a directorial decree which forbade me to teach during the official hours of the classes.

I worked in four different localities and everywhere interested myself in all educational methods, I encouraged or founded an independent school, a troop of Scouts, a cultural circle and taught in classes at the Mosque.

Later I was transferred by the administration to a village in the south of Algeria, a place to which politicians were exiled. This faced me with a dilemma of conscience: to accept was to encourage injustice; to refuse was to bring down sanctions on anyone who followed the same line of conduct as myself. I thought of resigning, but under pressure from my relations and friends, I asked to be given leave of absence. I learned several years later from an Examining Judge that this village appointment was made because I had not used my voting paper at the election.

What was important was that this made me see the contradictions in politics. I looked for a remedy. However, having to make a living, I undertook the running of the newspaper of an Islamic association for reforms, whose ideas for emancipation I shared. But I had to give up this job to devote myself to the Algerian Moslem Scouts, whose spiritual director I was. The French administration wanted to eliminate all Nationalist elements. The refusal of the great majority of the scout leaders to accept this produced a crisis. I was unanimously elected President. Then the movement was exposed to the hostility of the administration: subsidies were refused, permission to hold rallies and take collections was refused, there were expulsions of Scout camps by the police, and organisers of the Movement were intimidated or dismissed.

All this finally made me decide to carry the fight into the political sphere. I thought we could organise our society, in all fields, for the true interest of our people only if we were really free. My conscience called me to fight for the freedom of my people, unshackled by colonialism.

Not having been able to accomplish anything through the non-political Islamic organisation I have already mentioned, I started an independent newspaper with the help of one of the Nationalist parties and demanded a revision of the relations between France and Algeria on the basis of the charter of Human Rights.

I was exposed to vexations: the distribution of my paper in certain localities was hampered and I was summoned to meetings in the Offices of General Information. When the armed revolt broke out in 1954 I was arrested during the first week by the D.S.T. (Défense de la Sécurité Territoriale). These people tortured me. The torture consisted in applying to the nose and mouth of the victim, who was naked, a hose from which a jet of ice-cold water shot out with great force. When the victim had fainted he was revived with blows on the head and back. I had to submit to this three times. After this, electric shocks were applied to my kidneys which made me fall unconscious. This proceeding, which began again every time I recovered consciousness, was repeated until I could not come round any more. After this I received blows on my face, head and stomach. I saw Death. I prayed to God. The torturer said, 'Do not pretend you are dead. . . . You have faith. . . . Tell your God to deliver you.' Then he threatened to throw me into the sea. I learned later that a young Algerian intellectual from Oran suffered this tragic fate on this spot, as was reported by a Parisian weekly paper at the end of 1955. God saved me from this, as He saved me later in similar circumstances.

After this interrogation I was brought before the judge, who told me I was 'guilty of an attack on the safety of the State'. I was taken to prison and treated as a common criminal. After two weeks of solitary confinement I was allowed out for half an hour each day in a courtyard which the sun never reached. Gradually the numbers of those detained in prison increased. One day I met a young man in the courtyard who said, 'It's you who got me into prison.' 'But,' I said,

'I have never met you, nor told you to make any attack of any kind on anyone.' 'It was reading your paper that made my blood boil,' he replied. These words made me think, as did those of the Examining Judge who said to me, 'There are Scout leaders in the underground movement and you are the man responsible.' And yet my struggle both in the Scouts and in journalism had been inspired purely by humanitarian considerations. I had thought seriously on the best ways of teaching great truths.

After four months of detention I was granted limited freedom. When one of my lawyers, who was a Christian, asked me what steps I was going to take against those who had tortured me, I said, 'They are perverted creatures who have lost their humanity and all sense of the divine and their state needs more than anything else something to restore them and to get the poison out of their systems.' He answered, 'Do you know what you have just done? You have given me a lesson in Christian charity.'

A few months after I had been set free, I met a young man who talked to me of a fresh discovery: it concerned a journey he had made to Europe which had enabled him to find a revolutionary quality of life which was ideal for those who realised the necessity for a moral and spiritual renaissance in the world. Conscious of my anxieties on this subject, he said, he had come to find me so that I could partake of this knowledge. My curiosity was greatly aroused, and this impelled me to visit Caux in Switzerland in the early part of September 1955. I arrived very sceptical and suspicious. After all my enthusiasm for the United Nations Charter and the Declaration of Human Rights, I was discouraged to see that these were not being applied in my own country, and above all that those who clamoured for their application exposed themselves to government hostility.

When I got to Caux I found myself in the midst of people from all nationalities and beliefs. The first thing that struck me was to see the English and the Africans from South Africa united together and both prepared to admit to each other where they had been wrong. An African student said that his bitterness had been so great that the complete disappearance of the British Isles under the waters would not have been enough to satisfy him. Another confessed that he was studying physics with the object of learning atomic secrets so that he could one day make the British Isles disappear. A white couple from Kenya recognised their responsibility for Mau-Mau, and this in spite of the fact that the wife's father had been killed and sacrificed by the Kikuyu to their gods, because he was the worthiest white man they could find to offer up. A young black African and his sister, whose father had been killed by Mau-Mau, found they had lost their bitterness after they realised they themselves had no answer to division and hatred. All had found this secret of a change of heart which brought unity and peace. These living examples of real change of heart in men and women who found themselves in circumstances where it is usually very difficult to listen to the voice of God and the counsels of wisdom, bowled me over. I was convinced of the possibility of changing human nature and of the efficacy of the experience taught at Caux.

I had a meal with some French people and I told them my story and of the recent events in my country. They were deeply touched and begged my pardon for all that had happened. When I said that they were in no way responsible for the situation in Algeria, they stated that it was their way of life that had made it possible for their compatriots to get into this false position. A French Deputy, with whom I had an interview, wrote an article in his paper telling my story; this was reproduced in *Le Monde* of 2nd September, 1955.

After ten days at Caux, I returned to Algeria sorry that I had not had this experience earlier. Two weeks after my return the French police of my town came to tell me that I was to be subjected to an expulsion order under this heading: 'Presence likely to impede the work of the authorities.'

I left Algeria at the beginning of October 1955, and went to Paris, intending to go on from there to Cairo. I asked for a passport, and was required to wait three months for this in Paris. So I stayed in order to conform with this request. A few days later I met some friends from Caux. I learned that two hundred people from there were on their way to Paris. I had the thought to wait for them. It was then that I understood the importance of the work of Caux on a world scale; and I had the hope that this quality of life, which reflects the true values of civilisation, would become a reality everywhere. It could only be in a world living like this that my country would know peace and unity; realising that, in the age of ideologies, my country and the world were interdependent, I decided to fight with these men for a new era. The one thing that made me hesitate was my bitterness towards the West, because of Western colonialism, against which I had always struggled.

One can fight for what is right without bitterness. In our case I realised that to cure this bitterness already resolves half the problem; the other half, which is the source of this bitterness, lies in the spirit of domination, which is also curable. Having seen that a Western man freed from a desire to dominate, and an African freed from bitterness, can find unity, I discovered that to fight one for the other is more advantageous to humanity than fighting one against the other, and that to change enemies into friends is the highest moral service human beings can perform.

The living examples I saw of this change strengthened my confidence and faith. French and Algerians could, like other men, have this experience. From this, fresh regard would be born, and as a result a new Algeria would spring up. Finding myself in Paris, in a room full of people from all walks of life, I spoke and asked forgiveness of the French and the men of the West for my past bitterness towards them. I offered them my hand in brotherhood so that together we might battle for this spirit, which alone could achieve real peace. The audience was very moved. French people got up to express their feelings and to speak of their determination to fight for the same spirit.

The results of this decision when known in my country, where bitter passions had been unleashed, can be imagined. At this moment, my wife and four children were in Algeria. My eldest son, aged eleven, kept up the family correspondence with me. Two friends saw to their material wants. When they learned what I had said they withdrew their help. The letter from my son which gave me this news showed his great anxiety in the question, ' What are we to do? ' I replied, ' Do not think about money. Think about God and He will provide for you.' A few days later I learned my family had been offered a considerable sum of money from old pupils of mine who lived near by, and who had all made spontaneous contributions. Later my family became alarmed at the perquisitions being made in their neighbourhood by the army. I decided to move them to the home of my brother who had lived for twenty years in Morocco.

Then I went to the United States to take part in a conference for Moral Re-Armament to which I had been invited. While I was in New York in February 1957, the Algerian question came up before the United Nations. I went to listen to the debates. I met two delegations from Algeria. Each of these denied the rights of the other to represent the Algerian people. There was no link between them. I tried in vain to bring them together.

After four months in the United States I returned to Morocco. A few weeks later I was called up on the telephone at night. I went to the Post Office but no one was on the line. I returned home. I found a neighbour standing outside with someone else beside a vehicle. I shook hands with them and suddenly I was surrounded by five men pointing their revolvers at me. They fastened my hands behind my back with handcuffs and I was taken away in the vehicle to an empty farmhouse where I passed the night. The moon was up and I lay watching the rats jumping and listened to the hissing of snakes. At the point of a revolver I was made to write a letter to my brother saying I had suddenly left the house to serve my country. This was on the eve of the 14th of July.

Next day I was taken to Rabat and shut up in a cell. Someone who seemed to be the leader of the troop, and whom I knew was responsible for one of the big national organisations, came to greet me respectfully and to tell me that the heads of his organisation would like an interview with me. I objected to the way they had behaved in order to obtain this interview and reminded him that I had myself been to their office in Rabat to see them, but after a long wait had been unable to find the person with whom I had made an appointment, and that I had every intention of meeting them, as I had nothing to conceal from anyone. 'We know your high moral sense, your grand fight, your past which is without stain or blemish. All this will guarantee that no harm will come to you,' he said. He gave me some clothes, because I had been taken away in my 'gandura'. I said my prayers, and then was taken to Oujda. The driver turned to me and said, 'I am an old pupil of yours and I know your moral strength. We know how to appreciate men. We do not like injustice. You will be treated as a guest.' At Oujda I was shut up in a remote house. I received each day some bread and two sardines from a tin, but I preferred to have a glass of water and dip my crust in this. Five days later the Commissar of the group, with ten armed men, came and in a threatening way interrogated me on my activities, after removing my shirt and tying my hands together behind my back with handcuffs. Two weeks later the man who was responsible for this national organisation in Morocco, armed with a machine gun and a whip, came in his turn to interrogate me. He told me that he had received from his New York representative a letter alleging that I belonged to the organisation opposing them (although I was, and am, independent, without being for or against either of these adversaries, being convinced of the possibility of *change in each one which can bring constructive unity*). Then, having been tortured and threatened with death, I was asked where I would go if I were free. I replied, ' I would continue my battle for the Moral Re-Armament of the world.' I returned to my cell with my body covered in scars and pains in the stomach and head caused by the pommelling I had received.

Later those Algerians who were the leaders of the army of liberation were brought to this prison. After being detained for six months, one of them suggested we should escape, reminding me that our imprisonment was neither fair nor in the interests of the people and that it was the intention of our captors to do away with us. I answered, ' God knows better than we do what we ought to do and what is right. He has brought us here for a purpose which is not yet clear to us. We will pray to Him to ask to be shown what to do now : if it is right to escape, we shall escape : if it is right for us to stay, we will stay.' We prayed. That night I saw in a dream that I was escaping with a friend over ground covered with green grass, and that we were being pursued by a huge serpent who was unable to catch us. The following day I said to my friends that God gave us permission to go, that we should be followed by our enemies, but that we had the promise of divine protection. A few days later we escaped, in daylight, having disarmed and bound the guards. We followed a path that took us over desert land, clothed with green grass.

We separated in Casablanca, having met our enemies and yet escaped from a tragic fate. I went home and was received as though I had returned from the grave. A few days later I decided to leave Morocco.

While I was abroad I lived in a state of considerable anxiety over the friends I had left. I never ceased to pray for them. Later I learned that they had been able to leave Morocco a month after I did, and that they also were abroad. I saw clearly the truth of the divine promise and I understood the power of prayer and of faith in God, grasping this great truth that ' miracles come with unconditional obedience to God's will'. We learned, after our escape, that plans had been made to execute us two days later. Five weeks after, my friends were fired on at short range, but God protected them. How is it possible to explain this, except as a miracle?

Philosophical speculations are useless here. The power of prayer was shown on other occasions. We were held prisoner but constantly moved. Our quarters were changed four times. We were brought one night to a dentist's surgery from which everything had been removed. We were shut up in a room with all the windows stopped up. There was neither air nor light. One of us took a broom to sweep the floor. A great dust arose which choked us, and we asked the guard to let us out to the wash-place, that we might wash and get a drink. He simply banged the door. Someone suggested we should curse him, and I told my companion, we are oppressed people, and I recalled the words of the Prophet, 'Fear the curse of the oppressed because there is no veil between him and God,' and that we should not curse him but pray that he might go away and not return to be our jailer. We said this prayer. After that night we did not see him again.

Prayer was also our moral strength. Prisoners would be removed from the cells at night; in the morning nothing would be left but their clothes. We then suffered fearful emotions, thinking our turn would come next. I cannot express the sorrow I felt when I learned, from a fellow prisoner, of the torture and death in Morocco of an eminent lawyer from Oran, a true patriot. I thought I should suffer the same fate. It was prayer alone, and faith in God, that gave us courage and strengthened our hope that we should be delivered from our captivity. After a time of early morning meditation, I had the thought that the true prisoner is not the one held between four walls, but he who is the victim of his ambitions, his fears and his bitterness. I experienced a great freedom of spirit. All the prisoners to whom I confided this thought, much to their astonishment, experienced this same sense of relief. I encouraged them to pray and they decided to do this regularly. There were amongst our ten guards five who used to come and pray with us. The others were astonished to find that 'the prison was changed into a mosque'. Each new prisoner, whether he was simple or educated, came to say his prayers with us, and even those who had never prayed in their life, learned to do so with much confidence and faith in God. A young man who had nearly died under torture, came after he had recovered, and told us of his joy at finding himself in 'a school' and not a prison. He would pray fervently and recite the Koran.

I understood the strength of faith that is lived, and the dangers of having a spirituality which does not affect our living. There are people who believe it possible to act inconsistently towards God with impunity, because Divine Justice, which is immanent, often works slowly; yet this inconsistency with oneself, when it is deliberate, turns into a kind of moral cheating. Proclaiming principles of independence, and emancipation, and yet scoffing at them in practice; condemning torture and assassination, and yet coldly perpetrating them—these things have led us to an alarming situation. If the loss of human life and the huge expenditure of money are deplorable, the destruction of the values of civilisation is a more serious loss than all the rest.

Such is the end to which manners and morals have come in the service of the intellect. What would the world be like if the intellect was the servant of morals? It is only when we are sincere in our meditation that God can give us light. In my position, all that I had seen and suffered since my enlistment in the fight for national liberty made me reflect on this fight, and on the need to be consistent with oneself about one's fate and that of one's country.

How to bring true freedom to Algeria? Those who are enslaved by ideas of domination, exploitation, superiority, cannot give this. Only really free men with pure hearts and clean hands can bring this freedom to their country and the world. It is for this true freedom I have decided to battle. In my struggle for my ideas and convictions I have suffered greatly and been brought twice face to face with death. While waiting for death, this thought came to me, 'You are nothing and you have nothing: God is the only Truth. It is only He who gives meaning to your existence. Life has no value unless it is fed by an idea inspired by God.' The knowledge of this truth gives me the faith to live.

In the light of all this I must say that, in respect of all that has happened to me, from the French on the one hand and from the Algerians on the other, I acknowledge some responsibility for all this, because I have not known how to carry on the fight so as to bring unity. I know now that unity one with another comes from a change in each. It is said in the Koran, 'God only changes the condition in which men find themselves if those men decide to change themselves.' I know for my part that I have to begin with myself. I know how costly this is. I have decided to pay this price in order that the will of God shall be done.

MAHMOUD BOUZOUZOU

AT SESTO SAN GIOVANNI—
SOMETHING NEW IN THE PRESS

My life spans the last half century of the history of Sesto San Giovanni. They have been years of strife and division, ideological and industrial. I have seen the birth of Fascism and the rise of Communism during this period. I have seen our town grow from a population of 8,000 at the beginning of the century to 50,000. Another 30,000 swell these numbers during working hours, travelling daily to the town's huge factories. Sesto San Giovanni, so named from the fact that it lies six kilometres from Milan, is the largest single concentration of industry in Italy. Among the most important companies are Falck Steel, Marelli Electric, Breda Locomotive and Pirelli Rubber.

Looking back on my life today my most vivid memories are of the times I escaped from death. I was only four on the first occasion. I had fallen into the canal. The current was swift and I would have been sucked down into a subterranean passage had not my father succeeded in fishing me out at the last moment.

I have only one brother left, although we were a family of eight; six of my brothers and sisters died before any of them were a year old. Later, when I was an electrical technician in a power station I was twice almost killed by electrocution. Once I was left for dead but survived miraculously. Later still, when I was working in a steel factory, there was a serious accident in which several workers were trapped in a gas-filled tunnel beneath the factory furnaces. When I got to the scene one man was still lying unconscious inside. No one made a move towards him. A voice inside me said, 'Go down.' I went down and in the end was able to rescue the man, although overcome by gas myself before reaching the tunnel entrance. Finally, during the war, my life was in constant danger on account of the Secret Police.

When I was still at school my father wanted me to become a doctor, but my passion was to dedicate myself to the field of invention. By dint of experiment in many spheres I succeeded in establishing eighteen patents. Among my inventions during the Second World War was a torpedo of a special type. I went to the War Ministry and we tried it out. But one night in a dream I saw a sea full of drowning people, reaching out towards me and crying for help. Night after night I saw these figures pointing to me and crying out, 'Murderer, murderer!' Thank God we never put that invention into action! I felt that God had intervened, the God who has put His hand in mine, every now and then, all through my life.

I was head of the Boy Scouts of Sesto San Giovanni when I first came into contact with Fascism. We had a hall in a building which also housed the local headquarters of the new Fascist organisation. I was invited to join it. When I saw the constant bullying tactics and violence I decided it was not the right way for Italy.

I had always been an idealist and it was this which drew me towards Communism. When I was working in the Falck Steel Company, the class war was the subject of every discussion among the workers and I began to study the Marxist ideology. I believed in brotherhood and fought for it with the Communists from that time on.

It was during this period that I lost my faith. My uncle was a priest. It was he who baptised me with his own name. It was he also who married me, and the ceremony had been the most magnificent that the Church has to offer. My uncle was deeply hurt when he saw that I was losing my faith. Five years ago he gave me a pressing invitation to attend the celebration of his fiftieth anniversary as a priest. At that time he was a Canon of Monza Cathedral. To please him I finally consented and participated in the Pontifical Mass even though I was an atheist.

It was some two years later, I noticed some posters announcing a musical play, *The Vanishing Island*. It was being presented by an international group of Moral Re-Armament, of which I had never heard. As the owner and co-director of *Informatore*, a weekly newspaper I had founded some years earlier, I decided to go along and report on the play. A huge crowd, kept in order with difficulty by the police, blocked the street outside the Teatro Elena. I easily obtained entrance by showing my Press card.

At the start I was very sceptical and wondered what their game was. Could it be American propaganda? However, as the play proceeded I realised it was not propaganda at all, but the presentation of a new idea which moved me deeply. The first and second acts showed the fact of the world as it is today in stark reality. At the end of the third act it seemed that the public, composed mostly of workers, would never stop applauding. But I remained in my seat, lost in thought. One thing filled my mind: 'What a magnificent idea! If only it were true! If only men and the world could find understanding at last.' At the end of the performance, personalities from many nations and races came on to the stage. In themselves they seemed to represent the unity of the whole world. Their simple and convincing words proved that they had been liberated from all national or racial hatred. I went home that night deep in thought.

The following evening an irresistible inner force led me once more to the theatre. I took my seat as usual in the row reserved for the Press and I watched the play and was completely absorbed once more from beginning to end. I heard again at the end the introduction of groups of citizens from nearly every nation in the world, people who had been able to end the disorder in their lives. It was a marvellous demonstration of the best in humanity.

After the performance the cast came down from the stage and I gathered a group of them around me. They explained that a man can radically change his character and transform his relations with his fellows if he makes use of the following self-discipline: writing down early each morning the thoughts that come to his conscience and then putting them into practice. This will give him the strength he needs to put right the wrongs he has done in the past and to ask forgiveness from those he may have wronged. They said finally that the voice of God can be heard in the silence through the inspiration of these thoughts. 'What a splendid idea!' I answered immediately, but I laughed to myself at the absurdity of the idea of putting it into practice.

I could not help agreeing with them, but inwardly I began to feel very uncomfortable as I realised that there would be difficult decisions for me to make.

Before they left they said that if I had no objection they would visit me in my home. I replied that it was always open to everyone.

One day my door bell rang. I was in a very bad and sombre mood and was writing an article against one of the leading local Catholic newspapers and my article was written to attack the priest who ran

76

the paper. It was headed 'The Bad Priest' and replied to criticism of my paper. Without rising from my desk I called 'Come in'. In came three of the Moral Re-Armament force who had talked with me at the theatre: they greeted me politely and, seeing that I was writing, said in a friendly tone: 'Perhaps you are writing down your quiet time?'

'No,' I answered, rather annoyed, 'I am writing an article against a priest.' 'Indeed, isn't it difficult,' they said, 'to find the way to make peace with bitterness in your heart?'

These simple words of theirs, spoken with sincere regret at what I was doing, made me think of what I had heard at the theatre. These people were certainly better than I was.

I glanced at what I had written, and something I did not understand said to me, 'It is you who are bad.' I still hesitated a moment. The silence around me invaded my heart, and with a sudden movement I tore up my article in pieces.

We looked at each other and no word was spoken. The voice of my conscience showed me the fallacy of my poisonous writings and of my hatred against the priest. I remembered what they had said to me. 'Apologise to those whom you have offended!' But still my human materialism whispered to me, 'Not that! You are an atheist, and he is a priest.' An unequal fight between good and evil continued in me until my conscience revealed itself to me in a stream of memories of my relatives, of my uncle who was a priest. I saw their loved faces, showing me the good road and imploring me to follow it, the road that would make of me a new man and lead me to a new world.

The visit of these new friends and the disturbing stories of wrongs being righted that I had heard made me very thoughtful. I realised that as a man of courage I could not flinch from any challenge. In the end I telephoned the priest and asked to see him. I remember wondering what he was thinking when he asked on the phone, 'Which Rossi is it?' And I told him 'Luigi'. At the time I had a cold and added that I could not stay long. On my arrival I found a fire had been lit for my benefit. After I had apologised and told him my experience we began to talk. We went over much of the past including the inspiration that my uncle's life had been to me. We were together there for three and a half hours. When finally we parted, we had become real friends.

My wife had come with me to see *The Vanishing Island*. When I

77

decided to change she adopted the same course. We had always had arguments over the articles I wrote for the newspaper. She had always been against them. Now all quarrels were brought to an end because she had a new attitude and I found a new way of writing.

A flame of purity had come to win over Sesto San Giovanni. The light of this flame was felt by the 19,000 citizens who applauded the many repeat performances of *The Vanishing Island*.

Nor was the newspaper *Informatore* indifferent to the purifying flame. The first step was to clean up the newspaper by applying the four absolute standards. Inspired by this fresh start, we brought out a special ten-page supplement on Moral Re-Armament. It went into every home in Sesto, bringing an answer to many problems: 20,000 copies were printed and there was a reprint which was sent to all parts of the world, including India, China, all parts of Africa, London, Washington and Moscow.

Then my wife and I decided to accept an invitation to go to Paris, where *The Vanishing Island* was to be shown. I wanted to find out whether the people in the play really lived the life they spoke of on the stage. Watching them, I realised they did. I met industrialists who had changed their ways. They were honest with their workers, had improved working conditions and were paying better wages.

The journey we made to Paris was the first of many we were to make. As our conviction about MRA developed in the months that followed, we went to different cities in Europe with the international force which travelled with the plays. In this way I have had the privilege of meeting men from very different backgrounds and nationalities.

It was during my visit to Paris that one Sunday morning I felt the urge to attend Mass for the first time in many years. My wife and I went to the Cathedral of Notre Dame. To my surprise I discovered that a Pontifical Mass was being celebrated. I therefore took part in a ceremony like the one I had attended at the time of my uncle's fiftieth anniversary. I re-lived the whole experience in a reborn faith. I was so deeply moved that there were still tears in my eyes as I left the Cathedral.

It was in this way that I took my first steps towards a full return to the Church, after many years of estrangement. My uncle had died a year earlier. He had bequeathed to me a statue of the Sacred Heart and one of the Infant Jesus. I had put them away in a store room with other old household articles. One day, some months ago, during a time of quiet, I thought of them again. I had them repainted and regilded by the Sisters of a near-by Convent who specialised in this work. I then gave them to the new church in Sesto San Giovanni. The priest said that he would put the statue of the Sacred Heart in the Chapel, where it would inspire the faith of the young, while the Infant Jesus would be placed on the High Altar during Christmas week.

On 19th October, 1958, my wife and I celebrated our twentieth wedding anniversary. We were in Mackinac Island. It was a deeply moving experience for us both to receive in the wooden church on the island the blessing of the priest, following High Mass. God thus gave me a new opportunity to live through an experience with fervent faith that I had originally lived through as an atheist. The priest also blessed the ring my wife had given me. It was for me the seal of my new marriage in which God was the centre of our lives.

Many people often ask how it is that in this modern age human genius is capable of inventing such a formidable apparatus of destruction, but is unable to unite the world.

But there is a way. My experiences during these last years have convinced me that it would be difficult to find a more sincere fellowship of men, industrialists, bankers, professional men, men of all parties—communists, socialists, conservatives, all are drawn together in a joint effort to bring the cure to the materialism of both Right and Left.

It is the battle for a new world based on new men.

LUIGI ROSSI
Proprietor and Co-director of 'Informatore'

FROM THE COMINTERN TO CAUX
WITH A NORWEGIAN MARXIST

I was not born into Communism. My father and mother were comfortably off and deeply religious. They had a lovely farm with cows, pigs, and eight horses: with fields, a forest and even a fishing lake, in the agricultural and industrial district of Ostfold, in South Norway. I was born in 1892, the fifth child in what was to become a family of fourteen. Life on the farm was a daily adventure. We all helped. I fed the chickens, scratched the pigs on the back and played hide-and-seek in the barn. But my greatest joy was helping Dad with the horses. And then, in the long summer days, we boys played at police and robbers in the forest, went swimming, fishing and rowing, and came home hungry in the evening. Mother always had something good to eat in the kitchen : home-made bread, fresh butter, bacon and eggs, and milk straight from the cows. It was as if the whole world belonged to me.

Then one day something happened. I was ten years old at the time. Father was forced to sell the farm. He had lent money to business-men in the city. They went bankrupt, and there was no other way for us but to sell the farm.

I shall never forget the day we left for the town. It was as if the whole world had suddenly collapsed. We were twelve on top of the carts loaded with furniture, and some of the children were weeping. My eldest brother had to start work as a chauffeur and one of my sisters worked as a waitress in a café. Father got a job at the factory in Borregaard. The work was hard and it was painful to see him in such surroundings. When I stood waiting for him, I used to see hundreds of grey-faced, weary workers streaming out of this dirty factory. At the gate there was a policeman. I had seen the police arrest drunk people in the town. 'It must be awful in there,' I thought, 'and Father having to slave like this ! '

This new life seemed very strange to me. Seeing these hundreds of workers, I think I can say, was for me my first encounter with Karl Marx.

We lived in two rooms and a kitchen, and the three rooms together would have gone into our old kitchen on the farm. We lived on top of each other. Our diet was on the whole meagre, porridge, skimmed-milk and syrup. I remember that my brother and I went now and then to the café where my sister worked because the proprietress was a kind old lady who would say to my sister, 'See to it that the boys get something to eat.'

A few years later things improved. Father and Mother had saved every penny, and with some help Father was able to buy a small farm. He himself continued to work at the factory while we boys worked on the farm. We cut the timber, sowed rye and set potatoes. We acquired a cow, a horse and chickens. Mother went to the market every Wednesday and Saturday and sold fresh butter, eggs and wild berries which we had picked. When I was confirmed, in my fourteenth year, Father drove me to the church in a car.

Now it was I who looked after the farm and the two horses. We also had a small sandpit, and I sold several loads a day, which added to our income.

Then Father became ill. He had an accident in the factory, had to go to hospital and stayed there for a year and a half. Since the factory refused to accept responsibility for the accident, we were forced to pay the expensive hospital bills ourselves. We did not have enough cash, so the horses had to be sold. We lost everything a second time. I had to start working in the factory. To me it was as if evil had been let loose and I had been sucked into a maelstrom. At seventeen I took my first job in the huge Borregaard factory, and I shall never forget the steamy atmosphere, the noisy machines and the men who were like prisoners. I began to work at a paper machine on shift work; day work for one week, night work the next, twelve hours at a stretch and also overtime. The factory was owned by a foreign firm, T. Kellner Partington, Paper and Pulp. I felt miserable and physically ill in the factory and the whole social system made me boil with rage. This was my second meeting with Karl Marx.

My brother Kristian had also started work on the paper machine in the factory, and while the machine was running he would read the Communist Manifesto and other Marxist pamphlets with the help of a dictionary. I read them after him and was completely captured by Marx's criticism of capitalism, for it exactly corresponded with my own experiences. I enlisted as a Marxist and decided to fight with them. I went to a Communist Party school to receive a basic training in the theory of Socialism and I joined the trade union.

I married in 1914 just as the war broke out. During the war food prices soared, but workers' wages remained static. In my first negotiations with the English directors I made a demand for a weekly rise of two Norwegian kroner. This was refused. I met force with force and declared that we would leave the machines on the following Saturday. We got the rise. But although we had obtained satisfaction, wealth continued to accumulate in the hands of a privileged few while poverty increased among the ordinary people. I had to do my military service but Norway succeeded in keeping out of the war.

One day in 1917 when I was going home in a military transport, I read in a bourgeois newspaper that the Russian revolution had broken out. This made an indelible impression on me. In the Russian revolution I saw the realisation of my dreams for creating the new classless society: this revolution had started with a victory in backward Russia; in spreading to the whole world it must lead to the destruction of the capitalist system and the triumph of the labouring classes in every country.

I fought now on three different fronts; in the trade union, in the factory and in the political movement. The Russian revolution precipitated a conflict inside the Norwegian Labour Party between the group wishing to accept the twenty-one conditions laid down for membership in the Communist International, and those who wished to remain independent. In 1923 the extremists split off to form the Norwegian Communist Party, with myself as a founder-member.

The German working class had met crushing defeats in its struggle, but I was convinced that this was only a temporary setback and that the revolutionary forces would soon advance on a world scale. I therefore joined in the fight with great enthusiasm and joy.

My own factory employed two or three thousand workers. Our Communist cell of no more than seven was able to direct the development of the whole factory. We published a factory paper which had a circulation of one thousand with the guiding principle that mistrust against management is an essential condition for trust among workers.

In 1928 I was chosen by the Norwegian Communist Party to lead a delegation of seven men to the Sixth Congress of the Comintern in Moscow. As we got off the train in Leningrad the scene before me was very different from what I had imagined: many farmers were wearing strange uniforms, and masses of people spread out before me like a grey sea. However, I convinced myself that this was a necessary state on the road to progress, and the Russian revolution would become a blessing, not only for the Soviet Union, but for the whole human race.

Thus I found myself at the headquarters of the revolution with the men who were actually going to take the fate of the world into their hands. But the Congress was far from being united. In almost all the delegations there were rival factions.

At the hotel I lived alongside the German delegation, a small majority of which was led by Ernst Thalmann. The discussion in this delegation lasted far into the night, sometimes developing into shouts and brawls. I thought this odd, but that perhaps it might be a necessary means by which unity could be reached at the heart of the German delegation.

At the Congress there were arguments on which we were sometimes called to vote. We could vote for or against, and even those without a ballot were allowed to raise their hands, so from a democratic point of view there was no fault in the actual procedure. We elected Bukharin as Chairman of the Comintern by unanimous decision, but shortly after the end of the Congress he was deposed by the Comintern Praesidium without regard for the vote of the Congress.

During my stay in Moscow I also had the opportunity to observe a trial which formed part of a great purge. The leaders of the Don Basin coalfield were accused of sabotage. They received their sentence while we were there. Up to the podium marched the accused, each followed closely by a soldier with a fixed bayonet, and ranged themselves in a circle. Vishinsky was both supreme judge and prosecutor. He walked in as casually as though he were going to have a cup of coffee, lit a cigarette, looked at the audience, and nonchalantly read the sentence on each man. As all of them had confessed their crimes, none was acquitted, and none protested against the judgements. Some were sentenced to death, some received long-term prison sentences, some short ones, but the foreigners were judged much less harshly. Out in the streets there were masses of people patiently awaiting the results; as they heard them they protested loudly at the mildness of the sentences. The propaganda and previous similar trials had given the masses such a conception of these criminals that they could not imagine any other sentence except that of death being passed. I was wholly convinced of the guilt of the accused and could not imagine that innocent people might have been condemned as well. I held the same view later during the great purges.

My next visit to Moscow was in 1937. This time I came with a party delegation to negotiate with the Comintern about certain conditions in Norway and also to discuss tasks that the Norwegian Communist Party in particular had to carry out. The French Communist delegation also wished to present a report on the work of their Party. Many delegates from the underground German Communist Party also took part in the discussions. At one point a heated debate arose between these two groups. It had reached its peak when suddenly Stalin, who had been smoking his pipe in the corner without any apparent interest in the proceedings, mounted the platform and said, 'The French are completely right. I declare this debate at an end.' Such was the power and authority Stalin had acquired as a world leader that his word was law, not only in Russia, but also in all the Communist Parties of the world.

The Soviet-Nazi friendship pact brought confusion into many Communist Parties, including our own in Norway. When the German Army occupied Norway the Party suddenly found itself in a difficult and compromising position. Some days after the occupation of Oslo, as German troops were marching towards Ostfold where I was working, I summoned a meeting of all shop stewards in my capacity as Secretary of the District Trades Council to discuss the situation. I proposed that the trade unions and workers' movement should stand firm around the legally elected government, and denounce the Quisling government as a government of traitors, resting on German bayonets. The trade unions, I thought, should be at the disposal of the civilian and military authorities to destroy the Quisling government and expel the Germans from Norway.

A few days later I was visited by an envoy from the Norwegian Communist Party who told me that this resolution was completely wrong. It was the Norwegian Government in power at the time of the German occupation of our country which was to blame: according to them the Nygaardsvold cabinet was actually a cabinet of traitors. We had to fight Quisling and the Norwegian fascists with all possible means, but we also had to try to find an understanding with the Germans and to start to build a new workers' front that could be recognised as a temporary government in Norway. I protested that this seemed to me incomprehensible. I stood by my resolution and put it forward at the next conference with the Norwegian Communist leaders. Great strife resulted in the party ranks on the line to take towards the Germans, but we all agreed that we had to fight the Nazis and the Norwegian Fifth Column.

Despite the pact between the Soviet Union and Germany, the Norwegian Communist Party was dissolved by the invaders and was forced underground. The whole leadership of the party, myself included, were arrested. The Germans first surrounded my home and then broke in, armed with machine guns. It was 4 a.m. My wife and I had stayed the night in a hotel in Oslo, but the telephone had been tapped, and although our names had not been marked on the hotel register, they found us there and at seven o'clock in the morning I heard the sound of heavy boots in the corridor. There was a knock on the door and I said, 'You must be mistaken,' but the knocking grew louder, the door was roughly opened and in stormed Norwegian police and Germans. The room was ransacked. I was ordered to go with the Germans. I asked if I were under arrest. No answer was given, but I was taken to the Gestapo headquarters and immediately interrogated. Later I discovered that all my Party colleagues were there too. Most of the Communists were subsequently freed, but, when the war broke out between Germany and the Soviet Union, many of the leaders were again arrested and the Party was driven completely underground. But internal strife in the Party continued about our national policy. Unity was restored only after Hitler started his invasion of the Soviet Union.

After the Soviet Union was drawn into the war the Communists played an active part in the Resistance Movement. Communists met with Socialists and started to discuss the tasks that awaited them both after the war. One of the first was to find unity in the Labour movement.

When the Second World War ended with victory for the Soviet Union and the democratic powers of the Western world, we thought that we would move towards a quiet period and that it would be possible to build Socialism in an atmosphere of peace and understanding. Negotiations for amalgamation were taken up after the war, but proved fruitless. After the formation of the Comintern in 1947, ideological differences sent Socialists and Communists in opposite directions, thus showing our hopes to have been illusions.

It was at this time that I received my first impressions of Moral Re-Armament. At Christmas 1948 my youngest son gave me Peter Howard's book, *Ideas Have Legs*. In it, the author wrote about ideas on the march and I realised that Communism was not alone in studying the situation in the world and looking for a way to change it. Out of curiosity I read other MRA books and even attended MRA conferences, but I quickly came to the conclusion that the best solution was the one in which I had always put my faith. The class war had to continue; the road to liberation for the working class had to pass through a necessary stage of dictatorship by the proletariat, and that would have to go on until all opposition had been broken.

With this firm basic conviction, in 1950, I came to the ideological training centre at Caux. There I was faced by an ideology I had not reckoned with. In all the years that I had fought for Communism in Norway, members of my family had tried to make me break with the Party, but, because they had nothing to offer me that I could consider superior to Communism, all their good advice had had no effect on me. If anyone had countered my beliefs with an ideology capable of achieving the classless society I dreamed of, then I would have reconsidered my own convictions as to the means to this end. And I am convinced that, even today, had I not met Moral Re-Armament I would still be an active member of the Communist Party.

The way in which I came to Caux was in itself miraculous. I had already had my holiday for that year when my son Frank and his friend Lief Hovelsen came to invite me to Caux. 'Well,' I said, 'if I can go, it would be interesting to see this place, it would be an extra holiday, and if I can get leave from my work I will go with you.' Not for a minute did I think I could obtain such leave, but to my astonishment I was permitted to go with my son to Caux. Here I met Communists, trained Communists from Germany who had already experienced the great uniting force to be found in Caux. One of them asked me whether I considered the capitalist to be a human being. I answered that 'of course the capitalist was a human being but of a particular species who simply could not change his ways, and so had to be crushed and eliminated'. I mobilised all my Communist ideology, my philosophy and instruction in the class war in the sharp discussions that followed, but as I drew comparisons between the Comintern Congress of 1928 and the conference at Caux, I found myself forced to revise my whole conception of class war, to scrutinise the results of Communism so far, and to examine the world as it actually was. At Caux I felt an amazing unity based on love and understanding strong enough to break down all barriers of class, creed and colour. There were no factions in Caux; and even Communists and Socialists found unity.

I also met delegations from Italy, where the class war was extremely bitter. Reconciliations between management and labour took place. Even national frontiers were bridged. I shall never forget the French Marxist who apologised to Germans, of all types, for his hatred of them, and I started to see in practice the ideals for which I had struggled all my life. This inspired me with tremendous hope that true unity could be created on a fresh basis amongst the working

86

classes. I had to ask myself whether one could really arrive at freedom and democracy through dictatorship, whether one could establish understanding by means of hatred, or whether we could build a happy world by liquidating our opponents. Was there an ideology capable of mobilising all the energies of humanity, that longs to build a new world? We have arrived at a point of development where we are on the edge of catastrophe, for in this age continuance of the class war can only lead to a fatal atomic war. If, therefore, we are to realise the greatest hope of the working class, a classless society in which everyone will receive according to his needs and give according to his capacities, we must find a more effective way, a way of co-operation.

After some nights of personal inner struggle, and days of discussion with several German Communists, and with the comparison between the Comintern Congress of 1928 and the conference at Caux always before me, my resistance and reservations were completely demolished and I accepted MRA with all my heart. It was the only revolutionary idea big enough to bridge all differences, an ideology based on absolute moral standards and capable of dealing with human pride. I had spent my lifetime battling to make others change, but only now did I discover the key to that fight. I myself had to change in order to be able to inspire change in others. I had to accept the challenge of absolute moral standards, and give up my own self-will entirely. This is the deepest and most potent revolution, which frees the individual from himself and makes him a new force for the building of the new world.

Earlier I had always believed that, before people could change, a new system had to be created from which private ownership and the possibility of exploitation had been eliminated. It would be this new system which would develop the new type of man, capable of mastering the difficult art of living in discipline and freedom. Experience had shown that Marxism had completely failed on this point and that new systems do not in fact develop a new type of man.

One can socialise, nationalise and rationalise, but the nature of man remains the same—uncontrollable. New differences appear, new classes are created and new difficulties arise.

At Caux I made a statement to this effect which was released to the Press. On my return to Norway I was telephoned by the editor of the main Communist paper *Freedom*, who told me that he had received, through the National News Agency, the statement that I had allegedly made in Caux, and, thinking it was a falsification, he asked me to deny it. To this I answered that there was no falsification and that I stood by the statement as it had been published. He asked me whether I realised that this would hurt the Communist Party in Norway; and I replied that this depended on the way in which the Party received it.

As a member of the Central Committee of the Norwegian Communist Party I was also called in by the Party Secretariat to discuss the matter and seek to arrive at some agreement so that I could continue my work as a Party member. In this conference we discussed the world situation, different concepts of the class war and the dictatorship of the proletariat. It was agreed that I should write a document underlining the points where MRA and Communism differed and where I personally seemed to differ from the Party.

Examining the whole problem thoroughly, I came to the conclusion that nothing would be gained by putting up for discussion any deviations from the Communist Party policy. There had always been deviations and factions and a new round of discussions on this level would lead nowhere. So I came to the conclusion that I would give the Norwegian Communist Party an account of my philosophy of life, and also that of MRA with its absolute moral standards, and leaving no doubt about my own view. In my statement I also asked the question : Is such a way of life incompatible with membership of the Communist Party?

Thinking I should be called before a commission to explain myself further I sat down with several friends and we had a quiet time. The thought came to me quite clearly, 'Stand firmly by the statement you made in Caux. It is right. Stand firm.' And I believe it was this thought that gave me a tremendous power and conviction, as well as what I had seen at Caux, which was the source of an unshakable decision not to turn back. My written statement and question to the Norwegian Communist Party were never answered. However, I got an indirect answer at the next meeting of the Central Committee. I was not invited to the meeting ! Instead, my substitute was called to take my place. He came and asked me what this meant and why I was unable to attend. I said that I had not been asked to go to the meeting at all. He showed his loyalty to me by refusing to attend. The Secretary of the Party then called in a third man who had never been elected, either by the district leaders or by the National Congress.

The District Headquarters, insulted by this act, demanded that the Party leaders come to the District Secretariat to explain their refusal to accept my mandate in the National Committee, where I was an elected delegate. The Central Party leadership refused to do so. Finally I came to the conclusion that I had better leave the Communist Party.

My eviction by the Central Committee gave me proof that the Party did not accept the philosophy of life that I now proclaimed. I stated this as the cause for my resignation from the Party and gave the same reason in a Press statement, the text of which follows:

> My resignation from the Norwegian Communist Party results from my recognition of an adherence to Moral Re-Armament, and still further to the consequences which follow therefrom.
>
> The party received my view on these questions some time ago in a full written statement.
>
> Of course, I could not expect that the Norwegian Communist Party would accept right away as its working basis the policy, in my view a revolutionary one, which Moral Re-Armament represents, but I have always in politics and thinking, openly and without any digression, maintained fully my conviction. This I will continue to do.
>
> After serious and thorough consideration of all the existing problems I have come to the conclusion that the only logical and valid solution is to bring my membership of the Communist Party to an end.
>
> It is, however, my hope that in our country also many Communists, socialists, progressive and unprejudiced people generally will turn out pioneers in the fight for this new thinking, on which mankind and our own common future depend.

MRA was for me a challenge and a test. Again and again I asked myself whether I had failed the workers by embarking on this task of building a new society. But all the experiences I had confirmed that I had acted rightly when I associated myself with MRA and that Moral Re-Armament brings the solution to the problems of our time. I do not regret having fought for social justice and made use of the class war, but I see clearly that if I had met MRA earlier I could have done much more for my class and for my country.

My first meeting with Frank Buchman showed me a very humble man, a man gifted with exceptional affection and understanding for other people, a man who did not think of himself! Once when I met him he looked at me and said, 'I feel there is something left in you of your old life.' That was a very tactful way of putting it. The truth was actually that there was still left in me a great deal of my old life.

The analysis Frank Buchman gave of the world situation when he launched Moral Re-Armament in 1938 showed a unique foresight and this has already secured for him a very prominent place in world history. Karl Marx gave the idea for his time; Frank Buchman has given the peoples and the nations of the world the idea for our time, an idea which is deeper and more all-embracing than Marxism, and one which carries an indwelling power to change human nature. The human race has therefore got a great chance to fulfil its historic mission to turn the tide of history and to build a new world.

The West today is in a very weak position in relation to the East. Its past policies have created in the Asian peoples the greatest mistrust. But East and West need each other. America and Europe must be willing to pay the price for past mistakes, and renew their friendships with the peoples of the East on a new and more constructive footing.

The Asian and African peoples have deep needs and longings. The future of Europe depends on its ability to produce an idea whereby East and West can create a new future big enough to include all men. Nationalism is a mighty driving force for achievement of certain aims. But it is not enough by itself to assure independence, freedom and true happiness. Therefore the East, too, needs an ideological unity founded on absolute moral standards.

The strength of America lies in its economic resources, technological advance and great natural resources. But America's weakness is her lack of an ideology to answer the needs of our time. Only an ideology of world dimension will enable her to gain the trust of the Eastern peoples.

The present phase of Communist development is significant. Communism has the strength today to advance in many parts of the world. The weakness of the West allows this progress to continue, and indeed the inadequacy of the West provides Communism with its greatest asset. But Communism has completely failed to create unity in its own camp. Consequently world control by Communism would not bring eternal peace but constant strife. It carries many contradictions within itself, one being the fact that great material progress has not given birth to the new type of men who can master the situation. New classes come, new differences arise and new problems follow in their wake.

The events in Hungary, the Soviet attitude to Yugoslavia and the conflicts within the Communist parties have not only undermined any hope of peaceful co-existence on the part of the democracies, but disappointed many Communists too, causing them to relapse into apathy. But anti-Communism and apathy bring no solution for former Communists. Anti-Communism is reactionary and cannot solve the conflicts between the Communist world and the free world. To Marxists who have been disappointed by the development of the Communist state we must give a new vision of how they can continue to build a new world.

Inside capitalism also there are many contradictions, and even so-called modern capitalism has not been able to solve the basic problems. Class war will therefore continue with strikes, breakdowns and crises until the answer is found. Production must find a moral aim so that it serves not only the material, but also the spiritual needs of man. This is the preliminary condition needed to establish all co-operation and to eliminate classes and class war, and it is quite separate from the question of private property and altered systems. It requires a new type of man. We have, at all costs, to create this new man if we want to take up the challenge of Communism.

The world today offers great possibilities for good as well as for evil. Science and technology present us with a unique chance for a better future. But we live in fear of tomorrow. The age of the Sputnik, of technical and scientific progress can lead to war and catastrophe in view of all these contradictions, that not only exist but increase. It is man who is responsible for this dangerous and intolerable situation. Human wisdom by itself has not yet resolved the problems which have been raised by the atomic age.

The answer is simple. In order to reverse this situation a complete transformation is required in each one of us. This means our dedication in thought and deed to the four moral standards and the guidance of God. This is the solid foundation on which we can build a world freed from fear, where the needs of all will be satisfied.

HANS BJERKHOLT
Norway

'I DID NOT LOOK AFTER MY PEOPLE'

God in His power, who made the universe, created four things. One He called East, another West, another South, another North. From every quarter men are being brought together by the power which God has given us through the work of Frank Buchman. It is the straight and good road.

Last year I went to Mecca and was given the title of El-Haj. Now I have found this good road.

I am a Chief of the Hausas of Onitsha, which is a big market town situated on the banks of the River Niger, in Eastern Nigeria. I have also been a Member of Parliament, and now sit on the Municipal Council. We have many problems and difficulties in my region.

I had division in my own heart because I had no unity among my people or in my family life. As Chairman presiding over the Court, I have six men to advise me. These men used to quarrel between themselves and were in the habit of taking bribes. They would put off passing judgement in certain cases so that the opposing parties in the lawsuit would have time to increase the sum of money they were proposing to offer as proof of the merit of their cause! That sort of thing made me very angry.

One day, a group of men, Africans and Europeans, came to my home, the Chief's home, in Onitsha. They said they were making a film called *Freedom* which would speak from Africa to the whole world. They asked my help. I called my people together on the banks of the River Niger. The King of Onitsha was there and he also called his chiefs and thousands of his people. I mounted my horse and we spent the whole day helping with the film.

After that I asked the people who were making the film, ' What is it all about? ' I was told of four absolute standards, absolute honesty, purity, unselfishness and love.

When I went back to my home I could not sleep. My whole body was in torment. I got up in the night and woke up my wife. I wrote down these four standards and said, ' They are worrying me. I am not quite sure what is behind this, but look, here they are.' I used to drink beer and do all the things I wanted to do at night in the town. And all this made me restless inside whenever I thought about these four standards. I felt myself cut off from my people, my family and from my wife.

The following day I called my friend. I showed him this thing and he said, 'I have never seen this before.' And then I called four of my Moslem teachers. They started to debate among themselves about what these four things meant and they wondered how they would be able to keep them. They called in others, until there were twenty people. One of them, an old man of seventy-five, stood up and said, 'Yes, this is right. In the Koran there is a text which supports it,' and he quoted it. We were satisfied that this was the truth.

Then I called all my people and we had a mass meeting. I explained all this to them fully and they understood, and as it had worried me, so it started to worry them, and for two days the whole town was talking about it. They said, 'The Chief has brought something we all want to talk about.' After two days I called my people again and said, 'I must go and find out more about this and get to the bottom of it.' They supported me. Twenty-three cars full of people accompanied me sixty-seven miles from my town to the airport, and so I came to Mackinac.[1]

There joy grew in me when I saw men of many different nations who I never thought would agree. I prayed for them and I prayed for my people, that this would increase throughout the world.

After a while I started to hear the voice of God in my heart. When my father, the Chief, died, he left me some money. We were twelve children of one mother. The money was all left in my name. I had not shown my brothers the will. I made excuses and did what I liked with the money. I thought of all this in a time of silence and I wrote a letter to my brothers and for the first time told them the total of this money. I told them that now my heart was free and all that was unclean had left it, and that I felt this money should be divided in three: one-third for food, one-third for our family needs, and one-third to meet the needs of my people.

When I returned home from Mackinac, I called my family together and said, 'I want to be a different man now. I would like you to come along to the bank with me.' There are twelve of us in the family. I said to the bank manager, 'I would like you to give an account of the whole of the finances that my father left here.' And he gave me a full statement in the presence of my brothers.

[1] Where Moral Re-Armament assemblies are held in America.

I said to my brothers, 'Do you hear? Do you see? Now do you understand how much we have here in the bank?' On the way back one of my brothers asked me, 'Why are you doing this?' I said, 'I am doing this because God told me to. It is not good for me to use all this money for myself. You tell me your needs and I will deal with them right away.'

One of them said, 'I thank God. I had already had some thought of killing you. But now I see that you are a different man.' Another said he needed £200 to enable him to get married. A third needed £100 to start a business. They all of them now told me of these things.

When they had finished, I began to feel very sad and I wept, because of the past, understanding now how badly I had behaved towards them. I gave each of them a cheque. From that moment we have felt really united.

The next day they asked me what my secret was and how I had first heard of these four absolute standards. Then I began to translate them into my language so that they could understand. We began to listen together to the voice of God.

The next day this was reported in the newspaper, and the immediate result was that the following day five families ended their quarrels. From this a chain reaction grew throughout the whole town.

There was a certain Chief who was my enemy. If it had not been for the government I would have been at war with him. We were always getting furious with each other. Whenever his men came to my town my men would be straining at the leash to capture them and beat them up. I started to think about this, and said to myself, 'This is not good. Why are we enemies?' Then I took my courage in both hands and wrote him an apology. I wrote twenty-three letters of apology to all those people with whom I had not been on good terms. When I returned to Onitsha I visited them, each one in his own home, and we decided to be reconciled.

I met Frank Buchman several times in Mackinac, and we always talked of my people. I remember one thing which Frank said to me which struck me very much, 'If you want to save your country, you must give yourself to your people.'

As a Chief, I had not given myself to anyone at all. You ask me what I mean. Well, this man was my enemy, this other man was also my enemy, and yet again another man was my enemy too. So I took no trouble about them. When there was a dispute in the town I would send for them, but if they did not come, then I forgot about them. I did not know what was in the hearts of my people. Now I have apologised to all my former enemies and there is no bitterness any more.

Before, as a Chief, I never made any move towards my people. Now if there is any complaint in the town at all, I leave what I am doing and get into my car and go to them. So now, whether it is a young boy or an old man, I know what is in his heart.

One day I heard Frank Buchman say to the Prime Minister of Japan, 'The youth of Japan are learning to go neither to the left, nor to the right, but to go straight.' This troubled me, so I asked Dr. Buchman what he meant by these words. He said, 'You know how it is when you are judging in court and a man comes to you and says, "If I give you this gift will you judge our case favourably?" And another man also comes, and he says, "If we do such and such for you, will you favour us in your judgement?"' 'Yes, I know this,' I answered. Then continued Frank, 'Now, what you need is not to follow what any man wants, but to go straight ahead to what is right.'

Now I and the six men who judge with me listen together to the wisdom of God. We are united and can settle our people's disputes on the spot.

Other Chiefs have come to us from different places to ask how they can live as brothers and we tell them our experience, because it is this that will save my people.

In this way all peoples can find unity, from all the tribes, both Christian and Moslem.

I have told our story to the Federal Prime Minister, and the Prime Ministers of the Northern and Eastern Regions, and they have seen the change in me and know that it is true. God will help this work because it is not the work of our selfishness, but the work of God.

EL-HAJ UMORU YUSHAU
Nigeria

BUILDING THE AFRICA OF THE FUTURE

I've always been a very lucky man. Many have died without seeing history or making it themselves. A man like me has been able to have history recorded in his heart.

I grew up to hate imperialism. Bitterness was a heritage as far as I was concerned. My uncle was a Warrant Chief in 1900 when the white men came to Owerri in Nigeria.

He told me how they supplanted the authority of my grandfather, Chief Egwunwoke, with their own rule. They persecuted and imprisoned him and they used whisky and gin to enslave our people to their will. My uncle showed me the old gin bottles.

At college the attitude of the head teacher, a white priest, did not help to reduce the bitterness I had against the British. He often made use of the cane in punishing people who failed to come up to the standards set in his lessons. On Sunday mornings he said Mass and read the Gospel and said, 'Do unto others as you would have them do unto you.' I failed to identify the reverend father of Monday mornings with the reverend father of Sundays.

The Europeans in the Civil Service lived in what we mostly regarded as paradise. The people in the village had to borrow money to pay their taxes, and by borrowing they became slaves to the money lenders. None of them were able to explain why they had to pay taxes at all.

These things made me begin to feel 'There is no God'. I felt that if there was a God, punishment would come on these people, and it would be immediate.

I left the Church on account of certain atrocities in life that they appeared to condone. They never rose against the imperial power. I felt that as long as the Church did not take steps against these evils, they condoned them. For the same reason I had no use for the Western world: they always seemed to side with those who wronged us.

In 1942 I was near the end of my college course. My friends were moving out into jobs, some of them into the Civil Service. At that time the first Civil Service strike took place, over the demand for a bonus for the workers. Many of my friends were involved in the struggle. There came a day when one of them told me of an underground movement whose aim was Nigerian self-government.

The idol of the youth in those days was Dr. Nnamdi Azikiwe—
'Zik', as we all called him—whose writings and speeches inflamed
the nationalist ardour of Africans everywhere. His newspaper, *The
West African Pilot*, became our bible. After hearing him speak you
left the hall ready to shoot every white man you met. He told us his
own experiences in America and analysed the white man's attitude
towards Africans. A fire was lit in the heart of all young people who
had any patriotic feeling, and the Zikist Movement was born.

I left college to join the struggle, and took a job in the police force,
but at night I met and worked with the Zikists. Our fight was for
self-government, to improve the lot of our people, to build schools
and roads, so that the taxpayer would benefit from the taxes paid. We
felt that the things that had been badly done by the English would
be put right by the African if he governed himself.

We organised ourselves into groups and read the writings of Karl
Marx. We paid for the books by instalments. Marx first interested
me by his choice of words and turn of phrase. A good youth leader
must be able to speak fluently. The phrases in Karl Marx were more
important to me than his thesis.

Then I began to understand. He was propounding a cure. The
class distinction he wrote of I could see all round me. I saw European
hospitals and African hospitals: the 'Senior Service' and the 'Junior
Service' and noted the differences. I noticed that some worked like
beasts of burden while others behaved like masters, and if you said
a word against the imperial power you went to prison.

The jobs I had as a Civil Servant gave me several reasons for desir-
ing bloody revolution. Before my eyes, many youths suffered for
their convictions. Some were beaten with batons by the police to get
confessions out of them. This all heightened and deepened my
acceptance of Marxist philosophy, though I did not agree with some
of his conclusions.

It was unsafe even for two or three of us to meet without Government permission. So we never had a regular meeting place, but varied
it, at times gathering in the bush for fear of being rounded up by the
police.

One night in the bush one of my comrades stepped backwards and
gave a yell. He had trodden on a big snake. We took to our heels.
'We're not much good for fighting imperialism,' gasped one of my
friends as we ran, 'if a snake can scare us so quickly!'

Soon most of our leaders were being thrown into jail. I was in the court when one of my friends was sentenced. He called out to the magistrate, 'If the battle for self-government is a crime, then give me the greatest punishment!'

I had my house searched, but I was careful, and had no documents found with me. Soon I found myself in trouble in a dirtier way. First I was transferred from Lagos, the capital of Nigeria, to the Cameroons, an isolated area, at that time considered only fit for old people to retire to! I called it 'victimisation'.

They sent me first by sea to Port Harcourt in Eastern Nigeria, and then 200 miles inland to Enugu. When I got there I was sent by bus and motor lorry, then over the Cross River to Calabar. From there another lorry took me a further 100 miles to my destination. I was travelling for twenty-eight days. By the end of my journey my personal belongings, my cutlery, chairs and cooking materials, were all either broken or missing.

I felt lonely and destitute. So I took leave, went home on holiday and decided to get married. My people had long hoped for this, thinking it would slow down my political activities. My uncle had made a suitable match for me with the daughter of a neighbouring Chief.

On my return home he met me and made arrangements to take me to meet the family of my future wife in the town of Aba. He was to go by public transport and I was to follow on my motor-cycle.

As a little boy I had often seen my friends dressing up in their finest clothes to meet their brides. I said to myself, 'I won't do that. I'll wear a mechanic's suit when I meet my wife for the first time. Then I'll see whether she's ready to marry me, not just my fine clothes!' I did not know how nearly true this boyhood resolution was to prove. When I was thirty-two miles from Aba I got a puncture. I had in my pocket just four shillings and a jack-knife and at that point it began to rain heavily. For four hours I stood in the rain trying to stop a car and get help. When darkness began to fall I rode eight miles to the nearest police barracks on my flat tyre.

Next day, twenty-four hours later, in my muddy clothes and with a streaming cold in the head, I met my wife for the first time. She never said anything to me, but gave me a cloth to clean up. My uncle was not there, so I decided to go home, though her father tried to persuade me to stay. After four miles I began to run out of petrol, so I had to turn round again. I just got to my future father-in-law's house when the bike finally stopped. 'So you see, you were meant to stay,' he said, and he gave me a bath and a change of clothing.

I have often remembered that adventure since, whenever I have been tempted to wonder, 'Did I make the right choice?' Then I feel again that God had a hand in our starting life together, and that is the foundation of our marriage.

We were married in the Catholic Church at Umodu-Mbierri on 6th June, 1948. My wife was a teacher in a Convent School, and the Convent Authorities and my father-in-law insisted on the Church ceremony. But it meant nothing to me.

I returned to my post with my wife in July. In August, I found myself facing a trial which I felt had been planned during my absence on leave. I was falsely accused of receiving an over-payment of £10 13s. 4d.

Then began a long and bitter process of inquiries and hearings. At one stage a board of inquiry was appointed consisting of five Europeans, which sat for five days, each one receiving about £5 a day, to investigate this matter of the missing £10.

The Commission declared themselves unable to decide who was responsible for the deficiency in the fund. Nevertheless, I was finally brought to trial before a Magistrate. The evidence was only that of one man's word against another's. The Magistrate deferred judgement for three days. At five o'clock on the morning of the third day, a steward boy from the European Club came to my house and told me, 'You are going to be found guilty. There was a meeting in the Club last night. The Magistrate and the Resident were both present and they talked about you most of the time.'

When the Magistrate sentenced me to six months' imprisonment, I was not moved at all. But I was extremely bitter in my heart. As a Paymaster I had been handling thousands of pounds, and to suffer imprisonment over a matter of £10 was the greatest humiliation. Neither my wife nor my mother could understand it. I felt it was worse than to have been charged with sedition.

It was in the spring of 1949 that I finally went to prison after the failure of several appeals. Our first baby was born one week later. I served forty-nine days of my sentence before being released.

But soon I was off again to Lagos, the centre of the political life of Nigeria. My comrades in the Zikist movement were also coming out of prison at that time. We started a newspaper called *The Labour*

Champion, and I became acting editor. To do so I dropped my pay to £6 a month. I did so gladly.

At this point, in 1949, there took place the tragic 'Enugu shootings'. The miners in the Iva Valley were on strike near Enugu. Police turned out with tear gas, batons and rifles against a mob of unarmed demonstrators. The Superintendent of Police gave the order to fire, and twenty-one people were killed.

The ensuing Court of Inquiry declared it to be an 'error of judgement' on the part of the British Police Officer. His punishment was retirement. We of the youth movements felt this called for revolutionary action and that there must be another 'error of judgement' of another kind. It must be an eye for an eye and a tooth for a tooth. This led to the conception of a 'Mau Mau' policy in Nigeria and an ex-Servicemen's wing was organised to see how we could get materials and weapons to fight back.

The first attempt was made on the life of Sir Hugh Foot, then Chief Secretary of Nigeria (now Governor of Cyprus). It was unsuccessful, and the young man who made the attempt was sentenced to life imprisonment.

Our paper, *The Labour Champion,* criticised the findings of the judge. We were charged with sedition, and fined £200, which took every last penny the paper had in the bank and put an end to its existence.

I then determined to go into the trade union movement with a view to organising the working people. I cared about them, and I considered that they would play a decisive role in agitating for self-government in the country. This was also the action taken by most of my colleagues.

In the midst of these battles, my home began to break up. I had left my wife in the village when I came to Lagos. And one day I was shocked to receive a wire from her: 'No longer husband and wife. Your mother has driven me from her house.' I learned that she had gone to live with her father in the town of Aba. Later I heard that she had started teaching again and was living in great poverty. Her father had not been able to keep her and she was on her own, with our baby.

I was absorbed with *The Labour Champion* when I had a wire from my father-in-law saying that my wife was coming to join me at Lagos. I was unprepared and did not really want her to come. I had not enough money to support her. For this reason, after she arrived things grew worse. Our first child was terribly ill, and another baby was on the way.

Dissension arose between us. When she told me how her father had failed to support her, I hated him and wrote him a letter of hatred. The children's ill health, my busy life and lack of money made a breeding ground for misunderstandings. We had three years of mistrust, bitterness and family feud. My wife was suspicious of me, and I lost all confidence in her. When she went home to her family after the birth of our fourth child, our divorce seemed certain.

Meanwhile, the struggle for self-government was reaching a climax. The Zikist Movement was highly organised throughout the country, and we had our own code words and our secret system of communications. Many of us were passionately in favour of open conflict. Dr. Azikiwe left Nigeria to make a final attempt to wring from the British Government the recognition of our rights. The London Press greeted him with ridicule. The Colonial Office refused to recognise him as our leader or spokesman. He was told he 'represented nothing' in Nigeria.

With our full support, Dr. Azikiwe turned his face eastward and prepared to go to Moscow.

Suddenly we began to receive reports that instead of asking for help from the Communist countries, Zik had returned to Nigeria determined to unite with his former political opponents and find a road of self-government without bloodshed. His speeches changed in tone, calling for a renaissance in our people, and fresh slogans to bring unity, such as 'Not who is right, but what is right' were used.

Many of us thought he had been bought by the British. Others felt we should find out what it was that had influenced him so much. We discovered that he had gone to a place in Switzerland called Caux and had there met a new ideology called Moral Re-Armament. I was full of suspicion, and spread the view that a capitalist in America had started this in order to make his name known in the world: and I thought also that it was a new religion designed to put out the flame of nationalism in the colonial peoples.

I made up my mind to get all the facts about it. Then two men, one Scot and one Swiss, walked into my office one day. They told me they were part of the world force Dr. Azikiwe had met at Caux. We sat and talked for forty minutes. I was deeply impressed by the simplicity and humility of the Scotsman, and by the fact that he was a worker like myself, a shipyard worker from the Clyde. They spoke to me of absolute moral standards. I thought to myself: 'This may be all right for retired British officers or elderly people, but how can you expect a young man to live absolute purity?'

A few days later they introduced me to another of their friends, a young Englishman. He was so simple and so straight, I could easily see he was hiding nothing. So I said to myself, 'Yes, if this young man is living absolute standards there must be something in it.'

I accepted an invitation to see the play, *The Man with the Key.* This play challenged me. I saw the Russian ambassador in the play, Mr. Zenofors, refusing to accept drinks or smokes, and I heard the reason his wife gave, how drink makes people 'talk silly' and Government spies can use cocktail parties to pick up information from the 'silly talk' that goes on.

I thought this was the reason the Government asked us to so many cocktail parties in the Residence. I returned home and decided to stop smoking and drinking; these vices ruled my life at the time. I did this to preserve my trade union organisation.

Shortly afterwards, in July 1955, I accepted an invitation to go to Caux with a group of Members of Parliament and youth leaders from Nigeria and Ghana.

I was very sceptical for the first two days. But the longer I stayed the more I became convinced that these people at Caux were like me, thinking the world was in chaos and taking action to remake it. I read in a book which said, 'You cannot cure hate with hate.' I heard someone say, 'Although it may be an act of faith to expect a change in human nature, it is an act of lunacy to expect to change the world without changing human nature.'

I agreed with these two statements.

One evening, I found myself sitting at dinner next to a British Air Vice-Marshal; he told me he was not altogether convinced about the need for this ideology. Half of me hated him, because he was British: but the other half of me loved him, because his face had an astonishing resemblance to my own grandfather's, the Chief Egwunwoke. I felt impelled to apologise to him for my bitterness against the British. He said to me, 'Whatever you want me to do for you, I will do it.' We sat together in silence. Then I had this thought: 'Invite him to fight together with you, as a father and son should, for a new world.' He promised to join me in the struggle, and ever since he has kept his promise.

Next day the following thought came to me, 'Madman that you are, you have refused to believe in the existence of God, your Lord, and have left the Church of your fathers. Go back to the Church.'

When I went to the Chapel, I found the Reverend Father alone there. I had been wondering how I could make my confession for all my past faults. Then I noticed that he was an Italian Father and did not understand English very well; that was a great relief! He heard my confession, and I received Holy Communion.

After the service, my head quite cleared, and I saw I was dishonest towards my wife. At that point I became so happy and free in my heart. I realised the impudence of making speeches about liberty while I denied liberty to my wife at home, and felt the shame of talking on behalf of world unity when I was myself on the verge of divorce. Also I saw that in our youth movement we could never bring unity as long as we were always fighting about who would be the next chairman.

I wrote twenty-four letters of apology. It took me two nights. I wrote to almost every member of my family, to my in-laws and to my friends in the trade union and nationalist movements whom I had treated badly. My first letter was to my wife.

Frank Buchman was at Caux just then and helped us to understand the greatness of our destiny. He said, 'Africa must speak to the world.' He won my heart, for he symbolised for me peace and justice. After he spoke to the Assembly one morning, I tried to find out what work he did and what money he had. When it was clear to me that he had no money and had given his whole life to this work, I understood very well, because of what we were doing for Nigeria.

We Africans united from all parts of the continent and created the play *Freedom*, which gave the background of the African struggle for independence and for change. It was inspired by Dr. Buchman's faith in us. We presented the play first at Caux, and then immediately found ourselves invited to London, Paris, Bonn and other European cities.

When I made my apology to the Air Vice-Marshal, I thought my bitterness had left me. But one day at the Westminster Theatre in London, when we were preparing to give the play there, I remembered my court trial and what I thought about the British Judge who sentenced me to six months in prison. I was overwhelmed by the thought, 'Here you are working with the British in their own land in a play. Yesterday you were a convinced nationalist, and now you are a fellow-traveller!' I found myself plunged in the deep waters of bitterness. It was then that I knew my apology had not removed all the bitterness I had in my heart. I found myself sitting in the theatre, as though paralysed and in tears.

I told some of my colleagues of the torture in my soul and I said I was leaving. For their sake I struggled through that evening's performance.

That night I could not sleep. At the end of three hours I decided to listen to the voice of God. In the quiet of the dawn a clear thought came to me, 'What you are doing with *Freedom* is what is demanded by the revolution to remake the world. What you were doing before was merely to reassess the grudges and bitterness, which could not produce good results. This is the only thing capable of transforming the situation you have always fought to change. It is right. Go ahead.'

Then my leave ended and I had to go home. I wept when I said 'Goodbye' to those who were travelling with *Freedom*. They had become like my brothers and sisters.

My wife had never answered the two letters I wrote her from Caux. She told me afterwards that she thought I must have been drunk when I wrote them.

So when I returned to Nigeria I decided to go and find her. I got to the village, and her father and all her family gathered to meet me. I tried to tell them how my life had changed, but they would not listen to me. One of my wife's brothers spat in my face. She was standing watching. Something kept me from losing my temper. But I had to leave without her and travel the 500 miles back to Lagos.

Two weeks later I had the definite thought: 'Send a car for her, and ask her once again to return.' My brother went off in the car and returned with my wife. She did not bring any of her belongings, since she could not believe there could be a lasting reconciliation. Her father had instructed her to return to him if there was any trouble.

She watched me closely. The first thing she noticed was that I had stopped smoking and drinking. She suspected that I was only trying to make a favourable impression. Once, to try me out, she got some cigarettes and a bottle of beer and put them on the table. When I refused these, she began to see that something had happened to me.

The weeks went by, and she even forgot to write to her parents because things were going so well.

She, too, met my new friends in Lagos, my comrades who had helped me to change. Now she and I have begun to fight side by side to bring this answer we have found to our friends, our families and to Nigeria's leaders. People sometimes come and bring stories to each of us about the other, to try to sow suspicion and break our home again. But we have told each other all about our lives and the simple honesty between us, each day, builds confidence.

The harmony in my home gave me a new motive for my trade union work. I had only wanted to use the workers for the cause of the revolution I served: now I began to take trouble about them personally so that they should receive the wages and conditions they deserved.

When Queen Elizabeth was about to visit Nigeria in 1956 there was the threat of a big strike in the Lagos docks and there was much agitation for this.

We were negotiating for new conditions; and we felt the management were dodging us. The men issued an ultimatum: 'Unless we get our demands fulfilled by a certain date, we shall strike.' The date they mentioned was the day the Queen's car was due to arrive.

The management reacted in the usual way: 'We shall not negotiate under duress. Withdraw your threat of a strike.'

As tempers on both sides rose, I knew the small voice inside me was saying, 'Your job is to find what is right.' I told the management we would negotiate in that spirit. 'That's reasonable,' they said. We gave a film show at the docks to carry this idea to the workers. They gave me their full support. There was no strike; and Her Majesty's car was disembarked without trouble.

The negotiations took several months. But at the end of them we were awarded a ten per cent increase, retrospective for two years.

After that the men began to come and ask me, 'What is this new magic you have found?' We have been able to raise the standard of living of our members by about seventy per cent and the union membership has grown from 600 to 5,000 in the last five years.

In 1956, the annual conference passed a resolution thanking Dr. Buchman for what this ideology 'has done and is doing for the leadership and membership of the union'. And in August 1958, the union sent the 1954-57 President and the present Vice-President-General to report at Caux on all that has happened since the change began in me.

ONUMARA EGWUNWOKE
Nigeria

'I HEARD ABOUT IT AT STALINO'

When Germany surrendered I was with my regiment in Czecho-slovakia. We were taken to Russia as prisoners. My family thought I was dead. Not until a year later did they have news of me.

I had become a miner at the age of fourteen so as to save my family from destitution and in 1942 I had been called up in the Wehrmacht. I was sent to the Russian front, where I was wounded five times. As a general rule, being a miner, I should never have been called up. But my father was a Communist, and the government did not like that. . . .

The war did not change my father's political opinions. His first action after the end of the war was to form a Communist cell in his town in the Ruhr. For him, as for me, Communism offered the only way to avoid repeating the mistakes of the past.

As soon as he heard that I was a prisoner, my father wrote to the party headquarters in Moscow to ask for my release. All he succeeded in getting for me was preferential treatment and a permit which enabled me to move about freely. This made it possible for me to go to various schools to study Marxism.

The last of these schools was at Stalino, the big industrial town in the Donetz basin. This town was strangely like our Ruhr cities; everywhere there was nothing but pit-heads and blast furnaces, smoke and factory sirens. I knew that the workers of this region were in the forefront of the proletarian revolution. The party leaders receive their final training there before taking over official duties. That is why I was very proud to be able to attend the courses at the Stalino Marxist training school together with about thirty of my compatriots and fellow prisoners.

It was not easy to gain admission to this school and every application was examined carefully. We prisoners of war, on whom the party relied to advance Communism in our own countries, had to be able to furnish proof of anti-Fascist activities; we also had to be true

sons of the working class. They did not want to train at Stalino men
of whom they were not absolutely certain. The instruction which we
received was divided into four main subjects: (1) dialectical and
historical materialism; (2) the history of the Communist Party of the
U.S.S.R.; (3) the political and economic organisation of the U.S.S.R.;
(4) the biographies of Marx, Engels, Lenin and Stalin. Our instructors were all Germans, but their instruction was supplemented by
lectures from Soviet party leaders and scientists.

One of the subjects of discussion which often came up was that of
the change of behaviour in individuals which was necessary and
would one day lead to the establishment of the true Communist
society. None of us had any answer to this problem, and the living
of the Christians we had seen had not convinced us that change was
possible in man's way of life either.

We had a course on the ideological forces which were liable to sow
confusion of thought amongst Communists; in this framework we
were warned against Moral Re-Armament. It was the first time that I
had heard of it. Our instructors described it to us as a Christian movement, whose members suffered from the same defects as all other
Christians. Yet we were warned never to come in contact with Moral
Re-Armament people, a thing which we had never been told with
regard to Christians in general.

I often wondered why we had been given this course. I was to
discover the explanation later; at that time, Moral Re-Armament
had launched its first big ideological offensive in the Ruhr, and the
party headquarters in Moscow was uneasy about the way revolutionaries of long standing, survivors of the Nazi prisons, had started to
follow an ideology other than Communism.

Then I was released and returned home. At Bochum station I saw
my father again for the first time after five years of separation. My
sister was with him. She was a secretary in the mining company; like
me, she was a Marxist. My father was deeply moved and had tears in
his eyes. I had never seen him like that. Indeed I was surprised at his
behaviour. Many of his actions were inexplicable. He was thinking
and acting differently, he who had always been the Marxist revolutionary, the veteran of so many working-class struggles.

On returning home I could not understand either why a former
fighter in the Norwegian Resistance Movement was sleeping in my
room and seemed to have become the family's best friend. I soon

learned that he had introduced my father to the principles of Moral Re-Armament. But when I talked to him alone, I could not believe that this was the same thing we had been told about at the Stalino school.

There was no possible doubt; my father had come in contact with a new type of man, such as I myself did not know. Was this what we were looking for at Stalino? This did not mean that my father had given up the task which he had once taken on as a revolutionary, but he was trying to convince me that he had found a better way. We got as far as fierce arguments, in which other party leaders took part.

But my father knew that arguments led nowhere. Throughout my youth, I had always seen him behave like a dictator. He was a very excitable man, who expected absolute obedience from us all. Everything was different now. He sought each person's opinion on everything.

Accused of having had close contact with Moral Re-Armament, my father was expelled from the party. I myself voted at an official meeting for his expulsion, for we had to prevent the spread of ideological confusion in the party. At that moment the man whom I was voting to expel was no longer my father, but merely an ideological opponent.

Despite everything, I was much intrigued by his change and by his new friends. So one day I agreed to go with them to an evening lecture, at which a Swiss professor was to speak about the fundamental forces in European history. I was interested in that, but I had to go to the meeting secretly.

The penetrating ideological points made by that professor reminded me of the discussions on Moral Re-Armament at the Stalino party school. I was so struck that I asked permission to describe how I had heard of Moral Re-Armament for the first time. I was to regret it for months, because two days later the party, having heard of this, expelled me too. This was a very heavy blow, because everything in me drove me towards the class war; this expulsion caused me to lose my old friends with whom, at great sacrifice, I had so far worked to remake the world.

Then an encounter took place, which was to be decisive in my life, with a young French Jew. Most of his family had died in German concentration camps. I steeled myself to hear him bring a series of accusations against my nation. But nothing like that happened. He talked only about his own and his country's mistakes. This simple worker had only one desire, to put right the past. Despite the horrors that he had witnessed, he had asked God for the power to love the German people, knowing that hatred can cure nothing. 'To be able to help others,' he said to me, 'one must be able to recognise one's own faults first, however slight they may be.'

It was the first time I had talked to a Jew. The racialism instilled by Hitler was by no means dead in me; I had not succeeded in overcoming this prejudice in Russia. According to my idea, Hitler had treated the Jews unjustly, but I had never taken any interest in their fate and I refused to see that I was in any way connected with this injustice.

Max, my French friend, was a man like myself with the same faults and the same weaknesses. We had many points in common. I guessed that he had found in his life a force capable of overcoming hatreds that had seemed insurmountable. Here before my eyes was a factor in the transformation of society which we had not been told about in our Marxist schools in Russia, though it was of cardinal importance. I suddenly saw the limitations of a strictly materialistic ideology which could not cure selfishness and hate. And so I decided to follow my French friend's example. Through meditation and through absolute honesty about myself, I realised that the power which had changed my father, and which I had heard about at Stalino, could answer the anguish of our generation.

Robert Wegerhof
Ruhr miner

THE REVOLUTIONARY BUSINESS MAN

Born in the small village of Frittenden in the heart of Kent in England, my father was the youngest of eleven children. His father was a country parson. His mother's family were well established, with banking and brewing interests. Two of his ancestors were Lord Mayors of London. As a boy I used to sleep in a room in which hung a picture of one of my father's forbears, described as 'Charles, Earl of Romney, Viscount Marsham, Lord Lieutenant of the County of Kent and City of Canterbury, President of the Marine Society, etc., etc.,

etc.' I was most impressed by the three 'etcs.'. My father studied Latin and Greek at Oxford. He felt at home there, and his dry wit and cultured manner were nourished in the company of kindred spirits.

He loved travelling. In 1905 he went to Russia. He was to stay there over eleven years, engaged in various jobs which took him all over the country. When he first arrived he knew only five words of Russian, two of which were 'vodka' and 'samovar'. By the end of the year he was reading Tolstoy in Russian.

Russia won my father's heart. He travelled as far as the Island of Sakhalin off the Siberian coast. There he had journeyed in a sleigh drawn by reindeer; he had slept at night on pine branches laid on the snow; he had lived in Moscow and enjoyed its society, its cooking and its theatre.

He had also lived in Warsaw where he was employed as manager of a plant manufacturing soft drinks, 'made exclusively from natural products', said the advertisements. My father is fond of recalling that one of the chief ingredients was coal tar!

When the war began, my father went back to England to join the army. After a very short time he was chosen by the Secret Service for work in Russia. On 8th March, 1917, he was in the Nevsky Prospect, the famous main street of St. Petersburg, and there he saw two hundred people on a protest march, asking for bread. The crowd stopped when they came to a line of armed police. There was a short consultation. Then they moved forward. The police fired. A few days later the old régime was to collapse.

Shortly after the war, in 1920, my father left the army and was sent by a British firm to Canada. He soon married and settled there for good.

My father is a reserved man. Strongly built, tall, with great natural dignity, he is perceptive, modest and quiet. I remember one day discovering, quite by chance, that he had been awarded the D.S.O. during the war. I have never heard my parents quarrel. Nevertheless, they got on each other's nerves sometimes.

In 1932 North America was in the throes of a depression. To add to his business worries my father was concerned about my mother's health. Her nerves were not good and she was advised to get away from the house and go for a long cruise.

In October of that year my parents received an invitation to go to some meetings to be held in a hotel near our home by some people of whom they had never heard. They were to be there for a week. The meetings were to be about something to do with reform. Respectable people seemed to be interested. My parents, mildly curious, decided to go so as to be able to say they had been.

Both of them noticed that the people, ordinary enough, to judge by their appearances, looked happy, which in 1932 was not so ordinary. My father decided to go back a second time. It was suggested that the change everyone wished for in humanity would best start with oneself. This seemed to him perfectly reasonable.

My father was an armchair critic. He would amuse himself almost every day composing imaginary letters to the newspapers deploring every sort of situation. One of his favourite topics just then was the low standard of honesty in public life. A thought suddenly came into his mind: was it possible that his own standard of honesty needed raising?

He went home and did some serious thinking. Quick to notice the faults of others, he had never before been so conscious of the need to be honest about his own. He at once realised that my mother's health depended partly on his own willingness to alter his ways. He took the first step and spoke to her absolutely frankly and openly of all he felt most deeply. For the first time in their married life there were no secrets and no shadows between them: all had been said, nothing remained hidden.

The change in my mother was remarkable. Faith began to replace fear. Within a year her health had improved so much that she no longer needed to go on cruises. Within two years friends said she was unrecognisable.

The difference in her made a new man of my father. He was free now to think beyond the limits of his personal worries. 'I belonged to that army of people,' he says, 'who are quite ready to sack the office boy for pilfering but persuade themselves that their own fiscal irregularities are all quite in order. It cost me a lot of money to adjust these ideas!'

He took some paper and did a rapid calculation: what about that fur coat, those art treasures and jewellery which he had brought in without paying the proper duty . . . ? As a business man he knew that he also owed interest on his overdue debt. The cheque he wrote out represented a third of his annual income. He turned over the cheque to the Inland Revenue (Customs). The Press got hold of the story. Next day one of the papers put it on the front page.

The adventure was only beginning.

In 1935 my father took on the responsibility for the family's paper mills. He set out to run the business on a new basis. Despite the scepticism of the manager and the wariness of the workers he determined to put the interests of the men before the making of profits.

My father did not talk to the men in the mills about wanting to put people before profit in industry. He said, 'I have always believed that the fellow was right who said, "What you do speaks so loudly that I cannot hear a word you say." ' Men know at once whether you do things because you are trying to buy their goodwill and trying to improve production, or whether you care about them as men. ' A man's wife,' he says, 'always knows which of the two reasons it was which led him to bring her some flowers—because he cared for her and wanted to give her pleasure, or because he wanted her to close her eyes to a number of things. Workers are not fooled, either. Management almost always makes an attempt at material appeasement. Baths, bigger and better houses, gardens and hospitals will only achieve their end if the workers are included wholeheartedly in thinking through, planning for, and carrying out, such schemes.'

One day my father asked a miner what he most wanted in life. He waited for a reply about more money or better conditions. ' A man wants to be a man,' was the answer: an answer never forgotten. ' A great many strikes with demands for higher pay,' observes my father, ' are basically an expression of dissatisfaction with the attitude felt to be in the mind of the employer or his representative. Subtly applied social psychology is not enough. Conciliation and arbitration boards are really an expression of defeatism on the whole question of human relationships.

' Goodwill without a genuine personal interest in the people only creates distrust. To have trust you have to have honesty, not just the honesty which consists in keeping your word, but an honesty of purpose.'

It became clear to my father that the problems of industry were allied to the problems of the nation. Everything comes back to human relations. What was valid for the home and for the nation was equally valid in the international field. My father said, 'To attempt to conduct a business and ignore the problems in the world was simply painting your cabin while the ship went down.'

Just after the war two Indian newspapermen came to Canada to buy paper. They were invited to our home for dinner. My mother did her best to see they had curry cooked as they liked it.

The Indians were having trouble finding newsprint. There was none available in Scandinavia where they had formerly bought it. This was at the time when India's struggle for independence was approaching its fulfilment. One of the men who came to dinner was Devadas Gandhi, son of the Mahatma, who was the editor of the *Hindustan Times* of New Delhi.

The Indians left our home with a gallon of maple syrup from our farm as a gift for the Mahatma, and with the promise of 1,000 tons of paper at $30 per ton lower than that prevailing on the open market. My father had just concluded a very bad bargain, but he was building for the future. Next day my father also made personal representations to some of the other companies and got them to agree to supply the rest of the paper needed.

My father visited many countries in Asia and in Europe, convinced that the creating of a new spirit between nations was even more important than running an efficient business. No financial sacrifice was too great.

The year 1948 found him in the Ruhr, the centre of industrial German life. The country was not only a physical wreck, it was in an ideological vacuum. My father and his friends did not go there to tell people where they were wrong. They wanted above all to understand, not to criticise. The Ruhr was in the British occupied zone. My father went as an Englishman conscious of his own shortcomings and of his nation's, and willing to admit them. He often listened for hours to the pent-up feelings of the Germans, either in private interviews or in public. He felt they needed to be heard. It made him humbler too.

The Ruhr, of course, had been harder hit during the war than any other part of the country. Accommodation was scarce. Hotels were few and far between. Food was neither plentiful nor varied. My father and his friends gladly accepted invitations to stay in the homes of workers, managers, trade union officials, communists or capitalists. They remained in Germany for six months. Looking back on that time my father comments, 'My education really began to get going.'

A German who was there at the time has written an account of a meeting at Moers which was part of that education:

On a grey day in February 1949, people were streaming into the typically German beer hall. Outside in the mining town everything was grey, the houses, the leaves on the trees, even the faces of the people. Moers had become one of the major Communist strongholds in the Ruhr and the Communist party had just called a meeting. Two grim-looking characters, one on each side of the door, left no doubt that only Party comrades were to be admitted, but they did admit a handful of others who had begun to be well known in the town. For a week they had been producing the play *The Forgotten Factor* in the main beer hall of Moers. People had talked so much about them that the Communist Party headquarters in Dusseldorf had become anxious and given orders to the local comrades to put a stop to this foolishness. According to Lenin there was no ideology above class. This meeting was called to make sure there would be no alternative to Communism for the German workers of the Ruhr.

The 120 workers who sat down had been through fifteen terrible years. Hitler had killed most of their friends. Many of those present had been in concentration camps. Their wives and children had endured an average of 300 air-raids per year. Now there was starvation and occupation by the British forces. The British authorities had started to dismantle those industries which had been left by the bombs, and the threat of unemployment was very real to these men.

This meeting was their first chance to talk to people from the allied nations and tell them exactly what they felt. They talked without stopping for about two hours. The air had become thick with the smoke of bad tobacco and fumes of stale beer. One could feel waves of bitterness, hatred and even contempt flow from the speakers. The small group of foreigners around a table in the corner of the room had so far remained silent. At last the chairman of the meeting rose and said very politely that he doubted whether any of the foreign people would have anything to say but, if they had, the floor was theirs. Immediately an Englishman got up. 'If we British had lived up to what we had talked about after the First World War,' he said, 'you men would have been spared the suffering which you have gone through.' You could have heard a pin drop. 'God help the party and nation which does not fight to change these conditions,' the speaker continued. 'But we need the full dimension of change, based on the change of human nature.'

The next to get up was Bernard Hallward. He not only was, but he looked like, a capitalist. He spoke German. He told these men how he had been in Russia as a young man in 1917. He told them about his two factories in Canada, about his workers and their hopes and about his wife and their two sons. He talked to them about revolution. He agreed with them that men like him needed to be different. And he gave many practical examples from his own life as a husband, a father and an industrialist.

By the time Hallward sat down, there was a new kind of tension in the hall. Pipes had gone out, and people forgot their beer and began to ask questions relating to the deepest points in their own lives. Hallward stayed till two o'clock in the morning in that hall, and the Germans told him about their own hopes and fears. They had completely forgotten that he was a capitalist. In fact they met on a level beyond the front lines of capitalism and Communism, which seemed to be out of date that night.

At two o'clock the chairman called the meeting to order again and he was painfully searching for words when he said, 'Capitalism has been the thesis, Communism the anti-thesis: what you have brought tonight may be the synthesis.'

Five years after that meeting in the Ruhr I myself met the man who chaired it. His name is Max Bladeck. Max was one of the men who opened my eyes and gave me a new appreciation of my father. It had seemed an unusual thing to me that a man of sixty-six would go to a country like Germany for as long as six months under the conditions that prevailed in 1948. What did he expect from his visit?

Max Bladeck and others like him made me realise that a man like my father had done what no amount of dollars and no Marshall Aid could ever do. He was living proof to thousands that profit was not the only motive in business and that the pride and reserve of the British could be melted. He gave men hope that a better world could be created as workers and industrialists alike took on the job of re-making men as well as rebuilding the economy. 'If there had been even twelve more like him,' said Max, 'I do not believe Europe would be in the condition it is in today.'

It was hard for me to believe that the man he was talking about was the same man who used to spend hours with me trying very patiently to knock into my head the use of the ablative case in Latin; who once wrote some blank verse required for my English class (which the teacher recognised immediately as coming from a pen more practised than my own); whose steps on the stairs every evening when I was small always heralded a few minutes of jostling, wrestling, and laughing which were the climax of the day.

But I knew that this was the man with whom my mother no longer lost her temper; who, though widely misunderstood in Canada, paid no attention to the rumours circulated about him; who, with the advance of years, had, instead of retiring to the country, increased the time he spent away from the comfort of his home to make available his experience wherever it was wanted.

I had always respected my father. But I had not emulated him. I found it easier to drift with the crowd than to take a stand for what was right. In my ignorance I was often arrogant.

My father did not preach at me. He knew it would only put my back up. But he had a way, nevertheless, of making me feel that he was not too impressed with my haphazard style of living or my irresponsibility. In 1953 my parents invited me to join them at Caux in Switzerland. Caux represented a challenge to me. A big stake was involved for me in accepting, so I announced that, after I had spent forty-eight hours at Caux, I would leave to go behind the Iron Curtain.

I had long wanted to see at first hand something of life in the Communist countries. That summer I was given a chance of going to a youth festival in Bucharest and attending shortly afterwards a student congress in Warsaw.

I can see my father now at the railway station at Caux, his tall figure erect in the Alpine sunlight and his grey hair blown by the breeze as he said to me, 'Go, if you want to, but come back to Caux on your return. Come and see the answer to what you'll find in Bucharest and Warsaw. And stay at least a week when you do.' Hesitantly I agreed to do so. Then I set off.

In Rumania and Poland we were shown impressive plays and heard magnificent music. We attended seminars. We were given free beer, free cigarettes, at one point we were even given pocket money.

However, my aim in going there was not just to attend a youth festival. Above all I wanted to see how these countries had changed since the war.

So many of the people we met were in despair. On one occasion a doctor took me to his home, where I exchanged my obviously Western clothes for some of his. He invited me to accompany him on his rounds and carry his black bag as if I was his assistant. With him I saw the slums in which most of the working-class live, a marked contrast to the modern flats that were on show to students and tourists.

When I talked with the Communists, however, I felt like a school-boy with college professors. Whatever I might say of democracy, freedom and material achievements in the West made no impression whatsoever.

Those people had a discipline and a dedication to the cause in which they believed that I simply could not match. It began to dawn

116

on me that I had no coherent belief for which I was ready to make real sacrifices. I realised that, unlike me, my father had something to say to Communists that interested them.

Students told me how they risked their lives to listen to the radio from the West, but that the news they got gave them no hope at all. One said, 'While we live on the edge of hell, you indulge in the luxury of bickering amongst yourselves.'

One evening in the dusk in a park near the middle of Bucharest, a young student looked at me with supplication in his eyes and said, 'When you get out of here, at least do something!'

Leaving Prague one morning, I arrived in Caux on the evening of the same day. The first thing that struck me was the look of freedom on people's faces, after the bitterness and hatred I had seen during my six weeks' visit to the Communist countries. My father had gone back to Canada by this time, but so many people, industrialists and workers alike, told me how grateful they were to him. I knew that I was going to have to decide soon about my own life, about what I was going to live for.

But I was a coward. I left Caux determined to carry through my own plans of returning to Canada to make my name in journalism or business. I still remember, at the moment when the train left, saying to myself, 'You're running out on the biggest thing in the world, and on what you know is right.'

When I arrived in London on my way home I ran right into two friends of my father's whom I had got to know in Caux. They were men of the Labour world with first-hand experience of the trade union movement all over the world. We talked far into the night about the war of ideas, and about the motives behind men's actions: comradeship and sense of purpose, also the forces of lust, hate and fear. I could not sleep that night. I turned on the light and picked up a book which was on my bedside table. I opened it at a passage which presented an idea that my father and I had often argued about without ever reaching agreement.

This is what I read:

The remaking of a man is not a matter of self-effort, or pulling on one's own bootstraps, but of opening the shutters of the mind and heart in a time of silence to a new direction and the power that accompanies it. The process is very simple. The explanation of it, as in the case of electric light, may be clearer to some than others, and not fully understood by any. Yet only a fool would refuse to turn a switch in a dark room, because he cannot understand what makes the light go on.

Alone in my room I decided to do the one thing I had not tried. Having argued and discussed and theorised, I finally decided to try the idea. One of the first thoughts I got was to write a letter to my father. I decided to tell him how grateful I was for the kind of father he had been. I also had the thought to be really honest with him about the kind of son he had. Finally, I would tell him I was going to return with my friends to Caux and plan my next moves on the basis of how and where I could be most effective. Then I turned over and went to sleep.

In the morning I sat down and wrote him that letter from my heart. Shortly afterwards I learned that he had received my letter while he was flat on his back in the hospital after a serious operation, and that it had done more for him than any medicine could have done. The thought flashed into my mind that if I did what God asked me to do He would always do the rest.

It was on that basis that my father had made his fundamental decision about the business. Together as a family we decided that the best use of his time and now of mine was to give it fully and freely to build a new world. At a time when their prospects were better than they had ever seemed, my father sold the mills. He has never regretted it, any more than I have regretted following the advice he gave me on the station platform at Caux.

JOHN HALLWARD
Canada

A NEW FAITH AT THE SERVICE OF
THE WORKERS

My grandparents, who brought me up, used to live in a small town in the Lyon district in a kind of cul-de-sac where only men and women of the textile mills live. The cul-de-sac was like one big family, with lots of kids and we used to know everyone's private life. We lived in the street. Sometimes we got together for country dances and amused ourselves. The whole street, young and old, took part in these games, but a drunkard's shout or a fight between two women was enough to poison the whole atmosphere. My grandmother, who was like quicksilver, used to jump on people to separate them, which used to encourage my grandfather (a master-at-arms by profession!) to follow suit. That was my first school.

When on the point of taking my school certificate, I was sent away from the class because I had taken up the defence of a little comrade whom the teacher had treated roughly. This urchin was red-haired, sickly, and slightly deaf and I used to revolt against all the ragging that he underwent at school. After this incident I never again wanted to go back to school, although my parents did everything to convince me that education is essential if you want to find work.

After trying about thirty small jobs which I left on account of one thing or another, I wanted to work in a big factory where things get a move on and where you can go in and out without being beholden to anybody. I was twenty years old in 1927 when the secretary of the union in my factory died. The older of the militant members of the union proposed that I should take his place. They did not want that responsibility for themselves, because they were afraid, I think, of being sacked. They said to themselves, 'A chap who is only twenty will easily be able to find another job.' As for me, I accepted, saying to myself, 'I shall be going into the army in six months or a year, so I shall soon be rid of this job as secretary.' We each had our own ideas at the back of our minds, but finally I was convinced that trade unionism was one of the means of freeing the workers, of assuring them of better conditions, and especially of guaranteeing that human dignity which the employers had crushed in the preceding years. That is how I took on my first trade union duties. It was very tough. I had to relearn writing and arithmetic, which I had completely forgotten. I presented the books with our claim in them in fear, first of being sacked, and secondly of not having the backing of the working men and women.

The first time that I went, as part of a delegation, to the managing director, he treated me with a certain scorn; as if to say, 'This fellow is too young, he doesn't truly represent the workers' interests.' The attitude of this manager reinforced my trade union aggressiveness.

About 1930, three years after taking on these duties, the economic crisis developed and with it wage-cuts. Then the strikes began, becoming more and more bitter and lasting many weeks, even months. But the crisis got worse, and wages sunk still lower. That was when I learned strategy and dialectic. I understood that the strike was a struggle as important as war, a struggle for my own class, and that it had its own strategy and its own political line. The victorious issue of this fight would do away for ever with social injustices, would allow us to build a better society, and would satisfy our deepest hopes.

Before being appointed a permanent trade union official, I remained unemployed for eighteen months. I had been sacked from the factory. During the long days of unemployment I devoured Marxist books and taught myself all I could through my meetings with the best of the militant workers of that period. It is through the workers' struggle of these years that we perfected the tactics of united action which led to the unity in the trade unions and to the workers' victory of 1936. That year France had the honour of bringing to the world of labour great social reforms, the forty-hour week, collective contracts, holidays with pay. These reforms will remain an historic record to the victory of the French working-class. My generation carried through this action without wavering, and we sacrificed everything to it. This is what paved the way for the coming of the popular front and the practical application of these social achievements.

We made no distinctions between trade union struggles and our anti-fascist struggles, and the war of 1939 did not come as a surprise to us. At that moment I found myself, with some of my Communist comrades in the CGT (Communist trade union), under the threat of arrest. Faced as we were with the dilemma of the Russo-German pact, considerable uncertainties divided the ranks of the French Communist Party. For my part, I reported to my regiment.

In June 1940, as we saw Hitler's troops enter Paris, we felt rising within us all the traditions of France, of the country which had reared us, well or badly, but which was our own. It was with great satisfaction that we rallied to fight against the occupying power and to try to free our country and the world from Hitlerism.

At that time I decided to enter the underground army and I was completely in the service of the Communist Party. Our essential task consisted in organising the working men and women to enable them to carry on an underground struggle, both against the occupying power and the Vichy Government. This struggle might be of a

legal or illegal character. It covered everything from the battle for
social improvements, for wage claims, for bread, to sabotage and the
armed struggle against the occupying power.

We were always in danger of arrest. Many people refused to give
us shelter. We were ready to undergo torture and prison, but we did
not yet realise to what extent, and by what means, the occupying
power was also determined to break down our resistance.

It is then that an important event in my life took place, and I
understand it much better now that I know Moral Re-Armament.
One day in October 1941 I had to go to Toulouse where I had a
rendezvous with someone to help organise the district. At Avignon,
where I had just changed trains, I bought a paper. Opening it I saw
that twenty-two trade unionists had just been shot at Châteaubriand.
Among them were at least a dozen of my good friends, including my
dearest friend, who was with me in the textile workers' federation.
That day really was a black one for the Resistance.

The train was not heated, and I was cold and hungry. It was night.
The execution of my friends, the increasing toughness of the occupying power against the underground activities of the Communist
Party and of the French patriots, had considerably lowered my morale
and for some minutes I wondered whether I ought to leave the
Resistance Movement. I had suddenly understood that this commitment which I had undertaken was one that might demand the
supreme sacrifice.

I was silent, and in this quiet time, all at once, I made the resolution to fight whatever happened. Well, I felt that it was the right
decision, because immediately I became aware of comfort. I was
warm, I was no longer hungry, my morale was restored and my
strength renewed.

For the first time I discovered that there really is a higher power
and that, when you are on the right line for what is best for mankind,
then this superior force comes into action.

Another event came to add to this discovery. It was at Marseilles
two years later. There was a train of deportees at the Saint Charles
station and the Resistance had succeeded in helping them all to
escape from the train. The station is situated just beside a workers'
area which is called ' La belle de Mai ' and that is where I was. In the
middle of the night the people in whose house I was sleeping woke
me up and said, ' This area is being searched.' As they did not know

who the search was for, they were afraid, thinking it might be me. When I saw how agitated these people were, I said to myself, 'You must go. When the police come, the anxiety of your host and hostess alone will make them suspicious and you run a real risk of being carried off.' So I said to my hostess, 'Don't worry. I am going out into the street.' As the net-work of police drew nearer (there were at least two or three thousand surrounding the area), I sought to break out of the circle.

I had only my leather brief-case and my overcoat. It was six o'clock in the morning. The noose drew tighter and tighter. Then suddenly, without realising it, I found myself in the midst of officers and police patrols. I was so calm that they paid no attention to me. And that is how I came out of the cordon quite quietly to go to my rendezvous.

I could quote a whole series of similar cases, especially the six occasions when I crossed the border between the occupied and unoccupied zones without once being questioned. The only paper I possessed was a simple identity card, which, incidentally, was false!

More than a dozen times I found myself in real danger. Each time, as a normal reflex action, I thought of God and of my mother. I made a rapid examination of my conscience. I found in the justice of our cause and our action the link between my conscience and God. I have remarked, from what my comrades have told me in confidence, that when my fellow fighters, trained like me in the school of atheism, faced danger, they too sought help from a superior force. In such moments dialectic is deaf.

This battle brought us to the liberation of Paris. When I heard the last shot of the cannon that announced the surrender of the German troops in Paris, I remember sitting down on a bench and thinking of all my comrades who had fallen, and also of the methods used in the battle that had brought us to this day.

Before the liberation of Paris, I had been entrusted with certain tasks by the C.N.R. (the National Council of the Resistance). I was a member of the Interior Commission, the Commission dealing with the Committee of Liberation, and the Security Commission. It was this last Commission which was to put into camps all the collaborators, including those in the field of economics, industry, etc. I also assumed the functions of General Secretary of the Textile Federation in the C.G.I.

I was branded by the scars of a whole lifetime of union struggle, and battered and worn out by the four years of underground activity. The loyal comradeship that had existed in the Resistance was frittered away with the return of more normal times. I thought a lot about the past and about the struggle we had just lived through. I became sceptical as to the rightness of our watchwords and the means we had employed to carry through our tasks. Our wartime loyalties had given place to petty jealousies and pride, which created an atmosphere of distrust against which I no longer had the strength to act. I took the first excuse to abandon trade union and political activity. I found myself once more with empty hands and an empty heart. For a Communist who leaves the Party, this causes great suffering.

For a long time I had the impression of being alone. When you leave a great revolutionary movement, and you have nothing to replace it, you feel you are useless and ineffective. I listened to people, to tradesfolk, middle-class citizens, talking about their own little affairs, their political parties. I thought to myself, ' People are so busy with petty things and their own selfish interest.'

Then came the trade union split. Certain of my comrades from the textile industry asked me whether I would be willing to help them reconstruct the Federation within the ' Force Ouvrière '. I accepted.

In 1950 I made the acquaintance of Moral Re-Armament. We were discussing our national collective wage agreement. The employers of the north of France were proposing to us special arrangements for their region. Thinking it was better to have the discussions in a more favourable atmosphere, they asked us to come to Caux. We accepted this proposition.

At Caux I was deeply astonished to see hundreds of people able to live together without strife, with one common aim, and to discover the existence of such an ideology. I spent three days at Caux. I noticed there, especially among the youth, a faith and a dynamic quality comparable in several aspects to the ' mystique' and unselfishness of convinced Communists.

Further, I had observed that the employers of almost all countries, transported into this atmosphere, were reconsidering their original, out-dated points of view and were more easily becoming conscious of their responsibility as men and as employers in front of the problems with which the national and international situation faced them.

My friends of Moral Re-Armament saw me frequently and I accepted an invitation to go to another assembly which took place in Mackinac, U.S.A., where I got to know Frank Buchman. That is where I became aware of the opening of the second revolutionary phase of my life. I caught a glimpse of the whole struggle that had to be carried on to bring unity back to my country.

On my return from Mackinac I put this revolutionary action to the test by going to see several dozen employers and inviting them to come to Caux with the technicians of their factories and union delegates of all tendencies. In this way more than eighty delegations from the textile industry came to the Caux Assembly in the summer of 1951.

It was not always easy, but an atmosphere of trust was created. It enabled us to lay the solid foundations which led to our famous agreements of 9th June, 1953. The spirit of Caux has developed absolute honesty in the relationships between French union leaders and the employers. The referendum of 28th September, 1958, and the events which preceded it, give to one of the sentences of our textile agreements an even greater relevance: 'The textile industry intends to make an economic and social experiment in the interest of the nation, in a spirit of service, with a social objective.'

This experiment has given, in spite of the economic difficulties, at least an eight per cent wage increase per year to the textile workers. It has enabled the textile industry to support a third week of holidays with pay, the payment of five national holidays a year and the grant of an additional old-age pension for the workers. With the spirit of the 9th of June we were able to create an inter-union research bureau. With the help of this bureau we are making a permanent and honest inventory of the textile professions. We keep a check on the labour charges and the different methods of remuneration. One thousand four hundred militant union men have passed through our trades union training school.

A labour-management social committee composed of at least sixty people discusses in detail the wage situation. The debates of these committees have often been held at the time of social and political crises in these past years. All these meetings have given results. Our profession is amongst those with the fewest recorded strikes since 1951. The results of our discussions apply to 8,000 factories and 525,000 working men and women of the textile industry. Our agreements of 9th June, their spirit and their results, cannot be separated from the action that Moral Re-Armament has carried on in France during these last years.

Having fought and lived through the events of these last thirty years, I can divide my life and thought into three stages. The first, where I identified myself completely with the traditions of the French workers' movement: the second, the occupation period, which often made me think of the forces of good and of the existence of a higher power: finally, my meeting with Moral Re-Armament which led me to a total world concept.

I remember the Marxist forecasts according to which, when the conditions of human existence were improved, mankind's thinking was supposed to become better, more far-seeing, and of an untroubled serenity. Marxism says that a man is bound by fate, by fear, and by his needs and by his thoughts. I used to think for a long time that the material improvement of the condition of humanity would develop this elevation of thought and a reliable brotherly spirit, such as we had known during the struggles, when this had been our source of strength. But I had to take into account that the sacrifices made by some people for others were often repaid with ingratitude.

Working beside the men of Moral Re-Armament, I immediately understood that this ideology was going further than Marxism. It gave me the certainty of a better society, founded on perfect human behaviour. The type of man created by Moral Re-Armament is the torch bearer for a better civilisation.

The revolution of production is on the march. But the revolution of distribution needs Moral Re-Armament for its success; the producer and consumer have to fall in line with absolute moral standards. The history of the middle class demonstrates that men whose needs are satisfied are not necessarily superior men. If we want the men of today and the men of tomorrow to continue the forward march of civilisation, we must call upon a higher power.

The aim of the scientists of the whole world, and of the rival forces of East and West, is the conquest of outer space. Already you feel that the human spirit is, as it were, saturated with terrestrial experiment and the most audacious, the most intelligent and the most enlightened brains are turning towards space. Then one understands the imperious necessity for the spirit to venture forth beyond human thought and vision: and here Moral Re-Armament is the preface to a civilisation which is still impossible to measure by the standards of the one we know now.

The success of a revolution can be assured only by the combination of inspiration and realisation. Fifty years of struggle have had, as their starting point, the belief that economic standards lead inevitably to moral standards. These struggles were assuredly a necessity in the economic state of the whole world, but we are not less sure that the world of today will start from moral standards in order to assure the success of the economic standards. And that is where the ideology of Moral Re-Armament takes on all its revolutionary significance.

The inner change of men desired by Moral Re-Armament, that we have accepted, does away with the contradictions between self and our revolutionary aims. Our personal change is the preface to what the men of tomorrow could be.

To the action of the man of Moral Re-Armament, and to that of his whole team, is added the tremendous and mysterious strength of the invisible forces which work at our side to ensure the success of good against evil.

MAURICE MERCIER
General Secretary of the Textile Workers Federation CGT-FO

HUMAN TORPEDO

The family were so proud of me in 1943 when I was selected for the Naval Academy. And I was proud of myself! Three hundred of us boys from our area took the examinations. Each day some dropped out. Only fifty were left on the fourth day. And on 3rd November I was the only one who was given the choice between the Army and the Navy. I really studied hard in those days! As we Japanese reckon age, I was eighteen at the time, but that would be seventeen in the West.

I am Japanese, the oldest of eight children. There are three younger sisters and four younger brothers. We lived with our parents on Sakhalin Island. My father had money and position, and we had our own house and several farms.

The war was to put an end to all this. Our family lost everything, and in 1945 my mother fled with my brothers and sisters before the arrival of the Russians.

My father, who was Mayor at that time, had to remain under Russian occupation for two years, and I was living near Hiroshima, following a special training at the human torpedo school. They were called 'suicide torpedoes'.

The Naval Academy was an *élite* school, and of course we had special uniforms and good food, even in the last year after the American bombing raids began. I remember going home for the summer vacation, and travelling second, not the cheaper third, class on the train. The girls would turn to look at us in our smart short jackets. But we were under orders and did not want to commit any breach of discipline!

Then in a year and a half came the chance to volunteer for the suicide corps. There was no special pay.

I do not know if you can imagine the atmosphere in which we lived. It seems like a nightmare to look back on now, because of the reaction, but we took it very seriously in those days. It meant discipline and dedication. We were trained from childhood to be ready to die for the Emperor. We had learned to hate cowardice most of all. Our parents said they would rather have us brought home dead, than that we should return alive, having been prisoners of war. I felt the spirit of the old Samurai warriors within me, and was determined to fight for the Emperor.

You did not know beforehand which formation you were to be in, of course, because it was all secret until you started the special training. There were four suicide formations: the *kamikazi* plane pilots for the distant air strikes, the underwater *kaiten* torpedo men, the inshore surface boat pilots, and the men loaded with explosives who were taught to charge or dive into enemy troop concentrations if these succeeded in landing.

I was selected for the *kaiten* formation, the human torpedo pilots. *Kaiten* means 'reversal of fate'. We were sent a little way down the coast to a place about seven miles from Hiroshima.

For nearly six months we worked (up at 5 or 5.30 a.m.), all day long learning to steer those big cigar-shaped torpedoes which were destined for the vital parts of American warships. We trained in secrecy behind guarded walls, climbing down through a hatch which would be sealed from the outside. There, lying in the belly of our big fish (four times as long as we were), we used our hands and feet to work the levers which would steer us under the water towards the enemy.

There was a periscope for use near the surface, and of course we carried oxygen. The target, in the room where we had our training, was a warship which moved electrically across our field of vision in the periscope and the hits were recorded on dials.

One day, you knew the order would come and you would climb down into your torpedo for the last time. Your friends would seal you in, the water would rise above your periscope and your engine would drive you towards the enemy. You would have two hours of oxygen. This was enough, because if you missed your target, the warhead was timed to explode in two hours anyway.

Meanwhile, on Sundays during that summer we relaxed. I liked to read Hegel, Kant, Goethe and Plato. We could listen to classical music on the Japanese radio. I found Handel the most satisfying. Today it seems as if the radio is exclusively given up to hill-billy songs!

I remember one hot lazy day in August, I was standing in the shade of a big tree. The bombings were getting worse that summer of 1945. I was watching a Grumman fighter plane coming in. It was not a bomber, so I didn't run for shelter. Suddenly—br-r-r-rr—machine gunning! I jumped behind the tree. I had never been so close to death.

A few days later we were just getting up from breakfast. It was about 8.15 a.m. on a clear, warm morning. Suddenly the door was burst open by blast and a terrific wall of air rushed in on us. There in the sky over Hiroshima rose a 'nylon pink' mushroom-shaped cloud!

In the days that followed we were very crowded and all the time pushed into less and less space. More and more wounded arrived with terrible burns under their bandages, and we gave up our beds to them. We had to bury the corpses washed up on our beach, for many had tried to ease their pain by plunging into the river or the bay. I still have nightmares about those days.

For me everything began to go to pieces when the war ended. I could not get any news of my family and believed them all to be dead. There was no longer any reason for me to hold on to the old discipline. I began to try to make money in the black-market, and at various jobs.

I decided to continue my studies. Ten per cent of a college's enrolment was reserved for military or naval students after the war. The competition was frantic. I was lucky to get into an excellent school (now the university) at Kyoto, as a general science student.

After about two months I was walking back to the college one cold night when three American soldiers stopped me in the street and took everything of value I had, including the scholarship money I had been awarded. Soon afterwards the college bills came along. I could not pay and had to leave school.

When I could come by a little money, I would eat sweet potatoes and rice. Once, for a fortnight I had nothing to eat except horseradish and salt. And it was like that all over the country. We were cold and hungry and full of resentment.

I discovered that winter that my family were alive, except for my grandmother, whom we all loved. She had been on a ship that was torpedoed and sunk by the Russians. I hated the Russians because mother and father had to start all over again with nothing, and could not help me. I hated the Japanese Government who had brought us to war, poverty and despair. Finally, I hated the Americans because of the atom bomb, because they had robbed me, and also because with a box of sweets or a few cigarettes they could attract almost any Japanese girl.

For months I scraped and struggled. I would take a train to seek any job I could find. When the conductor asked for my ticket, I would jerk my thumb over my shoulder with an old ticket in my hand, to indicate I had already shown it in the next car, and get away without paying. My old Naval Academy discipline was swept away in hatred and frustration.

I began to earn a nickname of 'Deko', the tough! I organised the younger boys to barter rice, which was scarce, and American cigarettes, which were even scarcer, in the black market.

Finally, in April 1947, I was given a scholarship to Aoyama Gakuin University, a mission school, in the Engineering Department at Yokosuka. I had a secret hope that perhaps a Christian college would save me. After two dark years of disorderly living and trafficking in the black market, I was very unhappy. I remembered a Christmas party at which I had been present in the old days when I was twelve or thirteen. It had been so different from my present life!

I got a job as a washer-up at the American naval base next door to our school. They gave us one meal a day. We were so hungry that it was almost impossible to resist the temptation to pick up even the small scraps in the rubbish. Yet we knew if we were caught we would be kicked out. I did not want to lose this chance to study! I remember the anger I felt at the sight of good food being thrown out as garbage.

There was a political battle going on between rival student organisations for the control of the university. The school had a boat and I was a Naval Academy man. I still wore my uniform. I did not have the money for other clothes. If only I could get the boat going, everybody would look up to me. The only thing was that petrol was rationed. The Americans, I knew, had plenty. Why not try to get some? If I was discovered the guard would shoot: I knew that, too.

I chose a dark night to climb over the fence, and found a truck at the naval base. Just as I was ready to syphon out some petrol, I heard footsteps. My heart was beating fast and I was sweating as I crouched under the truck. It was a military policeman, but he never saw me and went on his way.

The next days I took many of the students out for trips in the boat. We tried to keep out of sight of the naval base. They might begin to wonder how we had come by petrol for pleasure cruises when rationing was so strict!

One night we ran out of petrol just as a storm blew up. A strong current carried us out to sea faster than our sail could take us back to the shore. We were all very frightened. At dawn I was at last able to bring the boat in on to the beach, and we knelt in the sand to thank Providence!

We learned later that the naval base had heard we were in trouble and had sent out a search plane. But they had not been able to find us. In spite of my hatred of the Americans, I had to admit that they had some good in them!

The cruises in the boat, and the way I had got the petrol for it, roused the students' admiration and they elected me their president.

I did not know much about the Communists then, but I remember one man who came to talk to me. He played on all my bitterness. Many of our best students at the Naval Academy listened to the Communists and are Communists today. The Communists won control of two of the national student organisations also.

As I look back on it, I think the only reason I did not fall for their line was that another man, with a big idea, was also fishing for me.

He was an American, Rowland Harker, the young Dean of our school. He spoke much better Japanese than I did English, so we could talk in a sort of mixture of the two. I could not help liking him, because he seemed really interested in us as individuals.

I had been made Prefect in our students' dormitory. He used to come two or three nights each week to see us. He cheered us up with lively games to help us keep warm and we enjoyed his company. He told us story after story of people like ourselves who had completely changed their way of living.

This interested us very much. For we did not expect very much from life, the way things were going.

That Christmas vacation I stayed in the dormitory, as I had no money for the journey home. New Year's Eve is a great occasion in Japan. Rowland invited me to supper, as I think he knew how lonely I was. We had hamburger steaks. What a change from my diet of sweet potatoes! We played games with matches on the table. He told me about absolute moral standards. That was not the way I was living! And he told me about listening to the inner voice to know what to do and how to do it. I had only listened up till then to the calls of ambition, popularity or other appetites.

What he said was a challenge to me. 'You gave your life to your country during the war, didn't you?' 'Yes,' I replied. 'Why not give your life now to create the kind of world you are looking for?' I did not answer that question straight away that day!

All I could think of was the stolen petrol. But I dared not say anything about that. The Americans might sentence me to hard labour in Okinawa, and I would certainly be expelled from the university.

But in the following weeks I began to 'listen', as he suggested. This was no discipline imposed by military training. It came from inside a man's heart and will, and that was its strength.

Rowland put us all to shame that spring. We found him, the Dean, in old clothes one day tackling the pile of bomb rubble in front of our buildings. Our immediate reaction was that he was crazy, but there was nothing to do but to pitch in and help. The school had little money, but this clean up did not cost a penny.

About this time I reflected on the four moral standards, and measured my life in detail by them. Yet still I could not bring myself to speak about the petrol.

Then Rowland invited me to share his rooms. That was wonderful for me. His place was warm, and I had not been able to eat so much for nearly three years.

A few weeks later there was a meeting for Moral Re-Armament in one of the big Tokyo Clubs. It was there I decided finally to take the step I had funked since New Year's Eve.

A former Prime Minister was in the audience and an uncle of the Emperor, along with other prominent people. I was one of the speakers. I told them what I had learned about MRA and afterwards some of them came to thank me. Right then I knew I could not put off any longer being honest about the syphoned petrol, whatever might happen to me.

I went to Rowland's room. He was sitting on the bed and I sat down beside him. My heart was pounding and I could feel my skin covered in goose-flesh. I was afraid he would say I could not stay with him any longer. Finally, I told him straight out that I had stolen petrol from the naval base, and why. I believe he had felt all along that I was hiding something. In any case he seemed to understand that I was the type who ended by wanting to be honest about things.

I knew that afterwards I should have to go to the Commandant of the Naval Base. I was almost more scared than when I had crouched under that truck. I blurted out to him that I had stolen the petrol and apologised. He was astonished. 'Good gracious, this is exactly the spirit we need!' And he let me go without punishment. It was pouring with rain as I went home, but I was smiling so much that everybody along the way turned to look at me.

And from that day my bitterness against the Americans vanished.

The next step was even harder—being honest with my parents when I went to Hokkaido that summer. We have a saying: 'A Japanese fears earthquakes, fire, typhoons . . . and his father.'

I began by telling my father all the things I had done that I was ashamed of. He grew pale and silent, and I did not know what was wrong. He was as though turned to stone with me for nine days before he found the courage to tell me about one thing he had been ashamed of doing during the Russian occupation. We have been true friends ever since.

Then I needed to go to the Tokyo station-master about the times

I had ridden on the trains without paying. He was surprised, but accepted my apology, though not the money I offered in repayment. He gave it to Moral Re-Armament, and since then has regularly sent a cheque.

The station-master took me to see the Governor of the National Railways: I told him how sorry I was about my dishonesty and how my way of life had been transformed. As a result, he offered the free use of their conference hall for Moral Re-Armament.

Since that time I have finished my university training and have worked with Moral Re-Armament in Europe and America, as well as in Asia.

My first real meeting with Frank Buchman was at the end of an assembly on Mackinac Island in the State of Michigan. We Japanese had had a dinner with him in one of the homes on the island. Personally I had only bowed to him as we met. This time we were on a train with him, heading West for Los Angeles. He sent an invitation one day to my coach asking me to join him at lunch. I spent several hours preparing what to say to this 'great man'. All through lunch he did not say a word except from time to time he made a remark about the scenery, which was superb. At the end of the meal he rose and cordially thanked the Negro waiter for the way he had served us.

That day I realised that I had been trying to put a 'great leader' at the centre of my life instead of God. It is a danger we easily fall into in Japan. I told Frank so the next day. He smiled and said, 'Fine, fine.' By saying nothing at that lunch he had taught me more than by thousands of words.

Another time I can remember he still said very little, but that little was very much to the point! We were in Madras with a large team of people, putting on our plays. I was ushering people to their seats at the theatre. We ushers agreed it was too hot to have people standing inside the theatre. Besides, it might make Frank and his guests uncomfortable in the front rows. So we turned away several hundred people.

Frank came out in the interval and remarked, 'We don't seem to have so many people today.'

We told him what we had done.

'What!' he said, with a voice like thunder. 'You sent them away! Those people who were willing to wait for hours in the broiling sun in the hope of getting in?' We said we were sorry. 'So am I,' he said.

Next day I was afraid to see Frank. I thought I had ruined everything and was very discouraged. But as I was trying to keep out of sight he came up to me. His eyes were twinkling as he asked, 'Well, how are you today?' and smiled. I felt his forgiveness. He hates the sin, but loves the sinner.

At another assembly I remember an airline executive coming to Frank's room to say goodbye. A task force was getting ready to fly to India. This man told Frank how grateful he was to have found a new understanding in his home and for the happy family life that resulted from it.

'What are you going to do to bring MRA to the world?' asked Frank.

'I'm going to give my life insurance,' said the airlines man. All of us in the room thought this was great, except Frank.

'And what else?' asked Frank.

'I'm going to provide seats for those who are going to India.'

By this time the rest of us were beginning to feel embarrassed and were looking at the floor.

'And what else?' Frank asked once more.

'I'm going to give myself wholly in this fight,' the man replied.

'Fine!' said Frank.

Another man who had a lot of influence in my life was a young Japanese, Yori Mitsui, son of Takasumi Mitsui of the well-known family in Japanese industry. In 1951 Yori gave all his energies and strength to help a delegation of seventy-five prominent Japanese, who were training in Moral Re-Armament in Europe and the United States. Finally he fell seriously ill, but, although he was dying, he continued to give the best of himself without counting the cost, to all the people around him at the Mayo Clinic. He was twenty-two.

As we lowered him into his grave in Pasadena, California, I decided to carry on his fight. Ever since then, when I am discouraged, I remember Yori and I know that I cannot betray the promise I made then. Many other Japanese have drawn fresh inspiration from a visit to his grave. On the tombstone are carved Frank Buchman's words: 'Gloriously Yori lives to bind together America and Japan for ever.'

I shall never forget the days we spent in Manila in 1955. I was one of the first Japanese to go there after the war. We were invited to the home of one of the most respected families in the Philippines, although it was unheard of for a Japanese to cross a Filipino threshold because of the violent hatreds left by the war.

A woman there told us what some Japanese officers had done to her family. Quartered in their home for many months, these officers had feared Filipino reprisals, as the American forces fought their way back into the Philippines. They had taken the woman's relatives with scores of other Filipinos, locked them in a church, poured in petrol and set fire to the building.

'How could you be so cruel?' she asked me.

What could a Japanese reply? In the end I said, 'I am very, very sorry. I want to dedicate my whole life to make restitution for the wrongs Japan has done to other nations. I will work and live so that the Japanese never again do such things.'

This is my commitment for the rest of my life, and my wife Yuriko has taken the same decision with me.

HIDEO NAKAJIMA
Japan

THREE BROTHERS WITH ONE AIM

People could not believe their eyes. At Atpadi, a village hidden in the heart of India, three cowboys and a big bass fiddle piled out of an old 1938 Plymouth. This old car had dodged bullock carts on the dusty sun-scorched road and further on had dug deep ruts in the marshes.

Rajmohan Gandhi, grandson of the Mahatma, was the companion and guide of us cowboys. We had been invited to meet Gandhi's great disciple, Vinoba Bhave.

Carrying on the work of Gandhi, this saintly man, Vinoba, has, during the last year, walked thousands of miles from village to village, asking the landowners to give land to those who have none. After washing at the well and eating a meal which the village women had prepared for us on banana leaves, we were told that Vinoba wanted to see us. We had written him a special song and the three of us sang it to him, playing our own accompaniment. He listened, smiling and tapping his fingers in time with the music. The words were in his own mother tongue. They said: 'There is enough land in the world for everybody's need but not enough land for everybody's greed. If

135

everyone cares enough and everyone shares enough, everyone will have enough.'

After we had sung several songs he asked us to come with him to his great public meeting. Outside, 10,000 people had seated themselves on the ground in eager anticipation of hearing and seeing the holy man. We sang for the crowd and Rajmohan translated. In his talk which followed Vinoba used as his theme the words of our song, and had the people roaring with laughter as he talked about Ralph's big bass !

Next morning at 4.30 we were striding along the road with Vinoba and his band of followers on our way to the next village, seven miles away. The entire population turned out to greet Vinoba and pay him homage. An arch of welcome had been put up. We wound our way between the rows of villagers who lined the gaily decorated streets. Again Vinoba asked us to sing and speak to the people.

Before we departed in our old Plymouth, which was waiting for us at the village, Vinoba called us and said, ' You and I must work together. We must form a great moral bloc and win the world to our side.'

As we drove away the villagers along the river bank looked up from their washing and waved us a friendly farewell.

There we were, three brothers in cowboy costume, three typical young Americans, singing in this far-away village so different from our home town, at the side of a holy man of India. What had brought us there?

Here is the story.

' I've got an idea. Let's start a band ! ' one of us suggested as we sat in the house one rainy day trying to think of something to stop us yawning from boredom. There were three of us—oldest brother Steve, aged fifteen; Paul, aged twelve; and Ralph, ten years old. Our fourth brother, Ted, aged two, was really too young to be included. This suggestion of a band caught on right away, so Steve took out his five-dollar guitar which he hadn't touched for five years and Paul persuaded Mother to buy him a cheap banjo ukelele. That was the beginning.

We had taken a great liking to American western and folk music, so that is the form our music took. Within two weeks our repertoire had grown to ten numbers. Our first public appearance was at our parents' cocktail party. At ten years old Ralph was the hit of the evening with his song 'Rye Whiskey'.

Dad, who was as eager as we, bought Steve and Paul new instruments, a guitar and a mandolin. Ralph had no instrument and with his natural flair for singing he was the featured vocalist. With his boy soprano he could yodel like anything. But there came a point where we felt Ralph should also play an instrument. Steve and Paul discussed the matter; we settled on the bass fiddle. Ten lessons and a few weeks later Ralph's bass fiddle joined us permanently. Named 'George', it towered above Ralph, who was only twelve at the time. So for a year or two it fell to the older brothers to carry it around.

Our musical venture developed rapidly. Our youthful enthusiasm and appearance won everybody. We found ourselves in demand to play at community functions, parties, benefits, hospitals, etc. We won an amateur contest in Indianapolis. We came out victorious over quite a formidable field of performers, including a spectacular jazz pianist. To out-dazzle this fellow we chose a very fast song called 'Freight Train Blues' in which Paul played both mandolin and banjo.

Our music was becoming a profession. Within only a year and a half of our starting we had broken into the professional ranks and were getting paid for our performances. Ralph recalls how our first cheque of thirty dollars began to whet his appetite for more. With that sweet smell of success we became more and more serious about our future as a trio. At the ages of eighteen, fifteen and thirteen we were given a weekly television show of our own.

Then we bought our own car. In succession we had a '36 Oldsmobile, a '36 de Soto and a '41 Ford. This last was turquoise blue. So our money mostly went into gasoline, cowboy costumes and instruments. At one time we had a maroon 'jeepster', a civilian-type jeep convertible. It had a musical horn which could play 'Mary had a little lamb', and one night in the garage this horn got stuck on the high note and just about drove the neighbourhood crazy.

In the spring of 1951 Dad changed his job. From Indianapolis we moved to Los Angeles, where he started a food business of his own. For us three California meant Hollywood and even greater prospects. Shortly afterwards we met the western star Tex Williams. He invited us to become a regular feature on his radio and television shows. The radio shows were broadcast over a national network. Then we signed a contract with Columbia records. The outlook was bright and promising.

We had begun our trio just for fun. Now, as our ambition increased over the years, it became more of a business and much less fun.

Paul: Rehearsing had become a duty. Ralph would put down his magazines and join us, dragging his feet. Each false note would make me furious and I often threatened to quit the whole thing. Steve and Ralph would argue who should sing the solo. I would cast my vote and settle the matter by the best democratic process, and we would press on grimly in a very bad temper.

Ralph: For us teenagers life in the entertainment world was something unique. Added on to all our other activities, it made us the busiest young men in town. We never had a moment to spare. Whoever didn't drive to the television show would study on the way. We had our school work and we held positions in our student unions. We were also active on our school teams—football, basketball, baseball, tennis and athletics. From an early age we were taken out each evening by Dad, who drilled us on the fundamentals of baseball. Then there were the clubs and dances, as well as the swimming from the beautiful Californian beaches, where all the kids go. We would take girls down, and just laze all day getting tanned by the sun. We would play a little volleyball, go into the surf and come out and lie in the sun some more, then roast sausages at night.

Steve: Everything was wrapped around our social life. At university I was spending so much time thinking about my dates that my grades weren't very high. It wasn't that I was stupid but I was always thinking about which girl to take out.

Paul: If you didn't have two dates every week-end, you were a social outcast.

Ralph: The worst thing that could happen to you was to have nothing to do on Friday or Saturday night.

Steve: We never stayed home. Mother would urge us to come in early, at twelve or one. That's pretty reasonable by American standards. So we would come in at three or so. Next day she'd ask: 'When did you come in?' So we would say: 'One-thirty.' Our parents were hoping against hope that we were going the right way.

Paul: They knew they couldn't say much to us, because we had been to parties where Mom and Dad were pretty high. That's the way their friends lived. Some of our parents' friends got divorces after being married for twenty years.

In July 1951 Mother and Dad were given tickets to a musical play called *Jotham Valley*. They came home from the play very enthusiastic and urged us to go and see it. Here was a chance to take our girl friends to something different, instead of the usual old thing—a movie. Besides the tickets were free—a real windfall. So we took our girl friends and we saw *Jotham Valley*. After the play we met some members of the cast. They were young guys like us, one from England and others from America and Canada. But, by golly, they had a smile, a clean, clear look and a sincere friendliness that we had never seen before. We were amazed to learn that none of the cast received any salary. The principal singer had a voice that the music critics compared to Ezio Pinza's, but he had turned down every offer of fame and fortune to sing in the MRA plays. When we first met these young men, it was a strange thing, but we felt we trusted them right away. We felt as though they were our best friends. The striking thing about them was that they knew what they were living for and where they were going, while we were just drifting along, trying to make life as pleasant for ourselves as possible.

A few days later we were invited to play at a birthday party for one of the cast, a young man from Scotland. It was a great party. We had never enjoyed ourselves so much—and we were used to parties! But this was different. There were over 150 people there, boys and girls, young and old, from many different countries. We sang a lot of our songs, which were received with great enthusiasm. The young Scotsman played some real hot boogie-woogie on the piano and we joined in with him. Great fun! But it was the atmosphere and the vitality of these people that made the party so much fun. There was always plenty of laughter and everyone enjoyed life to the full. It was 'good clean fun'. After the party was over we couldn't figure out how we could have had such a good time without all the usual accompaniments such as dim lights, dates and dancing.

Several days later we went to sing at a special luncheon. Just before lunch someone introduced us to Frank Buchman. He was seventy-three then and rather disabled. He was wearing a dark blue suit. He took one look at our loud California sports jackets and said with a twinkle in his eye, 'My, look at those beautiful coats, I must go and change right away.' He disappeared through a doorway and reappeared a few moments later sporting a bright grey-and-black checked jacket rivalled in gaiety and colour only by those we wore. An old man with such a young and gay heart knew how to win the hearts of rascals like us.

Jotham Valley was running at the famous Carthay Circle Theatre in Hollywood. We were invited back to help usher people into their seats. We did this night after night. It was great fun because it was done in complete teamwork, and nobody got a penny for it. That certainly intrigued us.

During the play each night we would sit in the lobby with our fellow ushers and talk with them for hours. They told us about the four moral standards. 'Wow,' we said, 'you guys must be perfect.' They laughed. We asked many questions about what each of these standards meant to them personally. Another thing really struck us. They said that the ordinary man can do the extraordinary thing, that as ordinary guys we could have a part in changing the world. We vaguely knew the world needed changing—but of course that had been well outside our range of interests! If we could help change the world then here was something big and important, and the most convincing part was that these guys lived what they talked about. Then came the day when they asked, 'Would you like to try it?' We said, 'O.K., what do we do?' They told us about listening to the voice of God in our hearts. One fellow explained how we are like radio sets. If the connections are dirty they need to be cleaned up in order to get good reception.

Our whole family was sold on the idea. Driving home one night, down the brilliantly lit Hollywood streets, we all agreed that we would happily give all our money to MRA and travel around the world with it—after we had become rich and famous!

However, we had all decided to give it a try. Our friends had said they had found that God had a plan for our lives and that if we listened we could find out what that plan was. In other words, if we listened God could speak. We were very sceptical. We had been an average church-going family and we knew how to pray, but that God could speak to us was going a little too far. . . .

Ralph: It was worth a try and there was nothing to lose, though inside I was scared stiff about what my friends in school would say if they found me out.

Even at fourteen years old I was struck with the thought, 'You've made a mess of your life, now let God have a chance.' It was a sunny Sunday morning. I sat on the edge of my bed and wrote, 'Say sorry to Mother, and help more in the house.' I went and did so. Mother immediately became more happy and cheerful. I was a real rascal at home. I was very lazy and indisciplined and never did my homework. Mother had a heck of a time getting me to school on time in the morning. She had a harder time getting me to do my chores around the house. 'Ralph, have you swept the driveway?' she would call. 'Yes,' I would call back from behind a comic book. Of course I hadn't swept the driveway. When Mother saw I hadn't done my job she would get after me and be very cross.

There were many things that the family did not know about me, and I made sure that no one should find out. I was just a young fellow with the usual problems—smoking in secret, girls, reading the wrong kind of books—but they ran my life. As everyone else was doing these things too, why try and do anything else? I was ashamed of some of these things, but was really licked by them. One of my new friends, a fellow from Canada, had cared enough to tell me about himself, about the things he had done wrong and what he had had to do when he decided to change. It was the first time anyone had ever spoken so frankly to me of his life, and for the first time I felt free to say what went on in my heart, especially all the things I had carefully kept secret. I poured out everything, and felt as free as air.

I told all these things to Steve and Paul, and then to my parents. This was the most difficult part. I was certain they would not understand, but they understood very well and were grateful. My new friends had given a modern teenager like me a great enough purpose to make me put things straight and live the right way.

Paul: It is interesting to get to know yourself and find out what makes you tick. I thoroughly enjoyed *Jotham Valley*, but throughout the performance I had an uncomfortable feeling. The play told the story of the reconciliation of two brothers and the benefit this brought to the folk who lived in the whole valley. This made me think, but I unconsciously tried to justify myself, saying, 'That's the way I've always lived.' But I should not have been so defensive if this had been true. I had the reputation among my friends of being a 'good guy'. If they told dirty stories I pretended not to be interested. The fact is I lived and thought as they did, or worse, but I liked to keep up appearances. So neither my friends nor my family knew what I was really like. . . .

I was greatly attracted by the size of the task that my new friends were undertaking. It hit me like a bombshell, and opened up a new world for me. It was logical and right, and seemed like the natural next step. We wanted to leap in with all the impetuosity and enthusiasm of youth.

We had an interesting life, we had money and success, but there was plainly something missing. For our lives completely revolved around ourselves.

One of the first thoughts I had when I was quiet was about my little brother Ralph, whom I had treated like dirt. I felt I should apologise, but hated to do it because I thought he would take advantage of me. The truth is that I was jealous of him. He was physically and intellectually all I would have liked to be. I did apologise and we became the best of friends.

One day I realised that I had always felt inferior because of my asthma. I had never been strong, and this feeling of inferiority had always run my life, though I had not seen it. To make up, I was a perfectionist in anything I attempted, whether schoolwork, sports or music, and when I didn't measure up to the inflated picture I had envisaged for myself, I got upset. My whole life was wrapped up in making a great impression on others, particularly the girls. What a relief it was when I could go to school without having to worry about what the others were thinking!

Steve: Probably more than Ralph or Paul I had great ambition for our music and visualised our names flashing in the neon lights of Hollywood. I did not know where it was going to take us—films, television or riding horses in westerns—but I liked the applause and success. They give you a feeling of getting there.

Our father, being a conscientious business man, drafted a fourteen-point programme, outlining ways we could reach the top. The plan included new clothes, publicity and correspondence with disc jockeys. During our school vacation we built a room over our garage which we set up as an office. We bought a filing cabinet for our fan mail and business correspondence. Pictures of our friends and idols in the entertainment field decorated the walls. As a guitar player, alone I could not be a success. We had to be a trio. Anything which stood in my way had to be eliminated. Paul was a real artist with his mandolin and banjo; he was my natural ally. Ralph, on the other hand, although he began singing before he could talk, found other interests in life, such as reading and sleeping. As a result great clashes occurred between us. Being the oldest brother I assumed the position of chief organiser and leader of the band. Generally I announced the times to practise and listed the songs to be rehearsed. This, of course, was natural; since I had the most experience in years on this earth, the last word should be mine.

Like my brothers I decided to take the plunge. I put things right, for instance I wrote an apology to my Latin teacher for the two years during which I had cheated in class.

Then we were invited to attend the MRA Assembly at Mackinac Island, Michigan. Everyone was for our going except my father and me. This summer I had intended using for intensive rehearsals, and I wanted to be on hand in case any promising offers came our way. Dad and I agreed that we could do much more for MRA if we became popular and famous first.

At that point one of my friends asked me why I carried on in music. 'Because I enjoy it,' I replied sharply. 'Steve,' he said, 'I think you are ambitious. Don't you ever think about your brothers?' I was furious. I shouted, 'If this means I have to give up my music then I am through with it. What's wrong with doing music?'

But after a few days a little voice deep inside me told me to go with my brothers to Mackinac. Besides, I had no alternative, as they had decided to go and I could not get them to change their minds.

That summer at Mackinac was a turning-point in our lives. We had found something to give to the world. I was shocked into the realisation that these absolute moral standards cut across every motive of life. My friend had a valid point when he asked me if I ever thought for my brothers. When Ralph enthusiastically played a rough game of American football my only concern was that he didn't injure his hands or arms, which would keep him from playing the bass fiddle. Just as I had organised our practice sessions I tried to organise my brothers' lives. I liked being the boss and being in control, because it gave me a feeling of security.

Unity for us came not by chance but by change. I decided first to be absolutely honest with myself. Then I apologised to my brothers for my domination. This was a difficult thing for an elder brother to do. My prestige would be shattered. Ralph said, 'Don't worry, we've never had much respect for you anyway.' The result was that for the first time we got to know each other and to trust each other. I decided to let God be the boss instead of me. Can brothers become friends? We have found that it is possible.

Driving across the plains in the far west of America, on our way home from Mackinac, we had written our first two songs in a fresh style called 'A Spanking New Day' and 'Come on Folks', which were recorded later for Columbia Records. We wanted now more than ever to use our talents to bring something new to people. Hollywood producers urged us to sing the popular songs of the day—'You can't have a popular show without them,' they reasoned. But we noticed that people enjoyed 'A Spanking New Day' as much, if not more, than 'Lovesick Blues'.

Of our list of 150 songs we weeded out all that were soft, shallow or suggestive. We used to sing them not meaning to do harm to people, but only to get appreciation and popularity. But that is not what music is for. It reflects the living and thinking of people; and it is also a powerful way of influencing them. Everybody enjoys it. Its influence can be good or bad. This specially struck us later, as we travelled in many countries. We saw the effects of Hollywood's films, particularly on the youth. So much that we export from America spreads the wrong ideas: and we are sorry that we were a part of it.

Our music took on a new dimension. Our old songs attracted only a certain public in America. Now suddenly the whole world seemed to open up for a new type of music. These songs spoke to the heart of every man. So our repertoire now includes songs in twenty different languages !

As summer 1953 came round we were as busy as ever. We had made the acquaintance of the best TV producers, and they had asked us to come and see them again to talk more seriously about the contracts they might give us. With these prospects we expected to earn about $2,000 a show. It was at this point that we were invited to go to the Moral Re-Armament Assembly at Caux, Switzerland.

It was the first of July. We were quiet and took time to listen as a family, and we all had the same thought: go to Caux.

We arrived there on 1st August, the Swiss National Day. A great celebration was going on in the meeting hall, which was packed. After our aeroplane trip we were very tired, had caught chills and were not at all in our best form. But someone announced to the big audience that three 'hill-billies' from Hollywood had just landed. So there was nothing for it but to take out our instruments and sing. Our first song was called 'The Caux Song'. We had written it just before leaving Los Angeles and had put the final touches to it over the Atlantic. This song described Caux—people had shown us pictures —and had a little yodel in it. It brought the roof down. We were gratified that our hill-billy music went over so well in Europe.

But the most important thing about our stay was what it meant for us as a family. At Caux our parents wanted to tell us about their past lives. It was really difficult, as they were afraid they would lose our respect for ever. The previous days they had found a whole new understanding and love for one another through each being absolutely honest.

We came into their room, from which we had a glorious view of Lake Geneva, the Rhône Valley and the Alps. Dad and Mother said, 'We just want you to know what kind of parents you have.' Then they told us about their lives, all the things they had not wanted us to know before. We were surprised; but we were so grateful. What a relief to know we were all so much the same! There were no more secrets, nothing more to hide. We were all human, and we needed each other's help very much. At this moment we knew in the roots of our being that God needed our family for His work in the world; that He was calling us, individually and together as a family, to be His instruments for changing the living and thinking of the youth of our generation. So we decided to commit our lives to God, and to obey His will and His plan, no matter what the cost, or where it would take us. We did this, on our knees, all together. We did not know where this would lead or what it fully meant, but we knew that it was the turning-point in our lives. Of course, there have been doubts, fears and hesitances since then, but God has never let us go. From each struggle has come victory and a deeper commitment. Today, looking back over the years, we are more thankful than we can say for our parents' honesty about their mistakes and for the encouragement they constantly give us boys to live up to the highest ideal we know.

Our parents returned home after three weeks. We were to follow for the schools' opening at the beginning of September. Then one day we heard that Frank Buchman had something very special to say to us. We were bowled over when we heard that he was inviting us to travel for a year with him and his friends. Immediately we cabled our parents to tell them. They replied, 'We back you up a hundred per cent in whatever you decide.' We were quiet and listened and all got the same answer, 'Accept the invitation. This is the most important thing you can do with your lives.'

We wrote our manager explaining our decision and asking him to cancel our contracts. Steve and Paul wrote a long letter to the President of their university telling him what they had decided to give their lives for. Ralph was to continue his studies by correspondence; so he completed his last two years of high school, studying in hotels, cars, buses, trains, aeroplanes and boats.

And we don't get a penny for our work.

Our young brother Ted also caught the spirit. When he was eleven, he came with Mother to Caux. One day he asked to speak in a meeting and said before everybody, 'Today I decided to get absolutely honest with Mother. And I also decided to stop smoking.' Everyone nearly fell off their chairs and then there was a burst of laughter.

Through all this we found a new scale of values. We saw ourselves for what we really were. Like so many in our country, we only knew about the pursuit of pleasure and how to suit ourselves and live comfortably. If we made an effort to be decent, it was only to get on better in life.

This has turned our ideas upside-down. The choice is clear: either we are part of the disease in the world, or we change and become part of the cure.

We were never interested in just 'being good', and we were really too busy to join a movement or organisation. But what our friends had given us was an ideology—not something to do in our spare time, but something to give our whole lives to. Now we could put the talents God had given us to effective and constructive use for the world. Not only have we found the answer to our own problems, but also, and this is more important still, we have found the people who can bring to the world the answer it needs and we have joined forces with them.

Our deepest conviction is that God has a plan to remake the world; and, in the same way as rascals like ourselves, every man can put his life straight and use all his energy to carry out this plan.

For us this meant that on a rainy October morning in 1953, with a group of thirty Asians, Europeans and Americans, we boarded the train bound for the Ruhr. This was the first leg of a journey that has taken us in the last five years to twenty-two countries on four continents.

STEVE, PAUL AND RALPH COLWELL
Hollywood

HISTORIC JOURNEY

A great crowd of pilgrims from the four corners of the earth filled the Basilica of St. Peter's in Rome. It was high summer, a few months before the death of Pius XII. Carried on the 'Sedia gestatoria', the Pope drew near to the High Altar and amid a storm of cheers from the crowd, mounted the steps to the throne.

On the left of the papal throne and facing the Holy Father on this day were two distinctive figures who had never before been seen in the Basilica. They were two Buddhist monks from Thailand, draped in their saffron robes with their heads shaven. One was His Excellency Phra Bimaladharma, Lord Abbot of Watmahadhatu at Bangkok, the biggest Buddhist monastery in Thailand; the other was his interpreter, Bikkhu Manas Cittadama, Dean of the Buddhist University in Bangkok.

The Holy Father greeted the crowd in six languages. He ended his discourse in English, saying, 'We are all members of the same family as we have the same Father Who is in Heaven, so let us strengthen our bonds of love and understanding.' Then, after the blessing, the Holy Father descended with firm steps to meet those closest to him. When he came to the Buddhist Lord Abbot, many wondering eyes were turned towards them. The Lord Abbot said to the Holy Father, 'I have come here to try to create understanding between Catholics and Buddhists. I believe that all the great religions have the same objective: although we have not everywhere similar ways of practising our faith, we should work together to assure the peace of the world.' The Pope answered with a friendly gesture, and, weighing his words, said, 'I agree and I want the same thing.'

The Lord Abbot presented the Holy Father with a gift of a saffron silk bag like the one in which every monk in Thailand carries his few possessions. The Pope tucked the bag under his arm and continued with his audience.

This meeting was first thought of by the Lord Abbot in his monastery many thousands of miles away in the suffocating heat of Bangkok. It was the eve of his departure for America to join Dr. Frank Buchman. It was the first time that a man of such distinction in the Buddhist hierarchy had undertaken such a journey to the West.

What are the origins of this extraordinary journey? At New Year 1954, an Asian Assembly for Moral Re-Armament was held in Bangkok, and the delegates were received by the Lord Abbot, Phra Bimaladharma, at the Temple of Watmahadhatu. After he had welcomed his guests, he generously offered the hospitality of his monastery to all who cared to come and live there. So it was that three young Westerners, who remained in Bangkok after the Assembly, and who had no funds for hotel life, remembered the Lord Abbot's invitation. Warmly welcomed, they shared in the food and accommodation of the one thousand monks and novices who lived in the monastery. For each was provided a teak-wood bed, softened only by the regulation mat of one-eighth of an inch thickness, and with a hard pillow. All three young men were taller than the Thais. One was a Dane, one a Norwegian and the other one an Australian, and the beds were considerably shorter than those they used at home! But the hospitality was generous and the monks shared all their food with them; food for which they had begged in their morning outing.

The three friends stayed six weeks. The Lord Abbot, who was fifty, was tireless in his questions. Sometimes they spent all night in these discussions. He is an 'illumined' man, according to the Buddhist expression, in whom deep peace and dignity are blended with a sparkling humour, and he is quick to sense genuine spiritual experience. These four men shared a common experience of moral change and spiritual enlightenment.

The Lord Abbot was a heavy smoker, but one fine day he stopped without saying anything to his guests, who did not smoke. The father of one of the young men was Minister of Foreign Affairs in his own country. One day the Lord Abbot wistfully observed, 'Here you are, the son of a Western Foreign Minister, living in my monastery. I wish I could say the same of our Cabinet Minister's sons.'

These friendships were maintained through the following years. In

May 1958, Phra Bimaladharma received the visit of friends bringing him news of Frank Buchman. While the young novices served tea and Coca-cola, the Lord Abbot got up suddenly to go and consult his calendar. 'The rainy season does not begin until 1st August. It is at that time the Buddhist Lent begins, and I would have to be back in my monastery.' This was the way in which he expressed his long-cherished desire to meet Dr. Buchman, the man of whom he had heard so much and who was at that time in the U.S.A.

In the next days he obtained the authorisation of His Majesty the King, of the Government, and of the Ecclesiastical Cabinet to take his leave. He invited as his companion Bikkhu Manas, Dean of the University, and also one of his pupils from the monastery, who had since become a successful business man. As monks are not supposed to handle money, this man would be responsible for finance on the journey.

By 6 a.m. the next morning there were five hundred saffron-robed monks at Bangkok airport. Someone said there would have been one thousand, but that it was difficult to get in from the country districts so early.

Planning the movements of a Buddhist Lord Abbot has not yet become part of the schedule of travel agencies. Buddhist monks must finish their last meal of the day before twelve noon, so throughout the next seven weeks of travel the airlines conformed to these hours and the days were regulated accordingly. But it was difficult to decide the hour exactly on a long flight from East to West. Then there was the question of seating. The Lord Abbot must not sit next to a woman, and had to be served by the steward and not the stewardess. But, long used to simple sleeping arrangements, the Lord Abbot and his companion curled up in their chairs and slept peacefully.

When he arrived at Mackinac, the Lord Abbot asked to see Frank Buchman straight away. The next day he was by his side on the platform with the other speakers. 'These absolute moral principles,' he said, 'will be the beacon that will guide humanity to its destination.' Then the Lord Abbot beckoned to his friends to carry forward the ceremonial gong with its golden scrolls, which he had brought from his monastery. Grasping the hammer he struck the gong four times, to symbolise the four absolute moral standards. Afterwards he pinned a gold medal, on which a portrait of Buddha was engraved, to Dr. Buchman's lapel.

The visit of the Lord Abbot lasted fifteen days. On the eve of his departure he came to Frank Buchman to say goodbye. 'When I have travelled in Asia, sometimes I have had trouble with my food,' he said, 'but here in Mackinac the food has been perfectly to my taste and I have felt really at home, just as if I were in my own monastery.' He continued, 'Dr. Buchman, I only wish that we could have met twenty years ago. Think what we could have done together for the peace of the world.' With a twinkle, Dr. Buchman replied, 'It is not too late to start. Let us do it together. I am so glad to hear you are going to Washington.'

On the way to Washington the Lord Abbot stopped at Detroit, where he toured the Ford factory, gave an interview on television, visited a Negro worker in his home and talked until midnight with a distinguished group of Detroit citizens. He told them, 'I have heard that ninety per cent of American workers are not satisfied with conditions and they always want more. This is a grave danger for your country. You think that the danger which threatens you is materialism from the outside, but this danger may be greater because it comes from within.'

Every evening the Lord Abbot would go to the National Theatre where crowds gathered to see *The Crowning Experience* which was being presented by a company, also from Mackinac, in Washington. This play is inspired by the life of a woman who had done much for the education of her people. A Negress, who, after years of struggle on behalf of her race, and years of perplexity over the problems of human relations, discovered the solution for which she and they sought. When the curtain came down, the floodlights were turned on the Presidential Box, in which the Lord Abbot sat. He rose, and, weighing each word, said, 'What you have seen on the stage tonight must be put into practice by the whole world.'

Many a Congressman and Senator had cause to remember the Lord Abbot's frankness. One evening a Congressman spoke with enthusiasm of the play. 'Then we count on you to carry this message to every member of Congress,' said the Lord Abbot and, presenting him with a tiny golden image of the Lord Buddha, he added, 'Every time you see this image it will remind you to live the four absolute moral standards.'

Before leaving the United States he spoke to all his MRA friends and thanked them. 'It is not difficult for me to understand the significance of the four absolute moral standards as they are also the same in Buddhism,' he said. 'The only thing is I find them difficult to apply. I admire the way you have of apologising when you are wrong. This is the way of real achievement for all true scholars.'

From the airport he sent a telephone message to Frank Buchman at Mackinac. 'I shall be by your side in the fight for the true peace of the world,' he said. 'The world must live by these four standards.' Frank Buchman replied by thanking him warmly for his visit and saying, 'You should go to visit Chancellor Adenauer.'

A few weeks later the German newspapers had on their front pages a photograph of the Chancellor receiving in Bonn the Lord Abbot of Thailand and his companions. Together the two men spoke of the fresh element that Frank Buchman had brought into the modern world. The next day the Lord Abbot said to the Lord Mayor of Bonn, ' We in Asia have looked to the West for technical help, but we never expected to receive spiritual aid or comfort from there. But Moral Re-Armament, with its four absolute moral standards, is the spiritual aid which Asia will gladly accept from you.'

It was in Switzerland that the Lord Abbot received the news that his old mother had died in a village in the north of Thailand. 'Now,' he said, 'I shall not be able to give her my present.' He had bought for her, in America, a wheel-chair.

As he left for Rome a telegram reached him from Dr. Buchman which read: 'My heart goes out to you in affection and sympathy. Every man has his mother in his heart. My own mother died while I was travelling in Asia. Her spirit illumined the whole railway carriage, which was as bright as day, and we were one. Your mother has given the world a great son. She lives on in what you are giving, by your courageous leadership, to all nations.'

In Delhi he was received within a few hours of his arrival by the President of India. Coming away from the President's palace, the Indian journalists assembled outside asked his opinion on the crisis in the Middle East. He said simply, 'The remedy lies in the four absolute standards. It may sometimes be bitter medicine, but it guarantees an effective cure. We have to accept and live these standards without hesitation. By observing them we shall end the divisions which bring about nationalism. Perhaps we shall arrive at a nationalism that includes the whole world. It is better to conquer oneself than to conquer others, because this victory brings peace and happiness to oneself and not suffering to others. If the leaders of every country learned this, there would be no wars.'

That evening, before going by air to his native country, he went on to say to a few friends, 'The world is like a clock. Within there are many different wheels of different shapes and sizes, some working quickly, some working slowly, but when they are working in harmony then we get the right time.'

PART TWO

The Universal Man—Frank Buchman

WHAT DO ALL these stories have in common? What happened in the lives of Iréne Laure, of the Nigerian trade unionist, and in that of Bjerkholt? What decided the three American singers, the Indian nationalist and the young Japanese to change course? How is it that a French industrialist and Maurice Mercier take the same road together?

What is it that these men, from different backgrounds, different races, different religions, and of diverse ages, find at a turning-point in their lives? What is the new element into which these people have plunged and which has suddenly altered the laws that governed their personalities and the whole trend of their existence?

We have a secret within the reach of everyone, a kind of public secret. What is it?

A definition would only be misleading, because we are here in the presence of an elusive reality, but one which is well known to those who have drawn near to it. Some live all their lives unconsciously turning aside each time it crosses their path. They pretend to deny the existence of something that has been there all the time, had they wanted to see. Others have realised the outline and dimensions of this reality, but have chosen to draw away from it. Some have never met it at all.

Let us try to grasp what this reality is, by studying the history of one man whose life has been wholly guided by it.

Recently he was celebrating his eightieth birthday. Hundreds of people came to him on that day from many countries. Heads of states and leaders of governments had sent their representatives. The Abbot of the monastery of Watmahadhatu, dressed in his saffron robe and with shaven head, came from the distant land of Thailand. There was also the ancient chieftain of a great tribe of Red Indians, wearing his tremendous head-dress, ornamented with feathers and horns. Costumes of the Japanese, Indonesians, Filipinos and Vietnamese, in their pastel shades, contrasted with the more vivid coloured robes of the Africans. Statesmen were there, and trade union leaders, ambassadors, heads of industry, serving officers in high commands, all men who, in their own spheres, had attained success, dignity or renown. Finally, there were hundreds of simple people and families with their children.

His eightieth birthday drew to him the gratitude of all the assembly. Letters and telegrams brought the congratulations of thousands of people, and of those friends he had made in all parts of the world during his long life. One of these was signed by a man a few years older than himself, Chancellor Adenauer. This is what the Chancellor said:

'On this day the wide circle of your friends will remember with great gratitude your sacrificial work in the service of Moral Re-Armament. You may be sure that a lasting memorial to your work is established in the hearts of mankind in this age. The way you have laboured to establish relationships between men and nations on the firm foundations of moral values will never be forgotten.'

In the modest family home of the man to whom this message came, which had been the home of his parents, are tokens of affection from all countries. Over the chimney hangs a sword, the Japanese sword of surrender, handed over in 1945 to the General commanding the Chinese armies. The General later presented it, in homage, to the man from whom he had learned the true secret of peace. A richly ornamented Greek Orthodox cross and various signed photographs bear witness to his long-standing friendship with certain royal families. Elsewhere there are preserved high decorations awarded him by sovereigns and governments. . . .

This man is Frank Buchman.

The message which Chancellor Adenauer sent was accompanied by the following call for help:

Now is the time to work more strongly than ever for European unity through Moral Re-Armament. A Europe in which freedom and brotherhood shall reign can only be created when the nations are mutually conscious of their moral responsibility. You have given most valuable stimulus to the great work of uniting Europe.

I am convinced with you that, unless this is carried forward, peace in the world cannot be maintained. Therefore I would be extremely happy if you yourself could give your own personal attention to it in the coming months, which are decisive for developments in Europe.

That evening, at the end of the eightieth birthday, Frank turned to those who, from all continents, had come to be by his side. 'I was dumb-struck when I first read the letter of the Chancellor of Germany. Ever since, I have been thinking how it could be done. . . . God will show us each successive step.

'The world is at the cross-roads. God has a plan and we will follow it.'

What secret is revealed in the life of this man who has given hope to a high Buddhist dignitary, to the Chief of a Red Indian tribe, and to whom is addressed the appeal of Adenauer to help reunite Europe?

Let us go back fifty years.

A doctor in the United States had advised Frank Buchman to rest and he came to spend some weeks in Europe. In the course of his journey, he found himself in Keswick in the north of England. He went into a small church where there were only a few people. Someone spoke of truths he had long known and they suddenly became alive for him. 'For the first time I saw myself with all my pride, my selfishness, my failure and my sin. "I" was the centre of my own life. If I was to be different, then that big "I" had to be crossed out.

'I saw the resentments I had against six men standing out like tombstones in my heart.

'I asked God to change me, and He told me to put things right with those six men. I obeyed, and wrote six letters of apology.'

These six men formed the committee of management of a hostel for young boys of which Frank was in charge. Frank had just left: his instinctive generosity towards the young people had clashed with the cautiousness of the committee who had cut down the boys' rations to balance the budget. 'Those six men may have been wrong, but because of my resentment, I was the seventh wrong man.'

Frank never had any answer to these letters, but this was not the important thing. What mattered was that something fresh had come into his life, something which was to determine its whole course. A new man had arisen in him that could not tolerate the mediocrity and compromise of the old, who could no more let his life drift on the whims of self-will, but was completely surrendered, as an instrument is, to be guided and tuned by a higher wisdom. A prisoner had escaped to become a free man. He gave his life in complete obedience to the service of this fresh inspiration.

The same day Frank found himself with a young man from Cambridge University, a pleasant fellow of good family, but who was nevertheless unhappy. Frank told him of the experience he had just had and the young man asked to speak further with him. They went for a long walk together by the lakeside. Frank listened while the young man told all that was troubling him, and that same evening, when they returned, the heart of the young man had been freed from its burdens.

All Frank's life changed from that day. Today, fifty years later, the statesmen come to him in the way the young man came long ago. Frank has nothing to offer except this one thing which is essential for them and for their countries.

'In 1915,' says a young Asian, 'two men, one a Westerner, the other an Indian, walked together on a beach in Madras and formed a lasting friendship based on mutual respect and a common love for people. During the next thirty years each of them became world famous. Each became the confidante of statesmen and a figure of tremendous influence upon millions of ordinary people. The Indian was my grandfather, Mahatma Gandhi, who died ten years ago. The Westerner was Dr. Buchman.

'Mahatma Gandhi,' continued young Rajmohan Gandhi, 'said of Moral Re-Armament that it was the "greatest thing that has come out of the West".'

Many members of Gandhi's family have the same affection for Frank that the Mahatma had. When Devadas Gandhi, son of the Mahatma (who had continued in New Delhi the journalistic tradition of his father), was in London, he came with his family to visit Frank Buchman as though he were one of themselves.

Manilal Gandhi, the Mahatma's other son, who had taken on in Durban the newspaper *Indian Opinion* founded by his father, always received Frank's friends as his friends. He opened his paper to the ideas that Frank sought to spread in South Africa.

It was on the platform of the Gare du Nord that Rajmohan, representative of the third generation, made the acquaintance of Buchman.

A year later they met at an international assembly. Rajmohan says of this experience, 'A large group of white South Africans particularly captured my interest. Ever since the days of my grandfather's struggle for the rights of the Indians in South Africa, there has been deep division between the two races. One morning the thought came to me. "There has been deep bitterness in your heart against these people. Apologise to them for this."'

Overcoming all the difficulty of obeying such promptings from the inner voice, Rajmohan spoke one evening from the platform. He said to these South Africans: 'I have been bitter. Will you forgive me?' The following morning a well-known student leader belonging to the South African group addressed the Indians in general and young Gandhi in particular, saying, with tears in his eyes, 'I must make my peace with the Indians and Pakistanis. Their countries are at diplomatic war with mine. I wish to ask the forgiveness of Rajmohan Gandhi because I have hated him for what his grandfather did in 1911 when he came across our borders and started passive resistance.'

A few days later in the middle of the night Rajmohan was to learn by telephone that his father had just died. 'It was a great shock,' he said. 'The man who helped me and was like a brother to me in that crucial hour was the young man who shared my room, a white South African. We prayed together. Immediately I flew back to India to join my family. Next to me in the aeroplane from London to Bombay sat a young Indian student who was going home to see his mother who was seriously ill. I had the thought to tell him the kind of fellow I had been and the new motives I have found for my life. "My life has been exactly like yours," he said.' Before the aeroplane landed in Bombay the young Indian student had learnt from Rajmohan the same secret that the young man from Cambridge learnt from Frank Buchman fifty years earlier.

Between the initial experience of Buchman and the like experience of Rajmohan Gandhi lie hundreds of thousands of similar experiences. They issue today in changed social conditions and transformed relationships between men and countries.

From his day at Keswick Frank learned a truth: that the remaking of the world must start from oneself, from the individual.

Nations desire the fruits of an answer without having an answer. We want production. We want peace. We want prosperity. We want a world organisation. We want a united Europe. We want a new national life. But we do not go to the root of the matter.

Nations fail because they try desperately to combat moral apathy with economic plans. Yet the material crisis may obscure the materialism and moral breakdown that underlie it, so that they do not know how to cure it.

The problem is not just an iron curtain which separates nation from nation, but steely selfishness which separates man from man and all men from the government of God.

All this could be summed up as follows: 'Human nature can be changed. That is the basic answer. National economies can be changed. That is the fruit of the answer. World history can be changed. That is the destiny of our age.'

For Frank Buchman, 'It is no good throwing eye medicine out of a second-storey window on to a crowd of people suffering from ophthalmia.' Each sick person must be treated individually. For Frank what counts is 'an intense preoccupation with the individual person', to which he has given his life.

One day when Frank was changing trains at Milan he had eleven minutes to wait. There he was greeted by a Communist, the head of the tramway workers of the town. The sister of this Communist, herself at one time in the Party, had, as a result of her contacts with Frank Buchman's friends, rediscovered a creative aim to live for and had made the effort to bring this to her brother. He was very ill and came from a hospital bed to take this opportunity of getting to know Frank. These two men found they were in perfect fellowship and their dedication became one. 'I only want to live for my little girl's future and the new world of Moral Re-Armament,' the Communist said to Frank. When the train left he said to those around him: 'My heart feels lighter and I am at peace with God.' The day before, he had had his civil marriage blessed by the Church in the chapel of the hospital. Making this contact with Frank was one of the last acts of his life, for he died a few weeks later, but he died in the faith that he had fought against all his life.

Frank's friends are always present in his memory. There had also been at the station, with the Communist, a member of an old and illustrious Italian family, Count Francesco Cicogna. Two years later Frank was talking of this occasion at the very moment when he got news of Count Cicogna's death.

In 1948 Frank spent a few days at Freudenstadt. It was there that, before the war, he became convinced that 'the next great movement in the world will be a movement of moral re-armament for all nations'. The family who looked after the hotel where he had stayed ten years before had just returned to their home, which had recently been relinquished by the occupying troops. They did their very best for Frank, but were limited by rationing. Frank complimented the old cook and took her out for a drive. When she returned in the evening she said to her employer: 'Well, I have made coffee for thousands of people in this hotel, for Kings, Princes and the most famous people in the world. Not one of them has ever thanked me. But today, this gentleman has taken me for a drive with his friends and given me the best seat in the car. This is the finest day of my life.'

This man who knows how to give the best of himself to others also expects the utmost from them. Although very indulgent in forgiving mistakes, he is also extremely exacting. Many remember his frankness because at a particular moment in their lives it has helped them truly to see themselves.

During the First World War he got to know Sun-Yat-Sen, a great man whose name is today respected both in Communist and Nationalist China. Frank said to him: 'The greatest evils in China are squeeze, concubinage and gambling. You must build your new nation on firm moral foundations.' Sun-Yat-Sen said of this conversation: 'Buchman told me the truth about my country and myself.'

In 1915, Frank went to Japan. He was received there by Viscount Shibusawa, the man the Emperor had sent in 1860 to Europe and to Napoleon III to bring back from the West those mechanical techniques which have created modern industrial Japan. Today Masahide Shibusawa, great-grandson of the Viscount, and his wife and two children, have all left their easy and comfortable existence to consecrate themselves in Frank Buchman's fight for the world. Keizo Shibusawa, father of Masahide and Minister of Finance, was one of the first to accept Buchman's invitation to join a party of Japanese who came to the United States after the last war. There was a power of friendship in Frank that drew five generations of this family to throw in their lot with his.

One of the veterans of American Communism said, 'I trained 300 men in Communism, and most of them have left me. What is Frank Buchman's secret, that the men he has trained remain faithful?'

Rajmohan Gandhi writes: 'Think of Frank Buchman and you must think of countless ordinary people of Asia, Africa, and Europe, of every colour, culture, creed and background who count him as their true friend. His secret has always been his intense care for people and for nations, and his ability to see what, under God, they can become.

'To be with him is an experience. You know that you are the only person that matters for him. So it is with nations. While others protest, criticise or are cynical, he has always had the faith, born of the experience in his own life, that the most difficult man, or the most divided nation, can change and demonstrate an answer.'

The generous friendship that Frank has given to all those whom God has put in his way is nourished by a penetrating perception of the profound longings in their hearts and a desire to respond to these; but, above all, Frank Buchman has a passion which cannot be deflected, that is devoted to helping each person fulfil their true destiny.

'The ordinary man, guided by God, can do the extraordinary thing,' says Frank Buchman; to each he gives the opportunity to enrol in the workshop of the new world.

In the years between the two wars, when the rearmament of Japan began to alarm the world, Frank said to a student, Takasumi Mitsui, the son of the well-known Japanese industrialist: 'You must become a peacemaker.'

One day Buchman found himself at a dinner-party next to an elderly lady from Edinburgh, whose life had been spent in good works. She confided in him that she was now 'getting ready to die'. 'Ready to die!' said Buchman. 'Why not start to live?' A few weeks later this Scottish lady reserved a hundred rooms in a hotel at Geneva for Frank Buchman and his friends. With the help of her son, who held a responsible post there, she invited them to come and speak to the statesmen at that time assembled at the League of Nations.

Introducing these men to a group of delegates from fifty-three countries, the President of the Norwegian Parliament, Carl Hambro, who was the League's last President, stated: 'These people have succeeded in fundamental things where we have failed. They have created that constructive peace which we have been seeking in vain for years. Where we have failed in changing politics, they have succeeded in changing lives.'

The reason Frank Buchman understands the men round him is because he decided, once and for all, never to think of himself. He is sensitive to the real needs of each individual. There is a story of a learned man who had talked long on abstract problems, to whom Frank suddenly said, 'You haven't told me anything about your wife yet.' Frank can tell who needs help and encouragement and also sometimes when a drastic warning is required. 'I asked God to make me super-sensitive to people,' he says, 'and there have been times when I have been tempted to wish I had never prayed that prayer.' To know men as they are, and yet to know what they can become, is to be committed to a life-long battle for their highest destiny.

So few people have this true sense of their destiny, and there are fewer still who are conscious of that of their country. They have, sometimes, a vague idealism combined with a sense of prestige, which draws strength from the past. Frank, on the other hand, has set out to give to each nation a real sense of its destiny.

During an assembly of European countries in Scandinavia in 1935 he said in a radio talk: 'Some nation must find God's will as her destiny and God-guided men as her representatives at home and abroad. Some nation must produce a new leadership free from the bondage of fear, rising above ambition, and flexible to the direction of God's Holy Spirit. Such a nation will be at peace within itself and a peacemaker in the international family. Will it be your nation?'

To the Swiss he said in the same year: 'I can see Switzerland a prophet among the nations, and a peacemaker in the international family.'

In 1938 he called Sweden to be a reconciler of the nations.

In the United States in 1939 he said: 'America needs a challenge to a new quality of life which will empower her to speak with authority to the world because she has an answer at home.'

To Mr. Hatoyama, Prime Minister of Japan, Frank Buchman said in 1956: 'Japan's destiny is to be the lighthouse and power-house of Asia. Japan can have an ideology which obliterates all the mistakes of the past and gives the certainty of an answer to every problem through moral and spiritual leadership.' A few days later this idea was put before the whole nation by Mr. Hatoyama himself, writing in the columns of *Mainichi*.

In the same way, in 1946, when Frank Buchman arrived at a great European meeting, he noticed that one nation was not represented at all. He at once asked, 'Where are the Germans?' Amongst those present it seems no one had thought, so soon after the war, of the place that Germany was to take in the new Europe. A Cabinet Minister, Heinrich Hellwege, expressed the opinion of the German Federal Government when he said later, 'We were alone, and it was one man, Frank Buchman, who brought us back into the family of nations.'

The Japanese Minister, Mr. Ichimada, said of Frank, 'What has struck me most is his understanding of the differences that exist in the thinking of different peoples, and because of that, his ability to bring a new spirit to each country.'

Modern man, ever since the Renaissance, seems to have lived in a kind of anarchy. The different parts of his existence, his personal, political, family, religious and social life, resemble semi-independent kingdoms ruled by different laws which, even if they do not completely contradict each other, yet have nothing in common. So twentieth-century man manages to be a rationalist in philosophy, practising in religion, a 'realist' in business, a democrat in politics and a dictator in the home.

All the success of modern ideologies can be explained by the inner desire of modern man to reach wholeness. But all that is most profound in man rebels against these efforts, because in all attempts so far some essential aspect of his nature has been left out.

For Frank Buchman all parts of life can be related to the central reality which governs all reality. A French trade unionist, trained all his life in Marxism, affirms that it is through his relationship with Frank Buchman and his friends that he has discovered 'a complete awareness of the world as a whole'.

Buchman offers to people and nations a quality of life based on standards which command the loyalty of individuals, families, communities and nations.

'What is the missing factor,' he asks, 'in the planning and statesmanship of the world today?

'We try to meet the united plan and passion of alien ideologies with talk and with lip-service to high ideals and with a last resort to force. And we hope to live as we have always lived, selfishly, comfortably and undisturbed.

'Statesmen talk about the answer. They talk of union. But disunity increases. They talk of moral values. But immoral policies prevail.

They use these words which the hard logic of events has proved true. But it remains words. These men do not face the cost in their own lives and the life of their nations of giving an answer.

'An extreme of evil must be met with an extreme of good. A fanatical following of evil by a passionate pursuit of good.

'That is why democracy fails. Only a passion can cure a passion. And only a superior world-arching ideology can cure a world divided by warring ideologies.'

Maurice Mercier, General Secretary of the textile workers of the Force Ouvrière, whose story we read earlier, states: 'What I have seen in the men round Frank Buchman goes further than Marxism: there is with them the certainty of a better society, a higher level of human behaviour. We have here a new man.' And he goes on: 'Man is not just a portion of humanity; he is made up of needs, of thoughts. He has to have a great hope. One can give him the hope of comfort, security, but still this is only a part of human life. It is necessary to reach the whole man, and there can be no complete conception of man without absolute moral standards.'

For Frank the way in which he lives in the familiar intimate daily round includes the way of universal or world-wide life and the universal or world-wide life comes into the intimate and familiar daily round.

When, on the island of Mackinac, he was preparing an international conference, he thought in the middle of the night of an elderly inhabitant of the island, a Red Indian, who had been an invalid since the First World War and was now seriously ill. Next morning, before dealing with his letters, telegrams or interviews, he first insisted that a good hot meal should be taken to this man from him. For him all life is indeed one, and private affairs should be the mainspring for action on a world scale and should give to them meaning and depth.

Shortly after the war, Mohammed Ali Jinnah, the founder of Pakistan, came to London to negotiate with the British Government. He took the opportunity, on his only free evening, of coming to a Moral Re-Armament play and afterwards he visited Frank Buchman's house. He came tired and worn after a busy day, feeling he had not reached his objectives. Frank received him with his characteristic friendly hospitality and offered him a delicious curry prepared with care by one of his countrymen. As time went on he relaxed and talked in a way which some of his colleagues declared they had never heard before. He said to Frank on leaving, 'I want you in Pakistan. You have the answer to the hates of the world.'

For many their happiest recollection of Frank is that of a Christmas spent with him. For Frank, Christmas begins on the 15th of December, and, sometimes at the end of January people still gather round the tree, if the branches are not bare by then. When the candles go out one by one and large shadows begin to climb the walls, Frank waits, as he did when he was a child, for the last light to go. Here again he is thinking of those round him and helping them to touch once again the mysterious reality that our world needs to rediscover. 'Ours is the eternal unity of being guided by a Star,' he wrote at one of the war-time Christmases, 'to give to every man and to the statesman the gift of a new world.'

On these occasions Frank invites everyone. One year, delegates to the United Nations conference from the Moslem countries found themselves united round the Crib. 'This is the best Christmas we have ever had in the West,' they said as they left. Their national and political differences have been set aside and their spirit has been enriched by a fresh element.

The head of the government of a Middle East country asked him, 'Dr. Buchman, you do great things for humanity, how do you do it?' Frank answered: 'I am a simple man and I do simple things, but they are the things the world needs.'

Today, fifty years after that first conversation between Frank Buchman and the young man from Cambridge, a great army of people has arisen from the ends of the earth, people who, with him and like him, have been drawn to rebuild the world through individuals. In the years between the wars, some would smile when they heard Frank declare in the various European capitals and at the League of Nations: 'You can plan a new world on paper but you must build it with men. Without an ideology democracy is doomed.'

Many put their faith in the success of conferences or intellectual exchanges. Others placed their hopes in the ascendancy of certain men whose very memory is now despised. Others clung to an empty idealism which was soon smashed like foam on the rock-like facts of everyday life. Everything has been tried in an effort to avoid a change in man himself. Buchman followed a way which looked longer, but was to prove more sure and which today, after fifty years of work, is more effective than any other because, from the beginning, he met the needs of the men round him.

In 1921 Frank was invited to Washington, at the time of the Disarmament Conference, by a friend, a British military expert. Of this conference, what is now left? The same problems remain. If one sure step has been taken towards a solution, this results from the decision Frank made, by himself, in the train on his way to Washington, in response to the persistent thought: 'Resign, resign, resign!' It was on account of this that he gave up the security of his position and, quite alone, with only his faith to give him courage, launched himself into the task of creating order in a world of chaos, through bringing the cure for the disorder in men's hearts. A new conviction came to him, 'We can, we must, and we will generate a moral and spiritual force that is powerful enough to remake the world.'

Other men followed. In the same way that one man received from Frank the secret which enabled him to start life afresh, so one day another was the first to decide to give up everything to fight at his side. Today there are more than a thousand; but what interests Frank is not their number, but the limitless work that is accomplished through them by that Greater Wisdom which presides over the destinies of the world.

Frank's humility has always prevented him from putting himself at their head. He has not wanted to create an organisation or a movement of which he could be proud. He often says, 'It is God who guides, it is not me,' and he adds, 'I have been wonderfully led.'

Without illusions about the weaknesses of human nature, Frank has an unshakable faith in its possibilities. He has no set plan to offer. He believes that each person, in the framework of his own faith, can discover what part he should play in rebuilding the world, if he accepts this faith to the end. 'To those of us who belong to Islam,' says a Pakistani, 'the work of Frank Buchman teaches us to rediscover and apply afresh the moral principles of our faith.' Christians, Buddhists, Shintoists, all maintain the same.

'I had given up Christianity because I had known too many Christians,' said Paul Kurowski, who had been more than twenty years in the German Communist Party. 'Then I got to know Frank Buchman. The atmosphere that surrounded him was for me something completely new. It was a real revelation. There was a peace, a love, a caring and a great humility. I had not met a man like this before. Frank Buchman listened very patiently to my ideas. He never tried to convert me. He never tried to answer my anti-religious point of view. He just had faith in the best in me.'

Frank never offered anyone a good position, security, or a future. He never asked anyone to join him. He placed each one face to face with the needs of the world and face to face with himself, and left him to the decision of his own conscience.

Some find a problem of definition in this world army united round Frank Buchman. They look for statutes, leaders, membership cards, slogans, and they find none. They would like to have discussions with persons authorised to speak for all those in Moral Re-Armament. Others would like to find a way of adapting to their preconceptions the exacting standards that hold these people. But we are here in the presence of a company of people who have each individually reached a basic decision, making a choice alone and freely before God, yet closely linked by their knowledge of the world's true problems and by their unshakable determination to bring to these a solution.

That is why men of all religions who have never known Frank or his friends, but whose faith has led them to live like him, immediately recognise in him a companion in the fight.

It is understandable that some religious leaders, who have the care of souls, should ask questions on the problems likely to arise in this body of people from so many different beliefs fighting shoulder to shoulder. They can be reassured by the fact that, in Frank Buchman's words, 'Moral Re-Armament enhances all primary loyalties', to nation, family or religion.

The Rector of El Azhar University, the thousand-year-old Muslim University in Cairo, Sheikh Abdel-Rahman Tag, said to some friends of Frank Buchman, 'I repeat to you the profound satisfaction which it gives me to see you bringing to mankind this ideology, which sets out to spread the principles of peace, love and morality amongst all without distinction of person or of nationality. The ideology you work for gives the essence of what Islam stands for and a true interpretation of its basic principles.'

The venerable U Rewata, one of the chief abbots of Burma, stated: 'In Buddhism we have the four moral standards which are the basis of MRA; the most important thing is that we learn to live by them all the time. We must bring Moral Re-Armament to every nation.'

Frank believes that God can use many, many more men—hundreds and thousands of them—to do much more and better than he has done. He often says, 'You have never succeeded unless you have trained ten men to do your work better than you can do it yourself.'

He believes in the value of offering to each person a tremendous task which seems far beyond his capacities. For this very reason, this task stimulates faith. Thus he could entrust the responsibility of a whole continent to four young men, when in 1952, Louis, the son of Madame Laure, went with three friends to Brazil.

Hundreds of men, stimulated and inspired by him, learn to work together as a team to achieve the impossible by their united action.

From the four corners of their continent Africans gather to go to the south of the United States. There they arrest the attention of the white people, win the interest of the Negroes and bring both parties to understand one another. In the same way, politicians, workers and industrialists from Western countries go as a united force to meet the men in corresponding positions in the countries of Asia and Africa. 'It is the first time that I have seen, from the West, a group of people from such a variety of countries and backgrounds who all pursue a common aim,' remarked one Communist ambassador who met them. Frank's genius is to see the solution of world problems in terms of men.

He has no preconceived notion of how a thing should be done. 'I do not know, but you will find out yourself,' is often the disconcerting reply made to those who hope to get a direct order from him.

Soon after the war, when an important team of his colleagues was about to start its campaign in Germany, he visited the head of the German Coal Board. The latter asked: 'Tell me, Dr. Buchman, what can I do for Germany?' 'I do not know, but God can tell you,' was the reply.

The next day the industrialist telephoned to invite Frank Buchman to come, with his task force from many countries, into one of the mining towns of the Ruhr, a principal centre of Communist activity. It was to be the beginning of a reversal of the ideological trend in Germany.

A Japanese says that one morning Frank came to him and said: 'Sumi, you must not depend on Frank's guidance, but depend on God's guidance.' The Japanese added: 'It is so typical of him that he has never drawn people to follow his leadership, but has always challenged us to trust God for everything.'

A Swedish journalist published these lines in 1938:

> It is not his lightning smile that forms his secret. His epigrammatic sayings, his mobility and flexibility, his power to hold an assembly in his hand and yet to submerge himself and disappear in the ordinary ranks, none of these even really tells you anything about the real Frank Buchman.
>
> Look closely at his pictures and you will see something in his very expression, something almost distrait, a sort of listening. For once the camera is telling the truth. That distrait listening glance exists in reality too, however closely he may be attending. It is constantly present. Sit a few days and study his face, and you will be amazed how often he appears almost at a loss, not to say helpless. He makes no secret of it.
>
> There is one basis only to his fabulously active life—guidance, for which he is openly on the watch at every moment. He is a sail always held to be filled by the wind, a man with a great and warm and humble heart, a democrat out to make men free under the dictatorship of God. (Herbert Grevenius in *Stockholms Tidningen*.)

'Human wisdom has failed. God has a plan.'

This is the attitude of Frank Buchman before the most serious problems. 'Everyone in every nation seems to have his own solution based on personal and national advantage. But the secret is, "Not my way, but God's way. Not my will, but God's will".'

This is not a theory but a practical daily experience that he wishes to share with those he meets. He believes that the citizens of the twentieth century can go to the same school as those men who have been, throughout history, the instruments of perfect Wisdom.

Returning from Rome, where he had been present at the canonisation of Nicholas von der Flüe in the Basilica of St. Peter, Frank Buchman put before the world the example of this saint, who was for fifteenth-century Switzerland a true statesman in the fullest sense of the word.

> Nicholas had this gift of divine direction. As he exercised it, he became the saviour of his country. He was a farmer who tilled his land well, a soldier, a magistrate. At fifty, oppressed by the problems of a warring world, he gave up much to follow radically the guidance of God. Soon his inspired good sense, knowledge of men and singleness of heart commanded the respect of his contemporaries, not only in Switzerland but in all Europe. He became the most sought-after arbiter in affairs of state. When the bitter quarrels of the Cantons brought his country to the verge of civil war, it was his God-given

answer which set Switzerland on the good road that gave her unity. It is most timely that this statesman of five hundred years ago, who listened for God's word and fearlessly passed it on to his generation, should today receive this supreme recognition. Truly he is a Saint for our times, a model for the United Nations.

This still small voice which Frank Buchman, alone in a railway carriage, had heard whisper to his conscience, 'Resign, resign, resign,' can, he believes, be heard in the heart of every man. 'Take the whole question of guidance, God's mind and my mind. The thought that slips in any time, day or night, can be the thought of the Author of mind. A thought comes, maybe just an arresting tick. One responds to it. And millions can be richer if it is effectively carried out.'

Not long ago, Frank was the guest of the Prime Minister[1] and Government of Burma. U Nu is a Buddhist, at the head of a Buddhist country, but there is for him, in the example of Nicholas von der Flüe, the same absolute reality that there is for the Christian who places himself entirely in the hands of the highest authority he knows.

U Nu asked Frank, 'Tell me about guidance. I spend much time in meditation. I have a house by a lake where I go to meditate. But I do not receive definite direction such as you describe.' Frank had just been telling him how, in spite of the many practical difficulties of the journey and the climate, he had been commanded by the Spirit to come from New Zealand to Rangoon to meet U Nu.

'Are your thoughts clear?' asked U Nu.

'Yes,' said Frank Buchman, 'so clear that I write them down.'

There was a long silence.

Then U Nu said, 'This is important for me. I am faced with problems as Prime Minister too great for the human mind unaided to solve.'

On meeting Frank Buchman, thousands of other men have learned, like U Nu, that there is deep in the conscience a voice that speaks, if we will listen.

'I was very busy,' says Frank, 'working eighteen to twenty hours every day. So busy that I had two telephones in my bedroom. Still I was dissatisfied with the results. There was a constant coming and going, but the changes in the lives of my visitors were inadequate, and not revolutionary enough to become permanent. So I decided on

[1] U Nu was Prime Minister of Burma when Frank Buchman visited him in May 1956.

a radical procedure, to give that hour of the day from five to six in the morning when the phones were unlikely to ring, to listen for the Still Small Voice to inspire and direct. . . .'

To this world of speed and hubbub Frank Buchman brings silence and reflection. He brings them out from monasteries and retreats to play their part in the industrialists' and cabinet ministers' office, in the classroom and the family kitchen.

'We may find this silence so satisfying,' he says, 'that guidance becomes the daily source of all our creative thinking and living; in this way silence can be the regulator of men and nations. For guidance comes in silence.'

He also maintains: 'Statesmanship without guidance and without change is like flying an aircraft in stormy weather over uncharted territory without choosing to use radio, maps and compass.'

On the eve of the Second World War, he presented this proposition: 'The choice is guidance or guns,' or again: 'The world's safety, your safety, the safety of your home, lies in God-control.'

All this comes from a central conviction of Frank's: God has a plan for the world and it is through those men who give themselves up to His will that it is realised.

He ended a radio talk made on his eightieth birthday with these words:

> A man of eighty is speaking to you. A man who has often been beset by confusion and gradually learned to know the answer for a nation. In every baffling problem of the statesman and the ordinary man the answer is given to those who listen. Only there must be the willingness to obey. It is not what we expect but what we allow God to give us. With all the sincerity of my eighty years and impelled by the urgency of the critical world situation, I say God is the answer to the modern confusion that dogs us. Go all the way with God and you will bring the answer to your nation.

From his trust in God, Frank has drawn the strength to face all the opposition with which he has clashed.

His words and his way of life bring a challenge which is disagreeable to anyone who tries to justify his weaknesses before the world. But what he and his friends are doing undermines even more the work of those who build on the foundations of hatred, prejudice or on jealousies or angry passions. The strangest alliances have arisen to block his path, alliances of people, who, although their interests are directly opposed to each other, nevertheless have weaknesses in common drawing them together. The charges brought against him have been most contradictory. They have consisted of whatever slander, at any time or in any country, happened to be the most damaging. The same men have first sarcastically criticised him for not attacking some world figure, and then tried to entangle him with this same person. Even men of good will, prevented perhaps by the smallness of their perceptions from seeing the greatness of the issues at stake, have been drawn in to lend support to this discreditable opposition, because they wanted to voice their own petty criticisms.

'Criticism is uncomfortable. I know that,' says Frank Buchman. 'It was like a dagger through my heart when I was first attacked. I suffered. I know what it means. But if you are a real revolutionary you always maintain perspective, no matter what people say about you. No matter how stones come, you go straight ahead. Stones of criticism are so bracing—they just set you up for the day.'

The unshakable faith in the guidance of God Frank applies to every side of life, including the material aspect of financing a vast work with no resources. When he answered the call to leave his university post forty years ago, he gave up his last paid job. He has since lived by faith alone: he is convinced that where God guides He also provides. Many thousands of people have since followed his example and learned to live in this new way. They have embarked on the boldest undertakings without any material security, only their deep conviction that they must quickly meet some clearly defined need.

An American business man wrote to Frank to ask his advice. He was one of those who had undertaken to put at Frank's disposal, in America, a suitable place where representatives from all countries could meet; he felt himself responsible for the financing of this; the bills were piling up, there were many workmen employed on the job who had to be paid, and there was no money. So, as a prudent business man, he asked whether it would be better to reduce the scale of the operation. Frank replied, 'I want you to move with me and the people of America in the dimension of what needs to be done, not what we think we can do. I want you to help me always to rely not on what I have but on what God gives. It is such freedom—and it works.'

This life of faith enlivens all the work of Frank Buchman. So many times his friends have seen him give back all he had received when it was a case of meeting the immediate need of the moment. A hundred Japanese youth leaders were ready to go to a fateful meeting which later events were to prove of vital importance to Japan. The date of their journey had been settled; the aeroplane to take them from Tokyo to the United States had been chartered; there was not a penny. There are no reserves to draw on for this type of need. Frank has accepted, once and for all, and in all circumstances, to count only on faith. This was one of the occasions on which he emptied his own wallet, and, following his example, hundreds did the same.

If these economic methods distress the prudent traditional thinking of Western business men, they meet with a very real understanding amongst working-class people, and also amongst others in all classes who are searching for a better way of life. And the greatest number of gifts come from thousands of ordinary people who make sacrifices because they feel it is essential to carry this work forward.

Frank was with a militant socialist one day, George Light, a man who had never had, even in his most prosperous moments, enough money to see him beyond the end of the week. It was at a time of inflation and George Light was one of the three million British unemployed. He was speaking to Frank of their sufferings and Frank took him into his room and said, 'My guidance is to share with you all the money I have.' He opened his wallet and showed him his bank account. 'He thrust into my hand,' George Light recounted later, 'half of his entire financial resources, and as I turned to go out of the room, he shook my hand and said with a smile, "We are both socialists now."'

The peasants of the Indian rice-fields understood the simple philosophy of Frank when he said, 'There is enough rice in the world for everyone's need, but not for everyone's greed.' And he added, 'Suppose everybody cared enough, everyone shared enough, wouldn't everybody have enough?'

Today Frank wants to use the vast technical resources that recent discoveries have made available in the battle to rebuild the world. Whether it is a question of aeroplanes to transport the big teams across the world to meeting points in distant lands, or the making of films and plays and the building of places where men from all continents can meet and unite, all this is for Frank a daily act of faith. Thousands of his followers now give to the world-work all that they have. It is in this way that they have seen vast enterprises develop before their eyes, and their own faith and also that of hundreds of others has been greatly strengthened. Family homes have been shared with others or used for encounters which lead to reconciliations. Others, who have only their hands, give their work; but all have given the most valuable gift—themselves.

'World problems remain the same because the root problem, human nature, remains unsolved. Until we deal with human nature thoroughly and drastically on a national scale, nations must still follow their historic road to violence and destruction.'

Frank Buchman knows that it is possible for a man's motives to change fundamentally; his own motives changed at Keswick fifty years ago. On that day a new scale of values was ordained for him for life. In an instant he had seen all that separated him from God in the way he had been living, although he lived respectably and according to good principles, and in conformity with the customs of his day.

In an epoch when selfishness and opportunism are accepted as normal by individuals and nations, Frank Buchman firmly restores absolute moral standards. During his time at Pennsylvania State College, he had the chance of sharpening his wits against the hard realities that face sceptical and careless youth. He grasped the fact that the highest idealism can be blighted from within because a slow rot sets in which propriety and convention are unable to stop. 'What you need,' he once said to them, 'is a good clean-up with a rotary street broom and a good wash-down with a fire-hose.'

For each man the starting-point is a change of heart, 'a return to those simple home truths that some of us learned at our mother's knee and which many of us have forgotten and neglected'. As the crisis is a moral one, the cure also is a moral one. 'It all goes back to those fundamental realities: absolute honesty, absolute purity, absolute unselfishness and absolute love.' Having said 'yes' to the absolute standard of God in his own life, Frank has the courage to ask the same of the statesman, the student and the docker. The great trade unionist from Berlin, Scharnowski, said humorously, 'Those four standards, they're in the Bible. They're in the Koran. But they are not in the trade unions, yet.'

'Making God the decisive authority, not saying "yes" with our lips only but with the discipline of our lives. It makes you natural, it makes you real. You need never try to appear wiser or better than you really are. This is the sort of person people will flock to and follow.'

This is what appeals to the French Marxist who meets Frank, the man hardened by the bitterness of the trade union fight; he asserts, 'What is striking is the personal radiance of the men who can look you in the eyes and say, "I apply these four absolute standards to myself." It is a new approach and there is a light in their eyes more effective than any speech.'

Frank knows that what the world needs most is not so much a new philosophical explanation, or sermons of high spiritual tone, or speeches rich with promises, but a quality of life lived out each day, year after year. Frank talks little, but often the little that he says goes deep into the lives of those he meets.

One day one of the great figures of the new state of Ghana was standing close to Frank at a meeting. He had a seat in his country's parliament, was the political leader of all the Moslem populations of the Northern Region and the religious head of his people; this man carried the dignity of a long line of rulers in his form and features. The Tolon Na today enjoys telling this story.

It was at one of the morning meetings in the main hall at Caux. Frank was there, and someone spoke about stealing and what it cost the nation. Then turning to me, as I was standing close to him, with a smile on his face, Frank quietly asked, 'When did you last steal?'

This struck me like a depth charge. My heart leapt into my mouth. I blushed and remained dumbfounded. That question was as simple as could be: yet I could not answer it there and then.

I retired to my room and prayed to Allah to take me into His loving care, repenting for all the evils I had done since childhood. As I lay there by myself I felt God was still waiting for a reply to Frank's question. I saw the whole world watching. It was the greatest challenge that I had ever faced in my life.

I thought and thought. At last relief came when I decided to write down the number of times (as far as I could remember) that I had stolen since my infancy. I made a note to return all textbooks that I had brought home from the schools in which I had taught; I also noted all the persons to whom I owed apologies for wrongs that I had done them. I decided to live Frank's way of life.

From his personal experience Frank had learned that it is not human effort towards absolute moral standards that brings personal release and change to man's inner being. Just as the Tolon Na had turned to ask for help from the highest power he knew, Frank had himself had to make his fundamental decision at the foot of the Cross.

The secret revealed in the life of Frank Buchman cannot be told in words. In the preceding pages we have traced a likeness, related incidents, told anecdotes. All these are but the stones of a mosaic before the artist begins his work.

For all of us there is a pattern in which every little fragment of the mosaic, each small stone, can find its rightful place in each one of us. We shall get the complete picture of ourselves if we have allowed the great disposer of all things to do this work in us, so that for each one the secret stands revealed in which, for thousands of years, so many people have found reality.

For each and every being has to become the artisan of whom the Creator has need, to show the full splendour of His work.

It will then be seen how far all this surpasses the limits of individual personality, to overflow into the world, into history, into eternity.

PART THREE

From the Personal to the Worldwide

A RELENTLESS FLOOD THREATENS to engulf many nations.

Men try here and there to raise a frail barrier, but their timid efforts only win them a little time before they are suddenly submerged.

In some countries the masses are taken over by a system of ideas. Suddenly there arises a revolutionary wind which with a single blast topples great structures, though men fancied that they were standing fast.

An idea invades a nation without the formality of a declaration of war. It takes prisoners without firing a single shot and conquers whole countries, while parliaments continue their debates.

Faced with these developments, governments take up opposing positions. Some encourage the revolutionary movement, because it is in line with their interests or their conception of history. Others consider that their task is to hold on to the existing state of affairs, feeling it their duty to defend certain 'values'—though these are sometimes only fine words hiding other interests. Yet each and all declare that their own political ideas are the right ones.

The Western world does not want to adopt the pattern of the Communist world, nor does the Communist world want the pattern of the West. Both offer their examples of living to the peoples of Africa and Asia, who on their side are determined to find their own destinies by themselves.

Is there a road that the nations of the world could walk together?

While the succession of international conferences and the disappointments that follow them seem to say that the answer is 'no', yet the work of Frank Buchman and the men committed with him proves

177

beyond question that this road does exist. Not only does it exist, but already men and nations have decided to take it.

Today, as the result of the ceaseless work of many years, abundant evidence—the repercussions on a world scale of what has happened to people, the boundless consequences of definite changes in them—has removed the last doubts from the minds of a growing number of statesmen.

There is a solution.

In his preface to Frank Buchman's book, Robert Schuman speaks of 'the beginning of a far-reaching transformation of society', whose fruits are already to be seen.

At a moment when, after difficult negotiations, important international agreements had just been signed in Europe, Chancellor Adenauer wrote a letter to Frank Buchman paying tribute to the force which had played 'an unseen but effective part in bridging differences of opinion between the negotiating parties, and has kept before them the aim of peaceful agreement in the search for the common good'.

The Communist world has itself for many years grasped the importance of this work. The following comment regarding Frank Buchman's friends was heard on the Soviet radio: 'For several decades these men have been in the vanguard of the ideological struggle. . . . They have established bridgeheads on every continent and trained teams capable of penetrating the masses with their ideology. They have reached the final phase of total expansion throughout the world.' (Radio Moscow, Home Service, 21st November, 1952). 'These men substitute for the inevitable class struggle the eternal battle between good and evil. . . . That is the heart of their action whose consequence is nothing less, according to them, than the transformation of the world.' (Same programme, 9th January, 1953.)

Asian statesmen appreciate these efforts. 'At this critical point in history this idea is indispensable,' declares the Japanese Prime Minister, Mr. Kishi. 'I have been impressed by the effectiveness with which these men create unity between peoples who were formerly divided.'

President Ngo Dinh Diem of Viet-Nam wrote Frank Buchman: 'I realise the tremendous repercussions which will develop from the mobilisation of the spiritual forces which you have undertaken throughout the world.'

The most typical evaluation appeared in the columns of one of the great American dailies: 'In America and across the world these men have changed the course of contemporary history.' (New York *Journal American*, 25th July, 1957.)

Which then is the road they offer?

Many have studied the world situation today. Many have given their diagnosis. Many have put forward as a solution a system of ideas affecting the conception of relations between peoples. Books accumulate on the subject. Plans pile up in the chancellery archives. One element, however, always seems to be missing: how to get these conceptions accepted by the governments, the masses, and the opposing forces? How to bring people with diametrically opposed viewpoints to share a common conviction?

The Communist world seems to hold the secret of the war of ideas. We see the infiltration of Communism, winning men in the ministries of the very countries which lead the opposition to it. We see it taking over the minds of a large number of young people. In order to try to regain the lost lead, the West hastily launches a so-called 'psychological offensive', without always clearly knowing what it is about.

Frank Buchman's work of Moral Re-Armament has been built on people. It is based on a profound knowledge of human nature, of the inner motives that control it, and of the spiritual and supernatural forces which can change it.

Because he knows personally the power that can transform a man's life, Frank Buchman has shown the way to make that power available to transform the world.

With prophetic insight he says: 'In my lifetime I have seen two history-making discoveries; the discovery of the atom as a source of energy and its mobilisation. That has given us the atomic age. The other discovery is of man as the source of untold energy and his mobilisation. That has given us the ideological age. It is the key to events around us.'

For the man of the twentieth century, the ideological conflict is too often presented in terms of false alternatives. He thinks he must choose between East and West. Those who refuse to let themselves be boxed in by one or other of the two systems try desperately to construct a third. They try to construct a coherent system by drawing on two completely contradictory sets of ideas. Frank Buchman offers a solution which means change for both East and West and in which

179

all can have a part—indeed, many are beginning to take part in it.

At the international meetings started by Frank Buchman one finds leaders of the young countries of Africa and Asia. They come eager to take hold of a constructive idea, one which fully satisfies them and which they can propose to their people. It is significant that the governments of Burma, the Philippines, Viet-Nam, and Japan have been the first to give their official backing to the international assemblies which have taken place these last years at Baguio in the Philippines, for the moral re-armament of nations. African peoples are ready to join in this initiative. A former Prime Minister of the Republic of the Sudan wrote: 'The destinies of Asia and Africa are linked by a common spiritual heritage. The leaders of the Sudan wish to associate themselves with Prime Minister Kishi, President Garcia, Prime Minister U Nu and other Asian leaders, whose initiative and wise statesmanship is preparing the way for the moral re-armament of the peoples of the world under the guidance of God, the common authority for all.'

In Nigeria, the Cameroons and Ghana the same note is to be heard, as well as from certain men in North Africa. For, indeed, these men have kept something which is almost wholly lost among Europeans, a consciousness of the bond that must unite politics and morals.

This perhaps explains why some politicians of the West watch the work of Moral Re-Armament somewhat sceptically. It also explains why those of them who are deeply concerned for the true destiny of their peoples see in it not only fresh hope, but the best hope of all.

How does Moral Re-Armament take hold of the thinking of a people? And once it has taken hold, how does it affect the destiny of a country, a continent and the world?

These are the questions which we will try to answer in this third section. A theoretical analysis could be attempted, but it will be more valuable to take one particular example. The facts will show the steady progress of this other rising tide which raises a people and sweeps it towards renaissance.

THE PRODIGAL SON

On 6th August, 1945, an explosion destroyed a whole city. In doing so, it shook the world and shattered the framework of history.

The atomic bomb of Hiroshima left behind not only hundreds of thousands of dead, and the charred ruins of a city, but also a spiritual void in a nation that had lost the will to live.

In a few seconds a nation that had engaged all its energies in total war—certainly a mad venture, but a superhuman one—was defeated by the most ruthless power that exists—the power of the atom.

As we look back years later, it is interesting to read what the first Japanese to leave their country after the war said. A Japanese girl—a student—said at that time: 'Up till the end of the war, young Japanese were taught to be ready to die for their country. Then came the end of the conflict and the collapse. People began to talk about democracy, but few knew what it meant. There was talk of freedom and the young people began to think it meant revolt against every law and principle. The present generation is very lost and easily becomes the prey of other ideologies.'

Many people abroad were conscious of the ideological void left in Japan by her sudden defeat. Some had ideas as to how to fill it. Each offered the service for which they were best fitted. The United States offered their advice, their dollars and a constitution. Russia, with her knowledge of training men, seized the opportunity given by the presence of many Japanese in her prison camps. As and when their indoctrination seemed satisfactory, she released them. 'We have a new constitution,' the Japanese began to say. 'It is like an empty basket. What are we going to put in it? We need an ideology which will make democracy work.'

The Western world was somewhat hesitant about what its contribution in the ideological sphere ought to be. The Communist world offered its ideas on a silver platter. One man, Frank Buchman, however, offered Japan something else to fill that empty basket. 'Moral Re-Armament offers the Japanese people a chance to live democracy and put it into practice,' declared an editorial in the *Nippon Times* of that period. 'The moral rebirth of one individual will influence his neighbours. Winning one person after another it can penetrate a whole country and mobilise it for action.'

This was the plan: to bring a moral renaissance in the lives of individuals; to proceed to win men one by one; through them to permeate a whole country; and to set this country on the move to alter the course of a whole continent's future. These have been the successive stages, and we will follow them in this and the succeeding chapters.

Providence had led Frank Buchman to the few people on whom all this was to be raised—in the years before the 1914 war. We have mentioned his first visit to Japan in 1915 and the friends he made there. We have told how at Oxford he inspired a Japanese to become a 'peacemaker' for his country. This man, Takasumi Mitsui, Chairman of the Mitsui Foundation, was among the first Japanese to bring a group of his countrymen to take part in an international meeting at Caux.

Here we must digress for a moment. Immediately after the war, a few Swiss, grateful that their country had been mercifully spared the horrors of war, decided to place at Frank Buchman's disposal a centre at which, in a practical way, good relations could be restored between the nations.

They had in mind, in the words of a French statesman, 'a school where, by a process of mutual teaching, we can work out our practical behaviour towards others'. Some Swiss gave all their personal fortunes, and many of their compatriots made contributions for the purchase of the hotels in the tiny village of Caux whose name is now known to millions the world over. The vision and the sacrifices of these Swiss have enabled the centre at Caux to play a decisive rôle in setting Japan, as well as many other countries, on a fresh course in the post-war years.

The first group of Japanese came to Caux in 1949. Three years later, in 1952, the nations of the world were assembled at San Francisco, for the signing of the Japanese peace treaty. There, the French representative, Foreign Minister Robert Schuman, expressed his gratitude to Frank Buchman in these terms: 'You have made peace with Japan two years before we signed it.'

What had happened during the intervening years? At Caux in 1949 those first Japanese saw a family of nations welcome back into its midst a country whose position was similar to their own, Germany. Many German delegates were present. A few months before Dr. Konrad Adenauer, the future Chancellor, had come with his family.

The Japanese saw this people discovering a purpose and laying the foundations on which the democracy of present-day Western Germany is built. Their example gave food for thought to Mr. Katayama, who had had the heavy task of being his country's first post-war Prime Minister. He said, on leaving Caux: 'If we have to establish peace and democracy in our country, we shall never do it through materialism, for that brings a conflict of interests, but only on the basis of a high level of morality, the only true source of spiritual regeneration.' Another Japanese spokesman stated the problem of the youth: 'Students with a sense of responsibility are anxious at present to organise an inter-university centre for the promotion of democratic principles. They say that they cannot find anywhere men of the moral quality to guide them along the right lines.'

Buchman and the men of many nations who were gathered at Caux offered Japan what she was unconsciously seeking.

Those first Japanese left Caux determined to persuade their government to send a major delegation, representative of the country as a whole, to meet with Frank Buchman. A year later, in June 1950, a special aeroplane landed at Geneva, carrying a delegation of seventy-six sent by the Japanese Prime Minister. It included the Governors of seven Provinces, members of the Diet, the mayors of Hiroshima and Nagasaki, industrialists and trade union leaders. Here is the message Mr. Yoshida, the Premier, sent through the delegation:

Japan expects a lot from Moral Re-Armament. First of all MRA can give moral content to Japanese democracy by restoring moral principles which have been set aside since the war. Then MRA can inject the nation with a stabilising force in regard to its ideas and activities by freeing men from rampant materialism. Lastly, MRA can give the foundation on which the Japanese can build a peaceful nation. I am confident that these Japanese delegates will bring back the good seed and that with the help of MRA friends all over the world, we shall see this bring forth a great harvest in Japan.

Only the future will show whether Mr. Yoshida's hope has been fulfilled. Today, some years later, the facts we record and the very real repercussions taking place in the life of other Asian peoples have given his words a prophetic ring to a remarkable degree. Addressing the delegation before it left, in a message the Prime Minister further declared: 'In 1870 a Japanese mission went to the West. On its return it changed the course of Japanese life by bringing about an industrial revolution. I believe that this delegation also will open a new page of our history by bringing us an ideological revolution.'

The stirring of this same hope was felt in the hearts of all the Japanese at Caux in 1950. In a statement to the newspaper *Le Monde*, the Mayor of Hiroshima, Mr. Shinzo Hamai, said, after describing the hell into which his town had been plunged, ' We say to humanity : " Let us be done with atomic arms; what we need is Moral Re-Armament. Japan is suffering from the demoralisation of political life. . . . Unless there is a revolution in the heart of every Japanese, of every human being in the world, this world will perish, every city will be in mortal danger of the terror and trial by fire that ours has suffered.'

Mr. Hamai carried a message from his city authorities: 'The rehabilitation of the individual and the establishment of a lasting peace : such are the objectives of Moral Re-Armament and are exactly in line with all our hopes.' A former Finance Minister said : ' One of the primary conditions of our economic recovery is the moral rehabilitation of the Japanese people.'

It is hard to assess exactly what happened to these Japanese at Caux.

They heard many speakers and met many people. One of these was Madame Iréne Laure. She told how she, who had fought in the French Resistance, had gone to Germany so that she could take a part in reuniting Germany and France. They also saw Communists and Marxists from different European countries recognise, in Frank Buchman's message, an ideology that went further than their own. They even saw leading industrialists of the West with such an urgent sense of the need for a revolution in their own sphere that their workers were ready to fight alongside them. Above all, the Japanese felt understood and loved, and found men ready to raise them up.

At this point some of them understood what an impact these experiences which they had heard might have on their personal lives. In the aeroplane that brought them there were two men who had taken places as far away as possible from each other. One was Mr. Suzuki, Chief of Police of Osaka. In his capacity as police chief he had been responsible for maintaining order during various strikes; faced with strikes in Japan those maintaining order had unlimited powers of repression. The other man was a trade unionist, a member of the Metalworkers' Executive, also from Osaka. This man, Katsuji Nakajima, was fiery in temperament but slight in build, his physique the opposite of the thickset and sturdy Suzuki.

One night, during his time at Caux, the trade unionist could not sleep. What he had heard the day before went round and round in his head. When he could stand it no longer, he got up, and went to knock on the door of Mr. Suzuki's room. He asked his forgiveness for the hatred he had felt against him. 'All my fine speeches about brother-hood are worth nothing,' he said, 'as long as I hold on to such hatred in my heart against you.' He returned to his room, his soul at peace. Now it was Suzuki's turn not to sleep. The next day, before a thou-sand people from many nations, the police chief apologised to Mr. Nakajima for his feelings against Socialists and Communists. 'I was bowled over by your gesture,' he said. 'You have started a reaction inside me. Thanks to you, I have been completely freed from my hatred.'

Those who have lived in Japan and know the great reserve and proper pride of her people would not believe such apologies possible. But they were followed by other apologies which were to echo round the world.

These Japanese had the courage to face squarely the immediate past history of their country. 'Japan is a prodigal son who abandoned the family of nations,' said one of them. 'Now he is deeply sorry for what he has done and wants to take his place again. Change for the Japan-ese is expressed in the cry of the prodigal son: "Father, I have sinned against heaven and before thee, and am no more worthy to be called thy son." Japan must begin by repentance.'

It was during this time at Caux in 1950 that, encouraged by Frank Buchman, the family of nations welcomed with joy the return of this prodigal son. The world was soon to follow along the road on which Frank Buchman had set out.

The Japanese delegation from Caux returned home by way of the U.S.A., stopping in New York, where they were the first group of their countrymen to be received by the United Nations. But the most significant event took place in Washington. The Japanese were received on the floor of the American Senate. The personal representa-tive of the Japanese Prime Minister was invited to address the Senators: it was the first occasion since the war on which a Japanese spoke publicly in the United States.

He offered the apologies of his people for what Japan had done

185   N

during the war. In that chamber, the scene of so many historic debates, for seconds his hearers held their breath. There was the most intense silence, and an Australian eye-witness reported that everyone was aware that something had taken place there which, a few moments earlier, no one would have thought possible. 'It was history,' he wrote, 'being made before my eyes.'

Then the Japanese speaker went on: 'We went to Caux in search of the content of democracy. We found the ideology which will feed democracy in Japan and which is at the same time the powerful answer to Communism.'

There was a similar scene in the House of Representatives, which broke with all traditions by receiving the delegation inside the chamber. A Japanese Member of Parliament spoke on behalf of his countrymen. He too apologised, as his colleague had done in the Senate, and added, 'We undertook the journey to Caux because the programme of Moral Re-Armament seems to us to offer the only possible basis for a genuine rehabilitation.'

The *New York Times* commented next day in an editorial:

> The enemies of yesterday may not be enemies today. Vice-President Barkley, receiving a delegation of sixty Japanese officials, business men, and labour leaders, could recall a long period of peace and amity that preceded the recent war and could hope for another such period. Mr. Chojiro Kuriyama, member of the Japanese Diet, had a particularly attentive hearing as he told the Senate of his regret for 'Japan's big mistake' and his recognition of 'American forgiveness and generosity'. All this in Washington, D.C., on 28th July, 1950, a little less than five years after the atomic bombs fell on Hiroshima and Nagasaki.
>
> The Mayors of Hiroshima and Nagasaki were among yesterday's visitors. . . . If they felt that they, too, had something to forgive they had achieved the miracle. For a moment one could see out of the present darkness into the years when all men may be brothers.

After the Osaka union leader had gone in the middle of the night and apologised to the chief of police, he went to sleep with peace in his soul, but the police chief had a disturbed night. Did the action of the Japanese have a similar effect on the American Congress? The *Saturday Evening Post* wrote: 'Mr. Kuriyama's statement would be hard for an American to understand. The idea of a nation admitting that it could have been mistaken has a refreshing impact. . . . Perhaps even Americans could think up a few past occasions of which it would be safely said, "We certainly fouled things up that time." '

Before returning home to Japan the delegation gave an interview to an English newspaper and launched an appeal which caught the attention of many Western governments: 'Russia has advanced in Asia because the Soviet Government understands the art of ideological war. It fights for the minds of men. We appeal to the governments and peoples of the West to do the same, to make themselves expert in the philosophy and practice of Moral Re-Armament, which is the ideology of the future. Then all Asia will listen.'

The Mayor of Hiroshima had presented to Frank Buchman a wooden cross carved from the still-living heart of a mighty camphor tree, a giant that had been blasted by the atom bomb. This tree had been planted at Hiroshima 400 years before when the city was founded. The Japanese delegation which came to Caux in 1950 took back a seed which was to take firm root in Japanese soil. From this was to grow another tree with the strength to withstand all the upheavals of the future.

NOT LEFT, NOR RIGHT, BUT STRAIGHT

In May 1957, a hundred young Japanese were about to pack their bags for Moscow. They were invited to the World Youth Congress there, and to Peking on their way home. Each one of them held a key position in the most influential of the Japanese youth organisations, the Seinendan. Its membership of 4,300,000 represents the most dynamic and progressive elements in the rising generation, and reaches to the remotest villages of the country.

The Seinendan is already three hundred years old. In the early days it was merely an assembly of young people who wished to take a hand in the welfare of the community. It was they who formed the first fire brigades of Japan. They also undertook large projects in irrigation and road-making. During the war the organisation was taken over by the military.

After 1945 the Seinendan had been reconstituted with the help of the American Occupation Authorities, in order to give the youth a taste for Western democratic principles. Political parties at once began to canvass for the support of its leaders. The extreme left set out to infiltrate the organisation at all levels, and one of their spokesmen was able to say with confidence: 'When the red flag flies over the Seinendan headquarters, we shall be all set to take over the country.'

When the invitation to Moscow was presented to the Executive Committee of the Seinendan only one objection was raised. It came from a vice-president, the daughter of a simple peasant family. When she stated her objections, she was greeted by vociferous protests from the extreme left: even her own friends shrugged their shoulders saying, 'What do you want us to do? Have you an alternative to the Moscow invitation?'

Two weeks later a hundred Seinendan leaders stepped out of an aeroplane after a 6,000 mile journey. A ferry-boat took them to an enchanting spot, Mackinac Island, at the heart of the American Great Lakes. An invitation, the only one of its kind to come from the West, had been extended by Frank Buchman and, thanks to the tenacity of the young vice-president, all concerned had turned down the Moscow invitation and come to Mackinac instead. In the space of two weeks the ideological balance had begun to swing in a different direction.

In the past, Mackinac Island had been a rallying point for the Indian tribes of North America. The possession of the island had been disputed by French, English and Americans, and their respective flags flew in turn above the wooden fort, which remains today a witness to the island's history.

Each summer, for some years now, thousands from all over the world have met in the new buildings of Moral Re-Armament. There is a legend that tells of the Great Manitou, the Ancient God of the Indians, who prophesied, 'On this isle the tribes will gather together to be reconciled. Later, the nations of the earth will meet here to establish peace.'

Into this melting-pot of the nations the hundred Seinendan leaders plunged. While their aeroplane was touching down on American soil other delegates were arriving from all five continents. There was Damasio Cardoso, the Brazilian docker with his comrades from the port of Rio. The young nationalist, R. D. Mathur, and Gandhi's grandson were joined by others from India. The Nigerian Chief, El-Haj Umoru, was there with Africans from all parts of their continent, among them a parliamentary delegation from Ghana. There were trade unionists, industrialists and politicians from Europe. Soon in the Great Hall, shaped like an Indian wigwam, a whole world was assembled.

The hundred Japanese themselves represented quite a chapter of human history. Most of them had come from farms or rice-fields and many had fought in the Japanese armies in China, Indonesia and the Philippines. Four of them had been at Hiroshima or Nagasaki when the atomic bombs fell and had lost their families there. Each of them had in his heart that day a profound hostility towards American policy. The little faith that they might have once had in Western democracy had disappeared.

The Japanese know how to organise. Within the delegation from the first days a right-wing and a left-wing cell were formed! At the end of each plenary session of the Assembly, the groups held council together and decided what their 'party-line' was going to be. Every evening and often until dawn one could hear passionate discussions going on in different rooms where little parties met. Everything was analysed, thrashed out, picked to pieces; when no conclusion seemed possible everyone went to bed!

Each day, at the main assembly meetings, no outward sign appeared on those hundred faces; yet the reality of a new world in the making was gaining ground in the thoughts of these men.

'Like many of those who had come with me,' a woman teacher from Hiroshima said later, 'I was rather sceptical and did not understand that minor questions of a purely personal nature could have the least effect on the world situation. But one day a Dutch girl who had lived in Indonesia with her family told how she and her people had been captured by Japanese soldiers and interned in a concentration camp. They had never had enough to eat and had been badly treated. Many people in the camp had died. She had hated us. "Now, however," she added, "I am no longer bitter because I know that you can't build peace with hate in your heart." Recently the Japanese Government had paid her some reparation money. She announced her decision to give that money for the work of Moral Re-Armament in Japan. In her view this was the only spirit which could create unity in Asia. Her story went straight to our hearts.

'I began to realise then,' continued the young teacher, 'what Frank Buchman meant when he said, "Peace is not just an idea. It is people becoming different", and "If you want to see the world different, the best place to begin is with yourself." I realised that I too had to begin with myself.'

One morning, one of the most resolutely anti-American of the Japanese was invited to breakfast by a New York surgeon, his wife and four children. 'Over breakfast with Dr. Close and his family,' he said afterwards, 'I told the story of how a Japanese woman was killed at an American base in Japan. They listened attentively and humbly apologised to me for what the Americans had done through such an act. The little six-year-old son said to me, "I have a little money saved up. Take it for those people who are in trouble."

'Up to that point I had loathed those people. But I had never understood that others too could hate me. And there was that child apologising for what the Americans had done!' This simple act melted years of bitterness.

At one of the dinner tables a Burmese lady was sitting with five Japanese. She told how, during the Japanese occupation, her favourite uncle had done his best to maintain decent relations with the soldiers who were living in his house. But senior Japanese officers were displeased by this. The uncle was arrested and died in prison some months later. This story left the five men in deep silence. Four of them had served as officers, the fifth as an instructor at the military academy. Suddenly the Japanese sitting opposite the Burmese lady could contain himself no longer; he broke down and sobbed. For the first time it cut him to the heart to realise the responsibility of his country. He recalled the day when, under threats from his superior, he had killed some prisoners. He began to speak of things he had never told anyone before and this, far from stirring up bitterness, healed the deepest wounds. For each one at that table, it was as if the weight of haunting memory and despair had dropped away and hearts were set free.

The Japanese did not yet know it, but these experiences were to make the deepest impression on members of the American Congress.

The Japanese delegation was invited to Washington. In the Senate restaurant a taxi-driver from Nagasaki described how since the time of the atomic explosion, from which he himself escaped, he had only two aims in life: to revenge the past, and to try by every means in his power to prevent an atomic war. For the first three weeks at Mackinac, he told them, he had never once agreed to sit down at table with a Westerner. But his stay had convinced him that it was impossible to work for world peace with hate in one's heart.

Senator Wiley, member of the Senate Foreign Affairs Committee, was so deeply moved by the words of this Japanese that he quoted them on the Senate floor some days later. He called this conversation 'an experience which he would long remember'. Speaking of the Seinendan leaders, the Senator added: 'They are discovering an ideology of freedom which can put an end to corruption and division, the trail which materialism leaves behind it in both West and East.'

Among the young Japanese was a chemist. During the first week of his stay he had proved to be the most violent advocate of anti-Americanism and of opposition to the atomic bomb. 'For my first month in Mackinac,' he said later, 'I slept during the day and felt wide-awake at night. My object was to make life difficult for the Moral Re-Armament people. My room-mate was a man called Leland Holland. He worked hard through the day and came back to the room about 11 o'clock in the evening. As I had slept most of the day, at that point I was full of energy. With the help of an interpreter I used to start discussing Moral Re-Armament with him. I imagined that the following morning he would sleep on a bit later, but he never did. His discipline made a deep impression on me. He used to get up at five-thirty every morning and bring me a cup of coffee; and that went on for forty days. Gradually I got the point that people in Moral Re-Armament don't talk a great deal but they put an idea into practice.'

One fine morning Yamamoto, the chemist, got to his feet during an assembly session. 'I have just posted a letter,' he said. 'It can alter the whole course of my life.' When he had left Japan the family quarrels had reached such a pitch that divorce seemed the only way out. In the letter he had admitted honestly for the first time where he was wrong, apologised and asked his wife whether she would be willing to make a new start with him.

A few days later Yamamoto woke up one morning, his head buzzing with ideas. The whole plot for a play began to unfold in his mind. Within seventy-two hours he had written *Road to Tomorrow* and the following week the play was performed. It had a great destiny before it.

The Seinendan leaders were at Mackinac when the Japanese Prime

Minister, Mr. Kishi, arrived in Washington on an official visit. There he received three of the young Japanese and some Japanese parliamentarians who came from Mackinac. From Blair House, official residence for American State guests, he telephoned Frank Buchman to thank him for the leadership he was training for the Asian nations at Mackinac. 'I believe that the sure way to lasting peace,' he said, 'is through a change of heart. What you are doing is more necessary than ever.'

'These youth leaders from Japan,' replied Frank Buchman, 'are learning to go not to the right, not to the left, but to go straight. That's the thing most youth throughout the world most need to learn —to go absolutely straight.'

Frank Buchman added, 'I ask that Japan will not only be the light-house of Asia but the power-house as well, and bring unity, purpose and direction to the whole East.'

Then the Japanese Prime Minister, through a loudspeaker attached to the telephone, addressed the hundred Japanese assembled with Frank Buchman. 'I expect a great deal from you,' he told them. 'I hope you are fully understanding Moral Re-Armament and will absorb its spirit in your whole being and take it back to Japan.'

'THE STATESMANSHIP OF
THE HUMBLE HEART'

The Japanese Prime Minister took up the thought that Frank Buchman had expressed in his telephone conversation with him. 'Our government,' he said in a public statement at Tokyo a few months later, 'is learning to go not left, nor right, but to go straight. I want to make this our national policy. We believe that Moral Re-Armament is bringing true and lasting peace to the world.'

Dr. Buchman's thought did more than describe the new course that the youth of Japan had begun to take. It was becoming the basic principle of the Prime Minister's policy.

Mr. Kishi was not the first Japanese Prime Minister to start on this road. Some of his predecessors have been mentioned on earlier pages of this book. The first post-war Prime Minister, Mr. Tetsu Katayama, went to the Caux Assembly in 1949. His successor, Mr. Yoshida, sent the delegation of seventy-six Japanese, whose visit to Caux marked a decisive point in Japanese post-war history. But Mr. Yoshida's successor, Prime Minister Hatoyama, was the first whose foreign policy was inspired by the principles of Moral Re-Armament. The honour goes to him for transforming Japan's whole relationship with one of her neighbours.

The time is July 1955, and the scene is a city where on every side stand the ruined shells of churches, gutted by Japanese bombs. There are huge gaps in the centuries-old fortifications which reveal a desolate open space strewn with rubble, where once had stood an overcrowded city. The survivors mourn 110,000 of their people, who died in air raids, in concentration camps, before firing squads or at the hands of executioners. Hundreds have sworn never to speak to a Japanese, or that they would kill the first Japanese they met.

Such was the atmosphere of Manila at this time.

The President of the Philippines, the late beloved Ramon Magsaysay, had just invited a group of men engaged in the work of Moral Re-Armament to come to Manila. On learning this, Mr. Hatoyama was eager that Japanese representatives should go with this delegation. As official delegates he sent two Members of Parliament, one a Conservative and an outstanding figure in the Diet, Niro Hoshijima, and the other a Socialist, Kanju Kato.

The great auditorium of the Far Eastern University was full to overflowing. Besides the students many of the country's leaders were there. Mr. Carlos Garcia, who was to succeed Magsaysay as President, sat in his official box as Vice-President. Hundreds of people were there who had suffered at the hands of the Japanese or lost their families during the war.

Mr. Hoshijima began to speak in Japanese. A murmur of protest could be heard in the hall; in a matter of moments there might be an uproar, but the voice of the interpreter breaks in and a deep stillness falls on the audience.

'The Japanese must pay war reparations. But reparations are not enough. First of all we must humbly apologise for the past. That is why my Prime Minister urged me to come with this delegation. Please forgive us . . .'

A thunder of applause shook the auditorium.

'Moral Re-Armament is already building a new Japan,' continued

193

the voice of the interpreter. 'With Moral Re-Armament all Asia can unite.'

This act of humble statesmanship marked a turning-point in the relations between Japan and the Philippines. Next day, President Magsaysay received the delegation in the old Spanish palace of Malacanang. Under its imposing crystal chandeliers he shook hands with the Japanese. Some months later, when he welcomed Frank Buchman in the same setting, he expressed his gratitude to him and added: 'Most people load me down with problems, but you bring the answers.'

Mr. Hoshijima's promise about reparations to the Philippine people was carried out. A few weeks later an agreement was in sight. Previously negotiators had spent months trying to reach a basis for agreement. The Japanese undertook to pay 550 million dollars in reparations. Shortly afterwards the Philippine Senate ratified the peace treaty with Japan.

In November 1955, Mr. Hatoyama made a statement which was published in the *Journal de Genève*: 'Moral Re-Armament,' declared the Prime Minister, 'shows us the practical way to re-establish relations with neighbouring countries. I am convinced that diplomacy needs this spirit if world peace is to be assured.'

Frank Buchman was to go to Japan a few months later, in April 1956. An incident took place during his visit which is best described in his own words. In a radio broadcast after his return to Europe, at the end of a journey which took him to Formosa, the Philippines, Viet-Nam, Thailand and Burma, he told the story:

One of the largest newspapers in Japan wrote of my recent visit that I had arrived in Tokyo at a critical time. The Diet was in a turmoil of deadlock and seemingly irreconcilable division. Each member took endless time to walk up and cast his ballot. They called it the 'cow's walk'. It frustrated and infuriated. Sleep and tempers were short. A new factor was needed. Leaders of Government and Opposition arranged a lunch in the Diet for me and the friends with me, men and women who live an ideology that unites. Said members of Government and Opposition afterwards: 'It was a miracle. You brought sanity where there was insanity. A solution was found. There was no riot. We found a way to solve our problems, not on the basis of any one Party's will, but on what was right.' Now it wasn't me. I didn't do it. It was the power of an ideology to change the thinking of men and women in the Diet.

It so happened that the Japanese Government seized the occasion of Frank Buchman's visit to express to him officially the gratitude of the whole nation. On the Government's behalf the Foreign Minister decorated him with the Order of the Rising Sun. Not long afterwards the Philippine people also expressed their thanks; for President Magsaysay, some months later, instructed Senator Lim to present to Frank Buchman the Legion of Honour of the Philippines.

Impressed by what had been achieved in the relations between his country and Japan, President Magsaysay, early in 1957, gave his full support to the idea of a conference which would bring together in the Philippines leaders from different Asian countries. Held under the auspices of Moral Re-Armament, it was to take place in Baguio, the summer capital of the Philippines. Magsaysay wrote to the three Colwell Brothers of Hollywood (Frank Buchman had got them to sing for Magsaysay the year before) inviting them to attend.

Unhappily, before the Colwell Brothers had even received the letter, the world was shocked to learn that President Magsaysay had met a tragic death in an air accident on the rocky heights of Cebu Island. And so it was that his successor, President Garcia, who, carrying out Magsaysay's wish, went to Baguio himself with three members of his government to support the assembly by his presence. There another decisive development was to affect two of the most implacable enemies in Asia, Japan and Korea.

At midnight each night, the mother of Choi Sang Woo woke her son, wrapped him in heavy blankets and took him up to the attic. There, night after night, she taught him his native tongue, Korean, which the Japanese authorities occupying Korea had declared illegal to teach to children. In this way, for forty years, hundreds of thousands of women, like Choi's mother, fostered in their children's hearts a love for their country and its culture. Because he was Korean, young Choi was not allowed to go to High School, although he was top of his class. A whole nation dreamed of the day when their chains would be broken and freedom won.

In March 1957, Choi attended the Assembly of Asian Nations at Baguio as a delegate from Korea. When some Japanese began to address the Assembly, he could not stand listening to that hated language, and he got up and left the hall. 'When I heard those Japanese speaking,' he said later, 'so many memories flooded into my mind that I was reduced to bitter tears.'

Such is the gulf of hatred between these two countries; very few people realise the extent of it, even in Asia. Some governments tried to remedy the situation, but in October 1953 all official negotiations between these countries were broken off. The Japanese Under-Secretary for Foreign Affairs, Mr. Kubota, tried to prove that the Koreans ought at least to have some gratitude to the Japanese people for the economic development which Japanese control had brought to their country. In this same statement Mr. Kubota asserted Japanese rights to almost eighty per cent of the privately owned land in Korea. In the face of such a claim the Koreans had broken off the negotiations, and no attempt to resume them on a diplomatic level had come to anything since.

Tension between the two countries was such that on international occasions the presence of the representative of one of these nations almost always led to the other one walking out. At the MRA Assembly at Baguio, Japanese and Koreans met again for the first time. Would this attempt also end in deadlock?

Leading the Korean delegation were Mr. Yoon Sung Soon, President of the Foreign Affairs Committee of the National Assembly, and Mrs. Park Hyun Sook, who had been a member of the Korean government for several years.

On the Japanese side Mr. Niro Hoshijima, who later became Speaker of the Japanese Diet, was once more in the Philippines. With him came Senator Mrs. Shidzue Kato, a member of the Senate Foreign Affairs Committee. These Japanese had arrived at Baguio wanting to admit their mistakes, and ready to recognise their responsibility for the acts of cruelty done to other peoples. But they found such an icy atmosphere at the start that it seemed impossible for them even to broach the subject.

One day, however, Mrs. Kato decided to address the delegates. She spoke to the Koreans from the depths of her heart and asked their forgiveness. The apology was accepted.

Mr. Hoshijima observed later: 'It was clear to me that we needed to do more than apologise to prove our sincerity. While in Baguio one thought kept coming to me: instead of waiting for a large-scale conference at which the Japanese and Korean Governments would discuss all outstanding problems, we ought immediately to tackle the essential questions and try to settle them on a basis of what is right.'

The Japanese invited the Koreans to tell them honestly all that they felt about the years of domination. They asked them also to indicate how they could prove the sincerity of their apology in a practical way. Mrs. Park Hyun Sook told of her years in prison, and of her husband's suffering—his vocal cords had been cut by Japanese police and he had been bed-ridden for eighteen years.

The next forty-eight hours were spent in long talks between the representatives of the two countries. They tackled the legal issues which divided them: the famous Kubota declaration, Japanese claims on private property, a thorny problem of fishing rights, a territorial question and finally the question of the exchange of political prisoners held by both sides.

At Baguio Mr. Hoshijima publicly expressed his personal conviction that Japan must immediately withdraw from her position on the first two points. The Korean delegates greeted this move as an important step towards a better understanding between the two countries.

Mr. Hoshijima undertook to see the Prime Minister about it as soon as he returned. Mrs. Kato, as a member of the Opposition, offered to make it easier for the Prime Minister to act by raising the question herself before the Senate Foreign Affairs Committee. The Koreans even agreed to go on an official visit to Japan on condition that they stayed in the home which some Japanese had given to Frank Buchman in Tokyo.

On 30th April, 1957, two weeks after the Asian Assembly at Baguio, the Japanese Prime Minister opened a fresh page in the history of Japanese-Korean relations. Speaking before the Senate Foreign Affairs Committee in answer to a question put by Mrs. Kato, Mr. Kishi declared: 'The most important point in our negotiations is not the interpretation of laws and rights, but to give priority to the creation of a right spirit between our countries. We on our side must take the initiative.' Referring to the two most difficult points at issue, the Prime Minister continued: 'I have no hesitation in withdrawing the Kubota statement. I regret that it has given Korea the impression of our people's feeling of superiority.' And referring to Japanese claims on private property in Korea he added: 'I have no intention of holding to our past legal interpretations. We should not hold to our past assertions but try fairly to solve these many practical issues on the basis of a humble heart.'

A few days later, Mr. Niro Hoshijima wrote in an article: 'I have seen fulfilled Frank Buchman's expectation for my country. Guided

197

by God, Japan is called to be the lighthouse of Asia. I feel humble and helpless before this call. But I have seen a light reaching other Asian peoples as we Japanese have opened our hearts in honesty and accepted our responsibility for the wounds and hatreds of the past.'

A Chinese delegate who took part in the Baguio Assembly, General Ho Ying-chin, a former Prime Minister and Army Chief of Staff of the Republic of China, declared: 'What we have failed to achieve in ten years of post-war diplomatic effort has been accomplished at Baguio.'

'Tension—Applause at Canberra—Kishi Apologises' was the head-line on the front page of the *Japan Times* in December 1957 above a news item from Australia.

'At the most important of his public engagements during his visit to Australia,' it read—a state luncheon given by Prime Minister Robert Menzies at Parliament House—the Prime Minister of Japan, Nobusuke Kishi, conveyed to the people of Australia from the people of Japan 'our heartfelt sorrow for what occurred in the war'.

Part of the story behind this move was not told by the Press. It was in Baguio that Mrs. Kato, the Socialist Senator, first learned of the official journey the Prime Minister was preparing to make to various countries at the head of a trade delegation. One thought came clearly to her: 'Go and tell him not to talk of trade but to offer sincere apologies everywhere he goes.'

On her return to Japan she made several attempts to have an inter-view with Mr. Kishi, but always without success. She was afraid of the thought of making such a suggestion to the Prime Minister and almost gave up the idea. As Mr. Kishi's departure date was drawing near, her conviction returned to her with renewed force, and she decided to go and see him without an appointment. She found him in the Cabinet room with five members of the Government, and went straight up to him. 'Mr. Prime Minister,' she said, 'God wants me to tell you this thought with regard to your journey. . . .' When she left, Mrs. Kato had no idea whether her words would be heeded.

Some days after his Australian visit, Mr. Kishi was received officially in the Philippines. President Garcia had arranged for one of his aides, Major Agerico Palaypay, to be in attendance on Mr. Kishi throughout his visit to Manila. One day, when there happened to be a free hour in the programme, the Major offered to show Mr. Kishi certain parts of the city. He took him inside the old city wall, where mounds of rubble still lie everywhere. He showed him the Manila Cathedral in the process of being rebuilt. As he drove him round he told him of his own wartime experiences. Major Palaypay had distinguished himself in the Resistance Movement against the Japanese, and then played a notable part in the struggle against the Huks, as A.D.C. to Magsaysay, then Minister of Defence. Palaypay had also made the acquaintance of Frank Buchman. He had been there when Magsaysay had received Buchman in 1956. Later, after the death of Magsaysay, he accompanied the new President to the Baguio Assembly. But it was at Mackinac, some months later, that Palaypay, for the first time since the war, found himself face to face with the Japanese.

'This scar on my hand,' he said before leaving Mackinac, 'has been the symbol of my hatred for the Japanese since the war. My mind told me it was wrong to hate. But my heart pulled me the other way. Here I have found complete freedom from all those feelings. If hate as strong as mine can be erased, then all men can change.'

As the car returned after the drive around the city, the Japanese Prime Minister remained silent. The same evening, at an official dinner, in the Manila Hotel, where a distinguished company of Filipinos was gathered, once more Mr. Kishi offered apologies on behalf of his country. There was a note of sincerity in his words which made a deep impression on everyone.

A German newspaper, commenting on Mr. Kishi's journey through Asian countries, had the headline: 'Kishi the Ice-breaker.' The *Washington Evening Star* of 18th December, 1957, carried an editorial of which here are some excerpts:

Premier Kishi is now back in Tokyo after having completed one of the most unusual missions ever undertaken by a statesman of his rank. All told, over the past three weeks, he has visited no fewer than nine nations that Japan occupied or threatened with conquest after the attack on Pearl Harbour sixteen years ago. And in each of these lands—including New Zealand, Australia, Indonesia and the Philippines—he has publicly apologised for his country's actions during the war.

Of course, since their defeat and unconditional surrender in 1945, the Japanese have made numerous gestures of repentance. But Mr. Kishi's tour has done more than any of their prior efforts to emphasise and dramatise their desire to bury the past and regain goodwill. Although bitter memories still remain they are now much less deep and widespread than they once were and he has done much to promote a further improvement in relations.

In March 1958 the Prime Minister sent a message from Japan to the delegates from Asian nations who were taking part in a second Baguio Conference. In it he said: 'In the course of the last twelve months I have had the privilege of visiting many of the countries which will be represented at your conference. I was impressed by the effectiveness of MRA in creating unity between peoples who have been divided. I have myself experienced the power of honest apology in healing the hurts of the past. We need the statesmanship of the humble heart in order to bring sanity and peace to the affairs of men. If we in Asia can achieve unity based on what is right for us all, then we will have something to offer in the councils of the world.'

THE ROAD TO TOMORROW

When the hundred young Seinendan leaders were back in Japan from the journey to Mackinac, they were conscious of the immense task awaiting them. For it was necessary to penetrate the whole country with their new way of life. To do something effective they had to reach the leaders and the masses. They saw in the play *Road to Tomorrow* a newly forged weapon adequate for the battle they were eager to wage.

Not one of them, however, was free to dispose of his time as he wished. Each had professional work to return to after two months' absence. It was in the hearts of some of these young Japanese that this battle for Japan had first to be won.

The play, written by the young chemist, was in the best tradition of Japanese drama. It is the story of a family of farmers who live in a village torn apart by class conflict. The son of the family goes to Mackinac, where he is seen a few weeks later writing a letter of apology. In a corner of the stage the spotlights pick out his brothers, sisters and parents, one after another as he addresses them in turn. The play also shows how a young Japanese becomes aware of his country's guilt and the wrongs done to the Filipinos, the Koreans, the Chinese and other nations. From Mackinac the son brings back to the village a seed of unity.

The rôle of the mother of the family had been played in Mackinac by a young woman, Tomi Susuki, who was President of the Seinendan Federation in her Province. She arrived in Tokyo deeply concerned for her parents whom she was going to see. She was the only daughter. Her parents, already advanced in years, had worked so hard all their lives, bending double in the ricefields, that her mother could no longer walk a step without leaning on a little cart. What was she to do? Had she the right to ask her parents to live in poverty and carry the burden of the farm? Her heart was torn as she left to see them. For three weeks she toiled night and day to try to get a little ahead in the farm work so as to free herself at least for a time. Her old parents saw how ardent her conviction was, and offered to take up the work again themselves so that she could leave again. Then her friends in the Seinendan came to her rescue and she was able to arrange with them that her parents would have regular help.

Another part in the play was taken by a young farm worker. He too had old parents and they needed him for the harvest. When he told them of his plans they backed him up and sold a piece of land in order to free him from any obligation towards them.

Each of these Seinendan young people suffered the same anguish on returning home. One of them was an eldest son and, according to Japanese tradition, it is the eldest son who decides everything once his father has retired. He dared not speak of the plans for the play. One day, however, he told his father what he had discovered at Mackinac and how he had decided himself to live differently. The father listened and questioned him. Finally the son spoke of the plan he had so much on his heart. 'If you think that's the most important thing you should do,' said the father, 'go and do it.'

Some weeks after the delegation returned to Tokyo, seventeen young Japanese, their family and professional obligations settled, met once more to launch together their assault on the country. They all held the view that the play had to be produced at once and performed in the capital before touring other cities. First they had to find all the equipment; for between them they had no resources whatsoever. A theatrical company decided to make the scenery for them and supply all the electrical equipment free of charge. One of the best producers in Tokyo, Sugawara, offered his talents to perfect the play. When one of the Ambassadors accredited ﾀ Tokyo learned that the cast had no place for rehearsals he offered them a reception room in his embassy. His son and daughter were so thrilled at the prospect of what the tour could do and also at what they learned from the young Japanese, that they volunteered to work backstage with the properties.

It was in this way that the conviction and sacrifice of those young people from the Seinendan fashioned an instrument, which, in city after city, was to bring to Japan a message of national renaissance.

One of the Japanese who was eager to join the Seinendan actors was a man who had spent eleven years in Russian prison camps in Siberia. Taken prisoner at the end of the war in Manchuria, Tatsuji Seki, with thousands of his compatriots, had been taken off to a series of camps in the bleakest areas of Siberia. All through their captivity he and one of his friends fought off despair by working to create a number of plays. He took the leading parts while his friend was the producer. They sought in this way to keep alive in the hearts of their companions both the love of their country and the hope of returning to a normal life.

Through all these years Seki had opportunities to observe the Russians. Although he submitted to their iron discipline, he realised that his guards were often divided by hatred and jealousy.

One evening in 1954, when he was resting in the smoke-filled dormitory scanning the Russian magazine *Culture*, he noticed the photo of a large building in Switzerland entitled 'Moral Re-Armament'. The article was written by a Russian reporter who had gone to Caux that year with a group of journalists during an adjournment of the Big Four Conference in Geneva. It was a violent attack which intrigued Seki. 'Moral Re-Armament,' he said to himself. 'That's what the world needs.'

To his amazement, a few days after his return from captivity, he received a letter from his sister and learnt that she was fully committed to the fight alongside Frank Buchman. Today Seki declares that he has lost his fear of the Communists 'because he has learned how to change the heart of a man, whether he is a Communist or not'.

Along with his former comrade in captivity he now plays one of the leading rôles in *Road to Tomorrow*, because for him the spirit of the play shows the only road to a better future.

After a première in Tokyo, arranged specially for Diet members, the stage was set up in the industrial city of Hitachi. This was the first contact with the world of Japanese labour. The success was so great that invitations flowed in from all parts of the country. In the course of the following months the play was invited by one town after another and went to the copper mines, coalfields and shipyards, as well as to the great industrial areas, as the enterprise started by those young leaders gained momentum in the country.

They played in well-equipped modern theatres, and sometimes, too, in ordinary halls where the audience, seated on the floor on Japanese matting, was so tightly packed that not one person more could have been slipped in. In all they gave seventy-six performances. At the end of each one many people stayed on to crowd round the actors, eager to learn more about what they had seen on the stage.

One freezing January day in Urawa, near Tokyo, the play brought together in the auditorium two men who were hardly accustomed to sitting side by side.

One of them, Mr. Sogo, holds one of the highest official posts in Japan as Governor of the Japanese Railways, with 45,000 railway workers under his orders. In Japan, the railway men are known as the most militant of the workers, and they are generally the leaders of the 'spring offensive' to force government and management to agree to wage increases. The latest of those 'offensives' had turned out badly. A strike had been launched and there had been a serious accident. The government had dismissed the union leaders and refused further negotiations until fresh union elections had taken place. There was total deadlock. The unions elected the same men again. The government refused to negotiate with them.

Seated in the front row of the theatre that night was none other than the President of the Railway Workers' Union, Mr. Koyanagi. He remarked ironically, 'The Governor's job is to keep the trains running. Mine seemed to be to keep the trains from running!'

After the play, over a cup of tea offered by the Mayor to everyone, the old Governor Sogo turned to the union leader. 'I was like the old dictator of a father that we have just seen on the stage,' he said. 'Often I have not done all I could to find a solution to the many conflicts that kept us divided. I am sorry.'

That evening the ice was broken by the Seinendan youth and negotiations started again. Some time later the National Federation of Railway Workers invited the same cast to put the play on at their

Tokyo headquarters. The guest of honour for the occasion was none other than Governor Sogo himself.

In Hiroshima there stands a new theatre only a few yards from where the atomic bomb fell. It was there that *Road to Tomorrow* was played.

Since the war, the hate aroused by the explosions at Hiroshima and Nagasaki has been effectively exploited by those who were trying to cut off Japan from the West, and especially from America. Day after day the Japanese Press gives news of men and women still suffering from the effects of the bomb. Each year, with demonstrations, congresses and resolutions, fresh attempts are made to intensify the hate and increase the resentments.

'I hated America,' wrote one of those victims. 'How many times have I wished and dreamed of the Americans being slaughtered as we were at Hiroshima. Violently anti-American as I was, I had no idea that the hatred in my life was creating hatred in my family, my trade union, my country and Asia; and that inevitably this hatred was causing disunity.'

Ayako Yamada, who was born in Hiroshima, described in her own words what happened in her city.

More than 2,500 people saw *Road to Tomorrow* that evening in the large municipal auditorium. The Mayor introduced the play. My brother joined the cast for that performance and greatly enjoyed his part as a village postman.

The same morning the sixty members of the cast went to the Park of Peace to lay a wreath at the foot of the semi-circular monument erected in memory of the victims of the atom bomb. On it are inscribed the famous words: 'Rest in peace. Never again shall we make the same mistake.' When the Mayor of Hiroshima had this engraved he was much criticised. Many took exception to the word 'we' and wanted it replaced by 'they'. But our Mayor, who had lost several members of his family in the disaster and whose wife still suffered from its effects, had been to Caux. 'We must blame no one for what happened,' he had said. 'We must together take responsibility to prevent anything like it happening again.'

As I stood before that monument to the dead [continued the young woman], many memories went through my mind, and my heart was heavy. I told my friends: 'Thank you for coming to Hiroshima. People come from many countries to see us, but no one has come with the cure for bitterness. You are the first to bring it. I am deeply grateful to be with you here today in order to be able to give it to the world.'

Osaka nearly closed its gates to Road to Tomorrow. In the story of the play there is a poor farmer who goes in the night to steal water from his more prosperous neighbour. This part was played by Kichizaemon Sumitomo, head of a great industrial family which, before the war, employed more than half a million workers. The head of this whole Sumitomo empire is at Osaka. It was reported to the Board of Directors there by a manager from one of their companies, that in Tokyo he had seen Kichizaemon Sumitomo on the stage in the rôle of a peasant. The directors were horrified. It was decided that the play would not be allowed to come to Osaka.

Two members of the board came to Tokyo to persuade Mr. Sumitomo to give up his part. 'It is too humble a part for you,' they said to him.

'I am playing this part, not for myself, but for the sake of the future of Japan, so that our children and grandchildren may be able to live in a truly democratic country. Many of these Seinendan youth have sacrificed everything to put on this play, and I am convinced that my place is by their side.'

'But think of the reputation of the Sumitomo family! It will be ruined!'

'I understand your reasoning, but it is normal for me too to think of the name of Sumitomo, for I was born into the family!'

'Very well,' said the directors, 'continue to play your peasant rôle, but don't do it in Osaka. It would be too distressing for us to see you like that.'

'If you were really thinking of your grandchildren and their future then you would want to see me in the play. If you do not understand, then I can only pray to go neither right, nor left, but straight ahead, so that God can use me.'

Mr. Sumitomo held his ground. The play came to Osaka, and these gentlemen came to see it, full of misgivings.

At the end of the last curtain call, Mr. Sumitomo stepped forward on the stage. 'After the war,' he declared, 'I lost everything which constituted my security. I lived my life without taking the least responsibility for the future of the country. Moral Re-Armament has shown me that I had to change my way of living if I wanted to build a new world. This ideology has brought a true perspective to bear on the future. That is why I gladly accepted a part in this play, even the most humble.'

One of the directors admitted, 'I wept like a child. . . . The play touches something deep in your heart.' At the following performance two of the most respected members of the board introduced the play and publicly told everyone they were sorry for the opposition they had raised against Mr. Sumitomo. At the end of the evening a man rose from the audience and began to speak. 'Mr. Sumitomo's objective in playing his part is to change the world. We can only pay tribute to the spirit he shows.' It was the former president of the Sumitomo Bank.

Once the doors opened in Osaka, those of the Sumitomo Industries throughout Japan were opened likewise.

'Within the Seinendan, 1958 was meant to be the year when the concentrated efforts of the extremists would be crowned with success in the elections and they would take over all the posts on the executive,' reports the young Vice-President, Miss Kinu Wakamiya. 'The most elaborate preparations had been made to assure victory. But those who were determined that the Seinendan should not be exploited by any exterior force were victorious at the elections, though by a very small margin.

'The real architects of this success in the elections were certain men who had been freed from personal ambition and had learned to have confidence in each other through honesty among themselves; these men had acquired in this way a genuine moral authority. They had thwarted the Communist strategy which exploits human weaknesses and ambitions.'

A few days before the elections another member of the central committee who had also been to Mackinac, had remarked, 'Previously the elections were always fought out between the right and the left. Now they are going to be between those who want to live Moral Re-Armament and those who do not.'

It was certainly on that basis that the problem was thrashed out in the general assembly of the organisation. There was no backstair intrigue, there were no violent speeches. But impassioned discussions took place amongst small groups of people seated on the 'tatami' matting. In each group there was a left-wing extremist, the bearer of precise orders, and one of the men who had been to Mackinac as well.

Shortly after the results of the election were announced, the Communist leader turned to the young Vice-President and said, 'We have been beaten by Moral Re-Armament ! ' She replied with a smile: 'It is not Moral Re-Armament that has beaten you, but the spirit of what is right.'

She summed up this success as follows: 'If we had lost it would have been a disaster for the country. It has to be recognised that what decides the future of the country is, in fact, the line taken by the SOHIO (Federation of Japanese Trade Unions) with its five million members, the Teachers' Trade Union with its 500,000 members and the Seinendan with its 4,300,000 members. Two of these organisations are now pro-Communist. That is why the Seinendan must continue its policy of going neither right, nor left, but straight.'

At the second Asian Conference for Moral Re-Armament in Baguio in March 1958, these Japanese were able, unitedly, to transmit to the delegates of other Asian countries their own experience.

The Japanese Prime Minister, Mr. Kishi, sent a personal representative, Kunio Morishita, to lead a whole delegation, which included the cast of Road to Tomorrow. The Japanese play, the first to be performed in the Philippines since the war, moved the audience there as deeply as it had done in America and Japan. But the keynote was struck by Senator Shidzue Kato, when she observed, 'This Assembly is creating a united group of Asians who are going to bring unity to the world.'

There were, in fact, delegates present from India, Viet-Nam, Burma, Formosa, Japan, the Philippines and Indonesia. One of them was Aryo Piereno, President of the Indonesian Youth Front, to which two million youth, some from the extreme left and also from the extreme right, belong. He had been twice condemned to death, first by the Communists and then by the Dutch. To one of the delegates in the audience, Senator Dirk de Loor of Holland, Piereno spoke one day from the platform, 'When I came here, I could not bring myself to speak to you, for you are a member of the Dutch Parliament. But when you admitted in your speech where you had been wrong, this helped me to see in you, not an enemy but a comrade-in-arms for remaking the world.' The two men shook hands. That handshake, and the Dutch Senator's speech which had made it possible, raised a storm throughout Holland. But there rose up in Parliament and Press more men to support the Senator's courageous act than the political experts had been able to foresee. At Baguio, Senator de Loor had said to the

Indonesians, 'There are black pages in the history which Holland has written in Asia. Together we can start a clean page. I ask your forgiveness for our past mistakes.'

The Indonesian youth leader summed up his sense of the significance of the assembly as follows: 'First, I have found the secret of family unity; then I have seen here Indonesians and Dutch finding an understanding of one another; finally, we have seen how, with the help of our other Asian friends and especially the Japanese, we shall be able to provide food for empty stomachs, work for empty hands, and for empty hearts the ideology of Moral Re-Armament.'

Another delegate, young Rajmohan Gandhi, declared, 'This conference has seen the birth of a force that will unite Asia, because it has brought a cure to the hatred that existed between the Asiatic countries, and between us and the West.'

And so the 'lighthouse' of Japan began to shine out in Asia.

But it was in the summer of 1958, on Mackinac Island, that this united force of Asia came to prepare the launching of an assault on the whole of their continent. Those who had produced *Road to Tomorrow*: Gandhi's grandson, the young Indian, R. D. Mathur, and Mr. Sumitomo, were joined by young Filipino musicians, young men from Viet-Nam and China, and finally the popular singing star of Japan, Minoru Obata. This last, after giving up his triumphant career, had just decided it would be more honest to resume his own name, Paul Kang, and his real nationality, which was Korean.

Together these men have created and produced a new musical play which is destined to do for Asia what *Road to Tomorrow* has done for Japan. One of the first performances took place in November 1958 at Seattle, at a time when the conference of the Colombo Plan countries was held there.

This was the start of work on a scale to affect the whole Asian continent.

AND NOW—WHAT IS THE TASK?

Throughout the preceding chapters we have seen how men, and also a nation, have found a fresh realisation of their true destiny. Where there was no ideal to live for, or only fallacious ideas to go by, fresh hope has been given which has re-orientated the lives, both of the individual and of the nation.

Already the main features of a new society can be seen emerging. It is coming into being. What is important is that the way is open and the stage of the architect's blueprint is past. What matters also is the range and effectiveness of the working out of these principles in action, as we have reported them.

We have chosen Japan as an example. But we could have taken another case instead, for the action of Moral Re-Armament is world-wide. The facts recorded cannot be discarded on the grounds that a Japanese or an Asian mentality is necessary in order to explain them. For the deepest things in a man are the same the world over.

Similar events have taken place on the continent of Africa. The African nations are giving to the world tangible evidence of their experience of Moral Re-Armament.

The most outstanding political figure in his part of Nigeria— Professor Eyo Ita of the province of Calabar—suddenly realised at a Moral Re-Armament assembly that the conflict between his region and the central government was, in fact, entirely due to personal rivalry. His conscience told him that his bitter personal antagonism against his Prime Minister, Nnamdi Azikiwe, had to be faced. The latter had been responsible for ousting him from his position as head of the government. He decided to go and see his former adversary, apologised to him and offered to accompany him on a visit to his province. Over the radio he made an appeal for concord: ‘ Let us be done with tribal politics which have divided our country ! Henceforth I shall set my face to a new national merger in which, with one mind and a new spirit, we, the whole nation, like one man, will rise and work together under the guidance of God for the freedom of the country.’ And so a nation begins to follow the road on which many of her people have already started since the day that Nnamdi Azikiwe first went to Caux in 1949.

Similar events took place in a neighbouring country, Ghana, at the moment when it was reaching independence. One of the leaders of the Opposition, the Tolon Na, averted a serious constitutional crisis by taking the same sort of action as Professor Eyo Ita.

In another of these countries bordering the Gulf of Guinea, there is a man who is today Finance Minister, and who, because he rooted out of his own heart that hate that he had cultivated against the colonial power, uprooted at the same time the elements of discord that had divided him from his family and his political colleagues. Now he is regarded as the pillar on which the national unity rests.

Even the most entrenched prejudices yield to this new conception of the relations between men. In South Africa black men who have led the struggle for the defence of their people's rights—such as William Nkomo, who was President of the African National Congress Youth League—and white men of the most extremest outlook—such as Jan Loubser, student leader from the Afrikaner University of Stellenbosch —have not only met and become wholly at one in their aims but, in uniting, bring to the world a new conception of racial relations. These South Africans, travelling together through the Southern States of America, capture the interest of American statesmen anxious to solve their own problems. 'You say what America needs to hear,' declared Commissioner McLaughlin when he received them officially in Washington.

These examples could be multiplied. But all these experiences have world-wide significance because the Africans are aware that they can also happen in other parts of the world. For this, in 1957, they created a film called *Freedom*. Its script is simply the expression of what they have tried, lived and proved. One of Walt Disney's cameramen, Rickard Tegstrom, nicknamed 'the camera Rembrandt', and other first-rate technicians of the moving picture industry, gave their services free of charge, and today this film, translated into many languages, presents to other nations the experiences of these Africans.

In Berlin, for example, *Freedom* was shown near the Soviet border, in a cinema where only East German marks were accepted as currency and men and women came in their thousands looking for hope. Whether it is shown in Finland, or in the black or white universities of South Africa, at Little Rock or in the Argentine, or to parliamentary representatives in the capital cities of sixteen different countries, this film revolutionises people's preconceived notions. 'Last night I saw a movie which may change the course of my life,' wrote a Hollywood film critic after a showing of *Freedom*.

These experiences resound from one continent to another and this is one of the characteristic ways in which the work of Moral Re-Armament goes forward. It reveals Frank Buchman's true genius. One day at Caux he had gathered together about thirty Africans who had come from twelve different countries and were just about to go home. He suggested to them that they put the fruits of their experience into *Freedom*. 'Africa must speak to the world,' he said. And so, Africa's voice has been heard in the furthest corners of the globe.

In the same way, at a Mackinac conference, six Members of the Ghana Parliament, from two opposing parties, wrote a play called *The Next Phase* and produced it with the help of other Africans there. At once Frank Buchman thought of the startling effect it would have in America. It had the simplest of themes: first of all it showed that a country which has just received independence must find a cure for internal rivalries if it is not to succumb to a worse form of slavery. It had an all-black cast and white South Africans volunteered to do the work backstage. Washington gave *The Next Phase* an enthusiastic reception. Citizens of Atlanta, the great capital of the South, came to see the play and invited the cast to present it in their civic auditorium. These Africans were in fact the only people who won the respect and affection of the white and coloured people alike. For the first time in history, the segregation ruling was waived in an Atlanta theatre.

Through their contact with Frank Buchman the Africans began to be aware of the part their continent is called to play in building the world of tomorrow. From their intellectual traditions, our Western nations have learned the habit of reducing every difficulty to problems of population, economics, finance and technique, which often still remain insoluble. They can learn from the African nations that a more effective way is by tackling and changing the motives of men.

'The demand of our times,' declared Dowuona-Hammond, Member of Ghana's Parliament, 'is for an ideology fundamental enough to deal with the problems raised by the human passions of hate, fear and greed, an ideology of freedom, that man's relations with man shall not be governed by how much we can get from one another, but how much we can selflessly give. That is the only guarantee that man's inhumanity to man shall end. Men shall cease to fear each other because their motives will have changed.'

These Africans still keep unimpaired a deep feeling—which today is sadly dulled in the West—that the human element must come first in every relationship between man and man.

During the last ten years men from these young African nations have come in hundreds to different Assemblies of Moral Re-Armament at Caux and Mackinac. They have been the first to grasp that a sound policy for their countries and their continent would follow only if they had a high standard in the conduct of their private and public lives. At the end of his stay at Caux the Minister of Works of an African Republic outlined for the Press the policy he intended to carry through on his return home. It had four points: to put things right in his family; to be reconciled with political colleagues in his region; to restore good relations between the Southern and Northern provinces; and lastly, to create unity at the heart of the government in which he served. 'I am very grateful,' he added, 'for Frank Buchman's thought that Africa can be a continent reborn. He is the only man to have thought in those terms. This Africa will be built up on the moral decisions taken in the hearts of our chiefs and our brothers. I want to make MRA's absolute moral standards the policy of my department, and I will fight to see that my government do not depart from these lines in national policy.'

If anyone were to smile at so courageous a statement, they might find they had condemned themselves. Which of us could look into ourselves and not admit that certain spheres of our life were kept in watertight compartments?

The Communist world seeks to woo and win these men of Africa. The Western world does its utmost to convince them of the soundness of its democratic principles. But it is to Frank Buchman that they turn with a greater hope. They have felt the need to meet together at an African Assembly for Moral Re-Armament. 'Through these assemblies,' the head of an African government wrote recently, 'new policies can emerge where man no longer tries to dominate man, or fears the loss of influence here or there, but where all men accept for themselves and their nations the dominion of the Almighty God and decide to live under His guidance.'

The experience of these men of Asia and Africa above all else gives food for thought to both the Western and the Communist worlds. Both see in it a challenge to the principles on which they have built their society. The most far-seeing on both sides begin to realise that Asia and Africa have a contribution to make to the world on which their own future may depend.

We can think here of what one of Mahatma Gandhi's companions, Governor Munshi, said when he was at Caux:

Are we going to accept the supremacy of the moral order, or the superiority of materialism? This is the conflict which underlies everything else. In our era, when notions of East and West have become largely outdated, our generation has tried to resolve this conflict through nationalism, different forms of democracy, socialism and other means. But it has scarcely helped us to advance towards a solution. The modern world is obsessed by the idea of a material standard of living; it has accepted the notion that if we change the economic conditions, this will automatically change men. In fact, higher standards of living have brought neither peace nor happiness. The time has come when we must learn to put first the absolute moral laws of Moral Re-Armament.

This eminent Indian's words parallel the thinking of Frank Buchman:

Communist and non-Communist have one fundamental weakness in common. They are not creating a new type of man. Consequently both lack the one essential for creating a new world. But there is a superior ideology which is giving men new motives, new character. It works! It is a new thinking forged by living absolute standards—absolute honesty, purity, unselfishness and love. With this ideology nations will begin to think. They will solve all their problems. Families will be united. Youth will find a purpose more dynamic and compelling than lawlessness.

This is the new statesmanship [continued Frank Buchman], a life commitment adequate to change the thinking, living and daring of the whole world. For everyone, everywhere, this is the future. This is normal living.

What might yesterday have seemed an empty dream to men without faith, has already today become reality. A rising tide of dedicated men—men of good will in the richest sense—is flooding over the world, sweeping away materialism, both the chaotic materialism of the West and the organised materialism of the Communist world. Thousands of people, because they have shed their petty concerns, are able to think for the world and today they concentrate their efforts wherever the need is greatest.

We think, for example, of these teams of trained people who have, in the past years, visited nearly a score of Asian capitals to help bridge the deep gulf which two centuries of commercial materialism has created between East and West.

We think of the work that goes forward in the Southern States of America. Since the Africans themselves began it with their play *The Next Phase*, this has been followed by another play, *The Crowning Experience*. A Negro lawyer of Atlanta, Colonel Walden, declared,

213

'A group of Moral Re-Armament people have spent five months in Atlanta, and from now on our city will never be the same again.' Two excellent American actresses played the leading rôles in this musical play: Muriel Smith, the Negro singer, and Ann Buckles, whose name has often figured on Broadway. Their presence, side by side, in the rôles which they played without salary and with such personal conviction, made a deep impression on America, which is in a state of confusion over the colour question. They were presented with the keys of the city of Washington at the end of a seven weeks' run when 83,000 came to applaud them in the National Theatre, a box-office record without precedent in the 123 years of the theatre's history.

We think of those hundreds of thousands of people who, wherever they may be, in their professional lives and the seeming humdrum of their daily existence, nevertheless live a life where all is orientated by a profound personal conviction which embraces the world and is rooted in the deep springs of their faith. John Riffe, for example, who was Vice-President of the CIO, an outstanding figure who is sadly missed today, waged a resolute fight for sound management and unity at the heart of the American labour movement. Riffe said to a Senator, 'You must tell America that when Frank Buchman changed John Riffe he saved American industry five hundred million dollars.'

We think too of these assemblies that are taking place at Caux and Mackinac and on Asian and African soil. There men are enriched by the pooling of their experiences, and they learn from one another how to settle the problems that weigh most heavily upon them. They are schools of statesmanship where politicians, workers, industrialists, learn to win to a better idea men who are animated by a materialist ideology.

In this whole trend, Europe takes her place alongside the other continents. Many more facts could have been given. We could have mentioned the incontestable part which Moral Re-Armament has played in the building of European unity. Madame Laure, whose story is told in our opening pages, has done, single-handed, more than any other woman for the reconciliation of France and Germany, and this is recognised by two men whose names will always be remembered when we think of Europe—Adenauer and Schuman.

We could have told of the many occasions when as a critical point was reached in negotiations between two countries—whether France and Germany, France and Tunisia, Holland and Germany, or Germany and Denmark—Moral Re-Armament played a decisive part by bringing together men who had no other common ground on which to meet. These facts have become history, and we have not reported them here.

We could have spoken of the meeting which Chancellor Adenauer asked Frank Buchman to arrange in 1951, at the moment when a Communist Youth Rally was staged in Berlin. A German newspaper reported it next day with the headline, 'Berlin a Washout—Moral Re-Armament the Basic Answer'.

We could also have described all that has been done in the field of industrial relations—in the French textile industry, the British coal-fields, the Italian chemical industry. Individual stories have referred to these, and other books have told what has happened.

It is for each nation to discover what her contribution can be to building this new world. Her traditions and her special genius oblige France to ponder this question.

For too long we have pinned our hopes on empty dreams: the man of genius, the international organisation, the plan conceived by some brilliant mind, an economic or political system. Each time we have believed that the object of our hope would solve our problems for us.

Time has passed, and our illusions have been swept away, leaving us cynical and bitter. But a new world is possible. The facts are there and speak for themselves. The facts recorded here are all simple: they are the result of simple actions. They are within everyone's reach.

Everyone, wherever he may be, can make the decision to be part of this rising tide of men and women.

There is nothing to sign, except for each one of us to put our names at the foot of the blank page of our lives, and so let the Will who presides over the world's destinies fill it in as He chooses.

There is no movement to join, but each of us can allow a movement to stir in us that breaks the bonds that bind us to materialism and make life stagnant.

Nobody receives orders from anyone, except those which he hears dictated in the depths of his own conscience. As it has been for hundreds of thousands, so for each one the starting-point is still himself.

Change in men opens the door to a fresh hope.

215

There is a network of people across the world already in action tackling this task. If we accept this new direction in our lives, we will quite naturally find our efforts joined to theirs. The world of tomorrow is in our hands.

What shall we offer our children? Will it be a world in disorder and chaos, built by the whims of our selfishness, conflicts, passions and fears?

Or shall we dedicate ourselves and our nations, so that our children can live in true hope?